Brawny Wycherley

W. Wycherley
Ætatis Suæ 28
Quantum mutatus ab illo Viro

P. Lely Eques pinx   I. Smith fec. 1703

WILLIAM WYCHERLEY

*From an engraving by I. Smith after the painting by Lely. Reproduced
by courtesy of The Players*

Brawny Wycherley

First Master in English Modern Comedy

by Willard Connely

CHARLES SCRIBNER'S SONS

NEW YORK · LONDON

1930

To

THE RIGHT HONOURABLE H. A. L. FISHER
WARDEN OF NEW COLLEGE, OXFORD

IN MEMORY OF
A WALK IN THE RAIN ON THE SUSSEX WEALD

———

Non invenies alterum
Lepidiorem ad omnes res, nec qui
amicus amico sit magis.
—PLAUT.

'Brawny Wycherley . . . Gentleman-Writer.'
—*The Earl of Rochester.*

'There is something brawny . . . in his step.'
—*Leigh Hunt.*

THE ADVENTURE

In my reading and travels while following the career of Wycherley I had the good fortune to work near certain friends and acquaintances whom I should like to thank again. They sustained me without fail. They helped to push forward my enquiries. And they were so generous of their time and so constant in their fulfillments that it soon became for me almost a matter of loyalty to them that I should carry to a finish what I had begun.

To the Right Honourable the Earl of Drogheda, descendant of the family into which Wycherley's wife first married, I am indebted for his kindness in opening to me the history of the Drogheda succession in Restoration times, as recorded in a privately printed book heretofore never quoted, by his mother, the late Dowager Countess of Drogheda.

The letters from Wycherley to Colonel James Grahme of Levens, Privy Purse to King James II, are here published for the first time. They were discovered last December in Levens Hall, Westmorland, by my friend Mrs. H. M. Gaskell, a descendant of the family of Colonel Grahme's wife (Dorothy Howard), to which family Levens passed from the Colonel. I have Mrs. Gaskell to thank also for her gracious permission to include in this book the first published facsimile, so far as I know, of a complete letter by Wycherley.

My conjectures on Wycherley in Spain (which I originally alluded to in the *Times Literary Supplement* for May 23, 1929), I should hardly venture to print were it not for the encouragement and support given them by G. Thorn-Drury, Esq., K. C., the final authority in England on the Restoration period, and by M. Charles Perromat, Docteur-ès-Lettres in the University of Bordeaux, who is the ablest living scholar in the subject of the life and work of Wycherley. These gentlemen also gave me the benefit of their judgment, and assisted me with references, upon several incidents whose dates have been difficult to fix.

Throughout the revision of parts of this book I enjoyed the aid of my fellow collegian, the Rev. Cunliffe Brookes, of Middle Aston, Steeple Aston, Oxon., and late of New College, Oxon. Mr. Brookes is a lineal descendant of Wycherley's great-uncle, Joseph Wycherley, and is the legal representative of the dramatist's family today. He most kindly made known to me unpublished circumstances of importance touching the long quarrel between Wycherley and his father, together with the hitherto unnoticed pedigree of the Wycherleys prior to the fifteenth century.

My stay in Angoulême and Saintes, where I walked the highroads of Wycherley's youth, became a fascinating holiday under the guidance and enthusiasm of M. Burias, Archeviste du Departement de la Charente. M. Burias set at my disposal his archives of the seventeenth century in Angoumois-Saintonge, including documents which he allowed me to borrow from an ancient tower of the Chateau d'Angoulême, and with daily eagerness he assisted my researches in every way at his command.

In Montpellier, though I was unable to find any further trace left by Wycherley himself, I lingered for a fortnight in order to begin to know old Languedoc somewhat as Wycherley knew it, and my reading in both of its libraries greatly profited from the suggestions of M. le Professeur Thomas, the distinguished historian (in the University of Montpellier) of the epoch of Louis Quatorze.

To Dr. Gerald B. Webb, of Colorado Springs (late of Guy's Hospital, London), I owe my information on physicians, patients, and medical practice in the time of the Stuarts. Dr. Webb I believe is one of the first to observe that modern biographers, tak-

ing too little account of pathology, often misinter-
pret ruling traits of character in their subject.

Publication by W. G. Hargest, Esq., of Derwent
Gardens, Ilford, Essex, and Miss Eleanore Boswell,
of Bury, Pulborough, Sussex (in the *Times Literary Supplement* for Nov. 21 and Nov. 28, 1929),
of new facts regarding Wycherley and the Countess
of Drogheda necessitated late revision of part of my
Chapter V. The discovery of the documents in the
case of *Barnaby v. Wycherley*, in the Public Record Office, was quite accidental, Mr. Hargest at the
time seeking material for his life of Richard Brome,
and Miss Boswell for her forthcoming extensive
work on the history of the stage. I am most grateful
to both of these authors for giving me valuable ad-
ditional notes on the case. Miss Boswell has been so
kind as to supply me with her complete bibliography
for it, which I have added to the reference list at
the end of my book.

At Clive Hall, Shropshire, I was charmingly entertained by G. Malcolm Watson, Esq., the present
owner, who showed me in all detail extant the relics
of the original manor-house and surrounding gardens as they appeared in Wycherley's time.

THE AUTHOR.

CONTENTS

CONTENTS

Brawny Wycherley

CHAPTER I

THE LADY OF THE MADRIGALS

ON a midsummer day in 1645, at Rueil, faubourg of the chateau of Richelieu, Julie d'Angennes languidly gave her hand to the Marquis de Montausier. He had besought her for it nearly fourteen years. The queen regent, Anne of Austria, sent to the wedding twenty-four brocaded violinists; poets who graced the salon of Hôtel de Rambouillet read new lyrics to the new marquise; fountains of fireworks showered yellow hail about the gardens. But round the table of the bride one might have felt something amiss: Love had not come to the feast.

The salt of life for Julie d'Angennes was to be adored not by one man, but by a room full of them. She was the eldest and wittiest of the seven daughters of Madame de Rambouillet, and from her girlhood had sat at the foot of her mother in the salon of the Précieuses. This had kept her young. There was mischief in her eyes—a glint of sun continually played against their blue. She used to wear her wild brown hair tumbled forward so that one saw, as if between curtains, only a triangle of forehead. But

3

what plagued every wooer was her smile, for it was the smile of a woman who at once gave and withheld: it was compact of adulation and irony, prudery and disdain, but in the end obdurate as the sphinx.[1] If a courtier who had got off with Julie stopped his career of laughter with a sigh, Julie stopped his career of sighing with a laugh.

'She would let die without pity a hundred men,' said the poet Voiture one evening, 'for love of her.' Julie poured a jug of water on his head.[2]

This inscrutable flirt gathered tributes as placidly as she might pluck flowers in a field. Chapelain had called her the Princess Julie; Corneille read his melodious verses to her; Richelieu asked her to his palace to dance for him. And then Montausier, a daring soldier and a fastidious dandy, came in his doublet of red velour[3] to lay corroding siege to her heart.

Julie, loath to leave her pedestal, put off the Marquis like all the rest, almost time out of mind. She did not dismiss him. That would have been difficult to do, for he was as persistent and laborious as a beaver. On her birthday, in 1640, he paid her the most glowing compliment of the century with his gift, the 'Garland of Julie,' a book with paint-

---

[1] Magne, I, 75.
(All names in footnotes refer to titles listed at the end of the volume.)
[2] Magne, II, 131.　　　　　　　　　[3] Roux, 26.

ings of twenty-nine flowers round which nineteen poets wrote sixty-two madrigals in her praise. Montausier on that day rather hoped to win the Princess. But he failed. Fourteen of the madrigals he had written himself.

Still the man loitered about Hôtel de Rambouillet. He was not the sort to bury his chagrin aloof. He paid court all the more, and his ardour revived in the very atmosphere of this citadel of the Précieuses. For there the last chapter in the literature of French chivalry was being enacted and written down. Year in year out it was the gayest house in Paris. It shone, it glistened, it palpitated, it mixed laughs with taunts, blew gallantry in bubbles, cudgelled all ears with preciosity, and at bottom insisted that the futile things in life were the most to be desired.[1]

Julie was a Catholic. She was given to the way of the world,[2] which was the way of the royal house, which was Catholic. Montausier had been brought up in Calvinism. With an austere gesture he abjured it. This was too much for Madame de Rambouillet to disregard.

'Julie,' said she, 'you are stubborn. If you persist in spinsterhood you will lead a dreary life. It would give me the deepest joy to see you the wife of so fine and good a man as Montausier.'[3]

[1] Magne, II, 345.   [2] Cousin, 407.   [3] Magne, II, 312.

5

It needed no more to make the Princess yield. Montausier did not count. But she loved and venerated her mother.

'I will marry him,' she said to herself, 'but only to avoid distressing her.'

She was then thirty-eight, three years older than her suitor, but she looked ten years younger than he was. Montausier bore the marks of war and of his imprisonment in enemy camps in Alsace; beneath that, his early years of Protestant discipline and self-denial had left him pious, parched, and crotchety; but he was a dogged lover, and he could woo a dogged coquette.[1]

The Marquis had bought the governorship of Angoumois and Saintonge, a province two hundred miles southwest of Paris, and two thousand miles southwest of the only life Julie d'Angennes knew or ever wanted to know. But she faced the break with spirit. Montausier carried her away to the Chateau d'Angoulême, a grim castle with walls ten feet thick, reared on a hill overlooking the valley of the Charente, a hill beset with winds which blew people into parentheses and with cold which drilled through to their marrow. Yet in one sense Julie was a most fit inheritor of this castle. High within its gray eastward tower, a century and a half before, had been born Marguérite de Valois, who

[1] Bourgoin, 232 ff.

6

had grown up to be chief patroness of letters in France, protector of Rabelais, and heroine of songs written by every poet the kingdom knew. Now Julie d'Angennes could kneel at the prie-Dieu of Marguérite, which stood (and still stands today, not quite against the wall) near the massive fireplace in the anteroom to her bedchamber.

The Princess Julie however professed devotion somewhat more than she practised it. Elsewhere in the chateau she was to have her fill of religion, for Montausier was a zealot, and he liked to think his eyes glittered. He had clogged the castle with eerie shrines, with Bibles in strange languages of Asia, and with tapestries of righteous scenes from the Old Testament[1]—bearded glaring patriarchs with set jaws, all of whom bore sabres thirsting to hew Agag in pieces before the Lord. If Julie had not possessed a genius for entertaining and a masculine skill in diplomacy she would have mummified in exile.

But Madame la Chatelaine at once bestirred herself to win cordialities in the province: chirped at the petits-maîtres, asked rural advices of the petites-maîtresses. She found Gombaud and Seigneur de Balzac living nearby, and she invited them together with pompous little personages of the town to soirées in the chateau. She had her youngest sister Angélique down from Paris, sarcastic Angélique who

[1] Societé Archæologique, lii ff.

7

tossed her head prettily and pouted. The company within the ramparts would be enlivened.

'I assure you one has great need of refreshment,' exclaimed Angélique one evening to a gentleman visiting from the Court, 'for without it one would soon die in this place.' [1]

A sensitive citizen of Angoulême overheard her. 'I shall not come to see the Montausiers again,' he sputtered, 'while that girl is staying with them.'

Julie toiled to restore good feeling. She called in more luminaries of the province. Old Gombaud, eighty years of wisdom, again limped over from Saintonge, bristling with his epigrams. The Marquis de Racan turned up, bearing a sheaf of his paraphrases of the Psalms. His very conversation was no less musical. Then Julie lured away her old friends from Paris. Godeau, the reverend wit who had married her to Montausier, came to join in the soirées, and Chapelain, who dressed like a boy of ten and always had his head full of unborn poetry.

But the master-stroke of the Princess was her treatment of the provincials. If she saw an unfamiliar gentleman arrive she covertly got his name and history; at table or while chatting she then called him by name and asked news of his family.[2] This charmed her guests. Without Julie, there would have been no men for her husband to talk to, since

[1] Tallemant., II, 313 ff.   [2] Ibid., II, 531.

8

he lacked all sense of the need of amiability. As the years drew on, in fact, the Governor became a library hermit, and often spent the whole night polishing his writings.

Madame de Rambouillet was obliged to revise her opinion of her son-in-law. 'He is foolish,' she admitted, 'by very force of being wise.'

In 1652–3 Montausier had to take the field again to put down civil war in the neighboring towns of his province—Cognac, Saintes, La Rochelle. Fighting was his natural occupation, and he flattened out the rebels with his usual thoroughness. But when he returned to the chateau, glum from conquest, morose in victory, he walled himself in more than ever behind his Bibles and parchments.

The gossipy Tallemant des Réaux was among others of the blue salon who at this period voiced his sympathy for the Princess Julie and his aversion for her husband. 'He shouts, he is rude, he contradicts,' wrote Tallemant, 'and when he disputes with anyone he marshals before their eyes all their past iniquities. Never has a man so served to cure me of the habit of conversation. When the Court relaxes, his piety redoubles. He has read the Gospels a hundred and thirteen times. His wife serves him tremendously in the province. But for her, the noblesse would hardly look at him. He rises at eleven in the morning, and shuts himself up to read, liking not hunting nor any popular sport. He makes translations: he has put Persius into French verse. He talks only of books, and sees mostly Chapelain and Conrart.'[1]

To escape by day from this Maecenas dipped in vinegar, Julie and Angélique, having assassinated Montausier in letters which they wrote to their friends, galloped their horses along the banks of the Charente. Sometimes they rode to hounds behind a pack which Monsieur de la Rochefoucauld provided for them in the neighbouring hills of Angoumois.[2] Hither and yon the ploughmen knew the cry 'Ho-la!' of Madame Julie as the fox was up and away.

After dinner, the soirées nearly always beguiled the time. Wifehood was not going to quench the blue which burned in the eyes of Julie d'Angennes.

It was in 1655, the beginning of a three-year period of comparative tranquillity for the Montausieurs,[3] that a young foreigner, without friends, arrived in the province. He was an English boy barely fifteen, called Will Wycherley, and because of political and academic chaos at home he had been sent abroad to study. He came of hardy stock. He was descended from the second oldest family in the

[1] Tallemant, II, 305, 529.   [2] Ibid., II, 313.
[3] Roux, 115.

parish of Clive, near Shrewsbury. His grandfather, Daniel Wycherley, who had married the daughter of a rich farmer in a neighbouring village, was master of the 'mansion house' in Clive. From his father, also Daniel, heir apparent to Clive Hall, William should eventually inherit this manor. The younger Daniel was ambitious for the family of Wycherley. He was not a scholar from the University, but he had picked up all the learning which the countryside afforded,[1] and dissatisfied with the extent of his son's Latin—no doubt soundly begun in a nearby Grammar School, at Wem—he amplified it with some rigorous teaching administered by himself. This father had didactic force. He was stern, thorough, and correct. And he was soon gratified to see that William could get syntax like a parrot and write Latin like a Roman reborn.

Will Wycherley at fifteen was in demeanour not a little ahead of his years. Daily training under such a magisterial father had brought to the lad inklings of manhood. He was of lithe and muscular frame, and strikingly handsome,[2] with a long face which gave prominence to his quick eyes, the eyes of one who pinioned what he looked at and who never ceased to look. He held his chin well back, his head slightly inclined right, and he had the gift of

[1] Shropshire Society, 337.
[2] Macaulay, Comic Dramatists, xxvii.

11

following any conversation with the most ardent interest. Sometimes too—for all his narrow experience—there was in his face the blank merriment of one who has spoken a swift jest and is amused by the imminence of his hearer believing it, or by his hearer's difficulty in quite comprehending it. Hardly any man, and certainly no woman, could resist his alert youth, his vivacity, his talent for companionship, his graceful, decisive, very masculine step.[1]

The boy had developed at home an avidity for literature, and his plastic mind was already enriched with the golden torrent of Athens and Rome. But in England the Cromwell regime, overthrowing the cherished pagan curricula of Oxford and Cambridge, had blocked the course of his further study. Daniel Wycherley thereupon lost no time in sending his son out of England, to the valley of the Charente, because the region was then noted for the excellence of its masters in the classics. It was a Catholic stronghold. The Wycherleys were Protestants. But to the mind of the elder Wycherley the distinction between Protestant and Catholic was evidently of somewhat less moment than that between Roundhead and Cavalier. He was an unflinching Royalist, he was contributing large sums of money to Charles II in exile,[2] and he looked to the eventual return of the Stuarts. Meantime he wished to

[1] Shropshire Society, 344.   [2] Ibid., 338.

educate the scion of Clive Hall as a gentleman.

Such a desire burned deep in the heart of the younger Daniel Wycherley, a man who had been the industrious architect of his own fortune. At thirty-eight, he was of massive stature, broad-chested as a police constable, and in countenance both comely and rugged.[1] His hair, gray early, gave him an imposing look of the judiciary, but in manners, as is often the case with those of new-made honour, he was a little more ostentatious than easy. Though Daniel son of Daniel was twelfth in descent from the original Wycherley in Shropshire, he was the first of his family in Clive who had risen above the yeomanry.[2] In the 'Visitation of Shropshire' for 1623 had appeared a list of those who 'disclaimed' their right to arms, and among the names therefore posted up as 'no gent.' was that of the elder Daniel, his father. The 'no gents.' were either those who could not trace their pedigree to any ancestor appearing in the Heralds' Books or those who were unwilling to go to the expense of entering up the pedigree. But the elder Daniel had married an heiress. Their son had read ambitiously. He had seen town life. He did not intend that any such disclaimer should be published in the next Visitation.

Great luck had befallen young Daniel as a student of law in a barrister's chambers in London: the

[1] Shropshire Society, 340.   [2] Ibid., 336.

Marquess of Winchester, a client, noticing Daniel's brisk intelligence, had made him High Steward of his estates in Hampshire. Once admitted to the intimacies of Basing House, country seat of the Marquess, Daniel Wycherley grasped and improved his opportunity for a lift-up in life. In this household he met and courted Bethia Shrimpton, favourite lady of honour and confidante to the Marchioness, Lady Honora de Burgh.[1] Bethia was a demurely beautiful girl of twenty-two, whose father was a Royalist of Whitchurch, Hants. In 1640, Daniel, then twenty-three, married her.

Five years later a Puritan mob stormed and burned Basing House, and bore away the Marquess, a Catholic, in fetters to the Tower. The estate they confiscated. Bold and decisive in this emergency, the High Steward borrowed £30,000,[2] bought the estate back, and provided subsistence for the nobleman's family. Winchester in gratitude made Wycherley his Steward for life, and from this time, in all administrative capacities over vast lands and manors, the Shropshireman became virtually the power behind the coronet. It was said of the family of Winchester that its representatives were alternately fools and wise men.[3] No excess of wisdom appeared to burden this Marquess. Daniel Wycherley feathered his

[1] Summers, I, 4.   [2] Perromat, 14; Gough, 150.
[3] Shropshire Society, 338.

14

own nest, though not by any palpable wrongdoing. But perhaps in order to guard the feathers he had plucked he developed an appetite for lawsuits, an appetite which a harpy might have bowed to.

Back in his own village of Clive, seven miles from Shrewsbury, Daniel Wycherley the younger, compared to his farmer father, was remarked as a gentleman who had got on in the world. Though he was annoyed if correspondents neglected to address him 'Esquire,' no fury distorted his lips if any one spoke of 'Lord Wycherley.' He did not suspect that villagers might confer such a title because his prosperity had made him a little overbearing. Having ridden so grandly and so very long over the estates of the Marquess, Daniel now coveted lands of his own, and he planned and plotted to triple the Shropshire holdings which he was heir to. In London and Hampshire he had taken by the forelock his chance of fortune, and ten years after he had achieved control of the Winchester demesne the yeoman from the Welsh border was able to send his son elegantly to France without noticing the cost.

Further life in Clive would only have stultified a boy of wit like Will Wycherley. Then, as now, it was a handful of ancient stone cottages, two handfuls of people equally stony and ancient, one street, which led up to Clive Hall, and a churchyard against a hill full of rocks and daffodils. The manor, built as an ell, had leaded windows in threes, and chimneys so high that they topped the old oaks in the garden. In front of it, a green plain fell away hazily to the Dee; in the back, beyond the pine woods of Grin's Hill, the Shropshire Hounds at long intervals started a fox. The rest was silence, and Clive Hall, except for clamour made by Will's brother George, aged four, was the abode of sleep.

But Will Wycherley, though his father desired to establish him as a country gentleman born, was not born to be a country gentleman. He was beginning life in France, where the English court was living, where young English noblemen were following the court, where young English gentlemen were following the noblemen. He himself was to live close to nobility, French if not English, as befitted a staunch Royalist. And he would study letters. He would be urbane, like his favourite Horace, the poet above all to whose wit and crisp philosophy he was singularly drawn.

Although Louis XIV did not revoke the Edict of Nantes until 1685, the ubiquitous Jesuits a full generation before had got their fingers into nearly all French education.[1] When Will Wycherley arrived in Angoumois the Jesuit fathers of the province were teaching boys to write orations patterned after Demosthenes and Cicero, and poems in the manner of

[1] Histoire du Lycée, 119.

Virgil and Horace. Geography and history they included only by way of explaining the authors read. The use of French, even in conversation, was forbidden by a Jesuit rule.[1] In such a programme, if his son should follow it, there was apparently nothing to be disapproved of by Daniel Wycherley.

During the second half of the seventeenth century, sons of English gentlemen studying in Angoumois were usually put in charge of private tutors. These tutors were Catholics. Masters of arts and other preceptors could take boys en pension and teach them Latin and French, but they were obliged to usher them into the Jesuit College Saint-Louis for all other training.

Wycherley however was to continue his education, indeed to learn French among other accomplishments of the age, in one manner little dreamed of either by his father or by himself. The story goes that he lived almost constantly in Angoulême.[2] At all events he was soon introduced to the Marquise de Montausier, who during her life in the province was generally to be found at the chateau. One may not say that this superb hostess made Wycherley feel merely at home; rather, she soon made him feel that his own home was a place he never again wanted to see. Away from the provincials Julie

[1] Histoire du Lycée, 121.
[2] Nouvelle Biographie, XLVI, Column 856.

seemed made for the court; far from the court she seemed born to please the provincials.[1] Thus by her the eager young man from rural England was smoothly lifted into the polite world, never to forsake it. Julie d'Angennes proved to be the first of three women who determined the course of Wycherley's life.

'I was often admittted to her conversation,' said Wycherley later (according to his friend, John Dennis), 'and was charmed, young as I was, by the beauties of her intellect as well as by the graces of her person.' [2]

But conversation in the salon through these years at Angoulême was not the only pastime for the Marquise and the visiting Précieuses. Julie and her 'illuminati' had always regarded the country unbearably dull unless they could transport to it the pleasures of the city—music, song, dance, even the staging of a play. In earlier days they had so whiled away sojourns at Chateau de Rambouillet, in the Beauce, near Versailles. Julie herself on one occasion had there enacted the part of Pyramis.[3] In Angoulême she revived such entertainments, and expanded them to include balls, masques, receptions, and promenades. The divine Julie, still adorable though in her forties, still vying with Helen in

[1] Flechier, 10. [2] Familiar Letters, p. 215.
[3] Magne, II, 146.

18

praises sung to her charms,[1] made herself a queen in the grim castle where her celebrated prototype had been born, and surrounded by the poets, the critics, and the dramatists, she created a second blue salon to glorify history.

Her husband month after month lurked in the shadows of his library, burrowing into Chaldean Bibles, or throwing up heavy breastworks of Vitruvius, Passenius, and the church fathers, from behind which he sometimes peered as if from behind a pile of wood. Tallemant tells us Montausier had a beautiful library in Angoulême. But the inventory of it[2] suggests that the bindings were often more arresting than the contents of the books. No doubt young Wycherley could have profited by occasional reading in the ponderous chronicles of Monstrelet or in 'The Games of the Romans.' Perhaps he did. No doubt, on the other hand, he was learning something to his advantage in a livelier room where he mingled with Princess Julie and the poets. They taught him the art of chiseling the spoken phrase.

About a year after Wycherley had begun his life in France, the Abbé de Pure published a work attacking the Précieuses, of whom Angélique d'Angennes was the acknowledged president.[3] The Précieuses were open adversaries of marriage. Many of

---

[1] Tallemant, II, 313.   [2] Societé Archæologique, lii ff.
[3] Roux, 115.

19

them were married, and therefore they advocated single life; the Abbé, unmarried and a priest, denounced it; the paradox dates from Adam. But Wycherley had filled his mind with the doctrines of the Précieuses. The Abbé's book and its subsequent storm could not soften him, and his early adherence to the coterie of Angélique and Julie bore a decisive influence on his career.

He acquired the taste of the language and the literature;[1] he drew into his ken especially the ways of the theatre. That little court in the chateau, so learned and so prudish, gave to the spirit of the young Englishman its rules of decorum, its irony of hyperbole, its dextrous turns of compliment, its art of insinuating more than is said, and best of all its utter absurdity. Thus while still an adolescent Wycherley formed one of his guiding principles of conversation and authorship: 'Wit is generally false reasoning.'[2]

As the acquaintance of Julie d'Angennes and Will Wycherley ripened one may picture the Marquise talking to her protégé somewhat after the manner of Madame la Vicomtesse de Beauseant giving advice to Eugene de Rastignac:

'You are only just come to Paris, and you are in search of some one who will give you lessons in good taste.'

[1] Quaas, 22.   [2] Letter to Pope, Feb. 28, 1708.

'Is it not natural to wish to be initiated into the mysteries that charm us?'

'Then you must deal with the world as it deserves. You are determined to succeed? I will help you. You shall sound the depths of corruption in woman; you shall measure the extent of man's pitiful vanity. You will be nothing, you see, unless a woman interests herself in you, and she must be young and wealthy, and a woman of the world. Yet if you have a heart, lock it carefully away like a treasure. Let no one suspect it, or you will be lost. . . .

'As soon as this woman singles you out, other women will begin to lose their heads about you, and her enemies and rivals and intimate friends will all try to take you from her. There are women who will fall in love with a man because another woman has chosen him. If the women credit you with wit and talent, the men will follow suit so long as you do not undeceive them yourself. There will be nothing you may not aspire to. You will go everywhere and you will find out what the world is, an assemblage of fools and knaves.'

The Marquise could not repress a fondness for her rapt young follower whom she saw maturing into courtly manhood.

'My little Huguenot!' she greeted him banteringly as Will Wycherley entered the great hall of the chateau.[1]

[1] Tinsley, 235.

Frequent repetition of this epithet must have worn the boy to sensibility of his religious isolation. As a Protestant, he was not quite one of the company. The Catholic atmosphere in all Angoumois in that day was as suffusing as the Moslem creed in Turkey. Apart from the influence of Julie d'Angennes, the town and countryside were overrun by Jesuits militant, whose avowed purpose was not alone to educate youth but to convert Protestants.[1]

But it was the Princess who directly initiated Wycherley to theology. He engaged in debate with her.[2] That was dangerous, as it is always dangerous to debate with a woman who joins beauty with understanding. It took thirteen years for the religion of Julie to gather Montausier within its fold, but impressionable Will Wycherley capitulated in less than five. The intercessor we do not know. It may have been either a Jesuit tutor or the almoner of the Marquise living in the chateau. In the latter case there would be no record of the conversion. But the immediate result was almost radical: in the first flush of his new faith, Wycherley wanted to become a priest.[3] However, the unrelenting conflict between Précieuses and priesthood seemed to deter him.

During the last two years of Wycherley's stay

[1] Histoire du Lycée, 87. [2] Cibber, III, 248.
[3] Granger, I, 238.

in France as a student, 1658–60, the soirées in the
Chateau d'Angoulême suffered some rather prolonged interruptions. Angélique, for all her railings
against matrimony, was married to the Comte de
Grignan in April, 1658. The arrangements for the
wedding and the ensuing festivities drew the Governor and his wife to Paris.

In the following year peace with Spain was talked
of at the French court. For Wycherley, this turn
of events meant that for the first time he was to
feel the nearness of the power of palaces. Cardinal
Mazarin found it necessary to go to the frontier to
undertake the treaty of Bidassoa, and Montausier
was in a great stir to welcome the dictator en route.
At the head of two thousand gentlemen in resplen-
dent array the Marquis led a cavalcade to a spot
within five leagues of Angoulême. It was a hot day
in May. The crowd was tormented by the sun. But
the Cardinal declined to proceed to the chateau for
refreshment because the least delay, he considered,
would postpone the amity of nations.[1]

Three months later, Will Wycherley was to see
the province again aroused by a visit of great personages. Louis XIV, a young man of almost the
same age as Wycherley himself, passed through Angoulême with his mother on the way to Spain,
whither they were bound for the purpose of celebrat-

[1] Roux, 115.

23

ing the marriage of the King with the Infanta
Maria-Theresa. With such a cork had the astute
Mazarin bottled up peace.

The Marquis and Marquise received the royal
party in Saintes.[1] Never since the time of the Romans
had the little town known such gilded pomp. The
first day—the day of tassels and trumpets—was
given over to the reception; on the second the King
touched the sick; on the third day he set out for
Bordeaux, having been so gorgeously entertained
by Princess Julie that he insisted upon her joining
his entourage in order that she might grace the wedding across the Pyrenees.[2] Wycherley, through his
friendship for Julie d'Angennes, stood thus early
in his life in the shadow of royalty, an experience
that was to serve him to no small end when he grew
older.

The return of the Montausiers to Angoulême in
October, 1659, was a fête for the nobility of the
province, for the reason that their presence was a
reflection of the court.[3] But the Governor and his
wife did not come back from Spain in the merriest
of spirits. They had taken their young daughter
Marie-Julie on the journey, and the child had fallen
ill of a fever. Her convalescence was drawn out
into months, while balls and soirées in the chateau
were perforce lessened.

[1] Vie de Montausier, I, 136.   [2] Roux, 117.   [3] Ibid., 117 ff.

Still, the intimacy between Julie and the young Briton who had now to be called 'her little convert' was unshaken. Throughout the winter Wycherley did not lose touch with the Précieuses. There is no difficulty in supposing that from time to time as he listened to conversations in the salon he heard spoken the name of Molière. For a decade Molière had toured the provinces with his company, was said to have played in Angoulême itself in 1649, by which time Julie had fairly collected her circle in the chateau, and he did play in Montpellier in 1654, where flourished a coterie of Précieuses, imitators of Julie and her mother.[1] But now, on the 18 of November, 1659, at the Théâtre du Petit-Bourbon in Paris, there was produced a play which so lampooned the clique of Hôtel de Rambouillet and Chateau d'Angoulême, that Wycherley, in the midst of that society, could not have avoided the prolonged disputes which raged over the author throughout France. Molière, inaugurating the comedy of manners, had written 'Les Précieuses Ridicules.' Such inebriates of elegance as Chapelain and Menage were converted on the spot.[2] The cult of the Précieuses had weathered the assault of Desmarets in 1637, and had only staggered from the blows of the Abbé de Pure, but now under the whip of Molière it succumbed, and Julie d'Angennes knew that after

[1] Demogeot, 361.   [2] Ibid., 418.

thirty long years she had outlived her sovereignty
of wit. As Molière at one stroke thus reformed literary taste in France, Will Wycherley, close to the
theatre of reform, learned while still a boy the
meaning of the comedy of manners. He remembered it.

The young gallant was soon to terminate his long
visit. Julie's retreat from letters did not in the least
bear upon his departure. Nor did the death of his
grandfather, in December, 1659.[1] The elder Daniel
Wycherley, 'no gent.,' last of the yeomen, left William's father sole master of Clive Hall, of the family farms in the next village of Wem, and of several messuages nearby, gathered in by the family
as property of old Daniel's wife. And Will Wycherley now found himself heir apparent. But it was
quite another cycle of events set in motion that was
to hasten his farewells. In March, 1660, news
trickled through to France that Charles II was on
the eve of recovering his throne in Whitehall. English subjects who had exiled themselves in sympathy
with their monarch cast their eyes toward London
once more. From England, Daniel Wycherley,
among other fathers of wandering heirs, sent for
his son to come home; the Restoration was only a
matter of days. With mixed feelings the young lion
of the soirées packed up his things, took leave of his
urbane friends, and recrossed the Channel.

[1] Perromat, 13; Shropshire Society, 356.

In the salon of the Marquise, Wycherley had
lived like an enchanted waif, or like a rather grown-
up only child who from day to day is fated to hear
the conversation of none but persons two or three
times his age. This coincidence taught the student
—the student of life—a valuable habit: he fell into
a way of never appearing wiser than his company.
But often when he did speak his tendency was to
twist the serious phrase of the moment into a quip,
after Horace's maxim: 'pleasant it is to trifle now
and then.'[1]

In the highly suggestive words of Taine, this finished young gallant returned to England knowing
how to wear well a perruque and gloves. That is the
real story of Wycherley's education in France. It
does not appear that the boy allowed his progress in
his studies to interfere with his constructive leisure
amidst the nobility of the Charente. Perhaps he had
observed in Montausier an example of scholarship
blistered. Behind those five formative years which
Will Wycherley had the capability to improve in the
wide halls and narrow highways of Angoumois-
Saintonge stood not a beetling tutor, not a desk and
books, not a new religion tried on like a crimson cloak,
but the queenly figure, radiant and ineffaceable, of
Julie d'Angennes, a woman great among men.

[1] Lansdowne, Memoirs, 13 ff.

27

CHAPTER II

A YOUNG MAN WELL-GLOVED

WHEN Charles the Second entered the City of London—it was on his thirtieth birthday, May 29, 1660—Will Wycherley was not among those who marched in the procession, danced round the bonfires, tossed coins to the mob for flagons of ale. Though he had arrived in England several weeks earlier he had posted with due obedience to Shropshire, where the silence was more startling than the din was in London, and within the sombre oak-panelled recesses of Clive Hall he was being inspected by his father, a critical man. One may surmise that Daniel Wycherley, as he beheld certain addenda of the foreign education acquired by William, was not altogether stricken with rejoicing.

The father, an Anglican churchman, found himself confronted by a son turned Catholic. That was a nuisance. And the convert did not even seem to be suffering from the approved pangs of conversion:[1] subdued eyes, a contrite heart, penitence and pallor. That too was rather irritating. The boy in fact was not unlike all spruce young Englishmen freshly back from France: the gallants who sauntered, who beat rat-a-tat on their snuff-box, looked ever so

[1] Quaas, 23.

slightly down their nose, and wore half a yard of lace handkerchief fluttering from their pocket. Daniel Wycherley was not amused.

He must pack airy Will off to Oxford, not merely to rid him of superfluous Gallicisms, if possible, but in any case to cleanse him anew in the sheep-dip of the Protestant faith.[1] Angoulême, as a school for the heir to Clive Hall, had proved something too much beyond Eton; it was Eton with a perruque. Was this yeasty surge the rivulet who had departed from England only five years before? He had brought back a freedom of manner almost oceanic. During the young man's absence Daniel Wycherley himself had moved on into the world a bit, but what was progress in the father of course was deviation in the son.

Until the spring of this very year Daniel, from time to time picking up bargains for his own profit, had been supervising sales of the lands of the Marquess. He counted up his swelling possessions, and he believed he ought to master the law if he would feel secure against the interference of busybodies. Whereupon, in 1658, he had got himself admitted to the Inner Temple.[2] He came to know men, among them, persons of power in the universities. Casting about now for a corrective agent in Oxford for his

---

[1] Anthony à Wood; Cyclopædia of Biog., II, 850.
[2] Foster, 'Men at the Bar.'

heretic son, Daniel at length secured the interest of Doctor Thomas Barlow, newly chosen Provost of Queen's College, a reverend gentleman who made it his recreation to pounce upon Catholics. It was morning exercise to him.

'I allow salvation to the Papists,' thundered Doctor Barlow till the pulpit quaked, 'only on the plea of invincible ignorance!'[1]

To Will Wycherley's father, Barlow for more reasons than the religious one must have seemed the ideal custodian for a son so alarming. The Doctor was both Royalist and Calvinist. He was the most learned of the Provosts whom Queen's had elected in the three centuries since its foundation. He was librarian of the Bodleian, and was called 'a library in himself and keeper of another.' Barlow moreover was shrewd and tenacious. Through the turmoil of the Protectorate he had set his teeth in his fellowship and had held on to it, though by the favour of Colonel Kelsey, deputy-governor of the garrison, to whose wife the Doctor was said to have presented certain gifts. But that was tact. Yes, Daniel admired a man like Barlow, ever strong upon the stronger side.

Will Wycherley went up to Oxford in the late spring of 1660.[2] The learned Provost, perhaps by whispered arrangement with Daniel beforehand,

[1] Magrath, II, 33 ff.   [2] Anthony à Wood.

30

took the wayward young man to live with him in
his own rooms over the great gate of Queen's, in the
High-street. It was not customary in that day for a
student to stay in the Provost's quarters; only highly
favoured gentlemen were there admitted.[1] Wycherley was to lodge where one who belonged to the ages
had trodden: within the triple-window of coloured
glass above the same gate Henry V had spent the
spring and summer of 1398, as a student, the year
before he was made Prince of Wales. He was under
the care of his uncle, Cardinal Beaufort, then Chancellor of the University. Prince Hal and Will
Wycherley—the one who had gone down to war in
Agincourt, the other who had come up from peace
in Angoulême. The newcomer, it seems, did not
make a point of talking about it.

Wycherley was entered as a gentleman-commoner, and having paid higher fees, he enjoyed privileges denied to ordinary commoners. He did not
have to matriculate. He did not have to put on a
gown. He wore a handsomer dress, in the spirit of
the time. Though he was supposed to be in residence
'for the sake of the public library,' he did not have
to read. Still the didactic Barlow had him listed in
the Bodleian, in July, under the title of Philosophiae
Studiosus.[2] Wycherley, like the exceptional and awe-
inspiring student of today, could revel in enumerat-

[1] Private information.   [2] Anthony à Wood.

ing to his college-mates in the cloisters of Queen's the things he did not 'have to do.' He was not in the roll of common men.

But life at Oxford in 1660 was hardly exhilarating. A university town could not cut away its Puritan cords as readily as London could. Even with the King restored and all England effervescing, dons down in the mouth, sour dons, and dons hawk-eyed with suspicion still trooped up the High and be-clouded the Cornmarket. The undergraduates, true enough, in their satanic pranks by night were about the same as in any generation. For a fellow-col-legian, Wycherley had Joe Haynes, the wit, actor, and dependable consumer of wine, who had entered Queen's in 1659,[1] and later sounded the keyboard of life all the way from being Latin secretary to Sir Joseph Williamson, Secretary of State, to posing as a Count while traveling, expenses paid, with a gen-tleman in France. Yet against such amusement as dear ruffians like Joe Haynes may have afforded, the stealthy shadow of old Barlow, just round a corner or across a staircase, was always elongating, shrink-ing, elongating. Wycherley at twenty, if not too old, was too knowing to be a first-year man in Oxford. As he went a walk through its alien summer mist he must have been sick for Angoulême—Princess Julie, the poets down from Paris bowing to her hand, the

---

[1] D. N. B. (Haynes); see also Haynes' 'Life,' *passim.*

pomp of the salon and its tinkle of wit. He was an outcast.

Doctor Barlow began to make his captive apostate see that it would be well for him to return to the religion he was born to.[1] The Provost, a blinking owl with the prey in his very cage, found he could be persuasive by hovering about the renegade, by appealing to him from day to day with a feast of reason if not with a flow of soul. Wycherley seems not to have bothered to resist. His thoughts were on the wing. If alluring femininity in Julie d'Angennes had won Wycherley over to the Romanists, prancing masculinity in Doctor Barlow may be said to have effected a right about face. Before the end of the summer the gentleman-commoner accepted reconversion.[2] What did it matter?

Apparently it mattered measurably to Daniel Wycherley. One can almost see him rubbing his hands when he got the tidings. The next event, now that the religious flurry was over and done, was that father and son agreed upon the reading of law as the wisest career for the heir to Clive Hall. Daniel did not insist that the young man remain at the university; on the tenth of November William Wycherley became a member of the Inner Temple.[3] Lawsuits were piling up; an able student of the codes could help his father win squabbles about property.

[1] Quaas, 23.   [2] Anthony à Wood.   [3] Perromat, 25.

33

So ended the Oxford days of a young man well-gloved, days he had been able to endure in the lodgings over the college gate hardly as long as Prince Hal himself had. London, not Oxford, was the place where things were happening, and Wycherley probably chafed to strut his French polish where it was better understood. The song of the tavern had drowned out the anthem of the college chapel. Nor if one may judge by an allusion in his plays did Wycherley regard undergraduates with any fevered fondness:

'I tell you this is Ned Harcourt of Cambridge,' says Sparkish. 'You see he has a sneaking college look.'

But in writing this line Wycherley at least discriminated, and remembered himself an Oxonian. He did more: he wrote the part of Sparkish for Joe Haynes.

Wycherley came up to London to live its life as eagerly as Will Shakespeare had come two generations before. He looked upon a London rejuvenated, a garlanded London, a London agog with jocund greetings. Barbers and perfumers were again making a living. The big May-pole at the bottom of Drury Lane again glistened with crown and vane, and again dances of old were being held round it.[1] Once more the King's head and the Duke's head adorned

[1] Cunningham, 7 ff.

34

signs over tavern doors, and men had died of joy from singing and shouting their sovereign's return. The young nobles who had followed Charles Stuart to France were back in gay dress, their spirits free and their tongues unbridled. Wycherley inside the gray walls of Oxford had breathed musty air, but now he found himself standing at the window of life with the sash flung wide, and when he saw gallants in buff coats and buskins, lace cuffs and red heels, chicken-skin gloves and ivory-top walking-sticks, he who so well knew those swaggering fashions felt he was in France again, sighed the unburdening of his heart, and leapt into the crowd to collect his good-mornings.

The work his father expected him to do in the Inner Temple Wycherley took casually enough; he dallied with the thick volumes of Coke, Plowden, Dalton, and other bugbears of the fledgling barrister, but he only dallied. It was too easy to walk out into the Strand. In his glossy auburn perruque, which fell well below his shoulders in front, Wycherley too paraded the Mall, chin up, amidst the courtiers.

The observed of all observers was of course the newly reigning monarch. Of the six or seven kings of England of abiding personality Charles Stuart was perhaps the last. Though the merriest, the laziest, and the most amorous of men, he looked nearly

as fierce and saturnine as the captain of a pirate ship.
He was so swarthy that General Monk before the
Restoration had toasted him as 'the Black Boy.'
Peter Lely had come over from the Continent to
paint his portrait.

'Is this like me?' cried Charles in his great throaty
voice when the picture was done. 'Ods fish! I am an
ugly fellow.'[1]

He could not act the part of a king either in words
or in gesture. In the House of Lords he would come
off his throne and stand by the fire. To the august
council-table he carried his dogs, black King Charles
spaniels which he bred in his bedchamber.[2] If he
rested indoors his mind wandered; but if he wandered outdoors his mind rested. Sauntering Charles,
sauntering like all his subjects who had returned
with him from France, set all London sauntering.
Little girls at play in Bird-cage Walk brushed their
hair away from their eyes as Charles strolled by in
the morning dressed in plain black velvet, with a
diamond star on a cloak thrown carelessly over one
shoulder, and wearing a long black full-bottom perruque. The King and his attending courtiers (and
spaniels) always made straight for the first pool
along the canal in Pall Mall, where Charles kept a
Balnearian crane with a wooden leg. Nothing during the walk was more urgent to the King than to

[1] Cunningham, 91 ff.   [2] Grammont, 448.

feed this crane, and to see if the leg made by the royal carpenter was working well.[1]

Wycherley looked upon this picture of original kingship—such as had not quickened England since Henry VIII had doffed the world aside—and was moved to write some verses, about twenty lines of doggerel 'To King Charles II on His Return.' It began, 'You come, Great Prince, at length Triumphant Home, Like Christian Constantine to Heathen Rome.' The young Templar perhaps meant to finish on a note of high compliment, but his last couplet was rather ambiguous: 'While every Mist that did obscure the State, Begins at your Approach to dissipate.' He seems not to have indulged again his literary urge for some years.

Covent Garden, a ten-minute walk from Wycherley's chambers in the Inner Temple, was almost as much the centre of London life as the plaza of St. Mark's was in Venice. In fact, it rather looked like St. Mark's. On the north and east sides Inigo Jones, a generation before, had built a Venetian piazza, within whose arcades he made fashionable promenades, and overhead, lodgings for persons of rank. The parish church of St. Paul's, also by Jones, stood on the west, while to the south the gardens of Bedford House bordered the square. Sixty feet from the houses, white railings enclosed this open space, in the

[1] Brett, 253.

middle of which arose a column topped by a great gilt ball, and a sundial with four gnomons. Round its base flower-girls and hawkers held forth, apple-women wrangled, and towsled gamins punched one another.

Londoners of fashion made quite another picture. Assignations, not confessions, were occurring almost from minute to minute in St. Paul's; the acts of private devotion and public worship seemed suspended. Tittering ladies tiptoed in and wrote epigrams in their Bibles. Or they met their gallants in the china-houses under the arcades, and received presents, then went along to a half-guinea dinner at Chatelin's, the famous French ordinary on the north side. Ben Long's tavern, the Rose, was a minute's walk off the Garden up Russell-Street; or by turning left into Bow-Street one arrived at the Cock, kept by Oxford Kate, and meeting-place of young noblemen of wit. These taverns were academies of ribaldry. There one learned to hit a waiter on the head with a candlestick, and to sing a bawdy song and drown out the rasping fiddles with hooting and laughing.

In this month of November, when Wycherley set about making his acquaintance with the town, arrived also the Queen, the dusky Catherine of Braganza, from Portugal. She was 'a very little plain old woman,'[1] with a set expression of disapproval,

[1] Pepys, Nov. 22, 1660.

and so short-legged that when standing she seemed on her knees. Her mouth appeared moulded in brass, and a projecting upper tooth and lip tempted observers to ask whether she was kin to Caliban. But the Portuguese Ambassador had worked like mad to arrange the betrothal: it was for the well-being of Europe. (Not many months elapsed before this poor Ambassador was ready to yield the ghost. What nearly killed him was to be assailed on one side by Charles because half of Catherine's enormous dowry remained upaid, and on the other by the Queen, because the Ambassador before the wedding had told her that Charles was virtuous.) On the day of the Queen's reception in England the King forgot to go; he was busy, in the house of Barbara Villiers in the Strand, where he and that lady were weighing each other.[1]

Such were the scenes, the happenings, which caught the eye and thought of the brawny young student of law as he took dinners with his fellow Templars, or walked with the wits, or tippled in taverns with other young men well-gloved. His manner, at once courtly and natural, soon recommended him to the beaux esprits. They swore the most embroidered oaths that Wycherley's talents definitely set him above the solemn and plodding harangues of men of the long robe. Just how far

[1] Pepys, May 21, 1662 (as of 1660).

above, or in what direction, these beaux esprits who advised truancy from the Inner Temple did not make quite clear. Wycherley himself was at the moment wavering between versifying life and codifying statutes.

His ambitious and acquisitive father kept an eye upon Will, for he frequently came up to town to fight a lawsuit and to parade his stalwart presence before the Templars. He impressed them. In his more jovial moments Daniel was not a bad sort. On the eve of St. Thomas the Apostle, December, 1662, the barristers appointed Daniel 'controller for the present Christmas,' and during a period of three weeks he enjoyed the distinction of sitting at the head of the table in the ancient dining-hall and playing host to the Benchers and the serjeants of the society.[1]

In the village of Clive, Daniel at the same time was working to solidify his position as a country gentleman. He ferreted out original deeds of his family and traced back his forefathers in Clive six generations, to the time of Henry IV. He produced these deeds before the College of Arms in August, 1663.[2] All of the preceding Wycherleys appeared to be merely farmers, though at least substantial farmers. But there was a Wycherley family dating back still another century, to the time of Edward I, as

[1] Inderwick, III, 72.   [2] Harleian, 1396, fo. 328.

early as the year 1300.[1] Its founder was Roger of
Wycherley, and the family seat, Wycherley Hall,
was a fine old black and white house with six gables,
near Baschurch, several miles west of Clive. This
house was a landmark of importance, and Daniel,
as anxious as the father of Shakespeare was for
family arms, claimed the arms of Roger of Wycherley on the ground that the first of the name to live
in Clive was the founder's great-grandson.

Opposition flared up. Certain gentry of the
county headed by the Corbets, of Acton Reynald,
petitioned the Heralds' College against admitting
Daniel's contention, saying that he had no right to
claim descent from one of the West Salop families,
that he was but a yeoman, and that he used to go off
to his farm with his basket on his shoulder like a
workingman.[2] Daniel indeed had come up in the
world since his connection with the Marquess of
Winchester. But the Heralds admitted the steps in
the pedigree going up to 1300. In Clive, at all
events, Daniel was to stand supreme.

How far beyond his pretentious father in the
country was Will Wycherley to climb in town? It
was not yet a question. In five years of living in
France he had certainly acquired more gentility than
could be proved in five generations of Wycherleys.
His manners were sustaining him well. He was now

[1] Harleian, XXVIII–XXIX, 500.
[2] Documents in Heralds' College; private information.

reaching a point where he was beginning to read men, not books. No one could live in London in the early years of the Restoration and avoid the brilliant throng in Covent Garden. That meant that one quickly ambled on to the theatres, for the court itself lived more in Drury Lane than in Whitehall. A new theatre was licensed in Portugal Row, Lincoln's Inn Fields. It came to be known as the Duke's Playhouse, and was managed by Sir William Davenant, the poet laureate. But the theatrical event of the time was the opening in 1663 of the King's house, in Drury Lane, which was dazzlingly lighted with thousands of wax candles on cressets, and which included in its company of players Joe Haynes, Wycherley's fellow Oxonian, as low comedian, and Nell Gwyn, who in 1650 had been born in a coalyard in the same street.[1] Thomas Killigrew, the court wit, was named manager. Between these two theatres Wycherley probably caught the fancy of an outlet for his satires on contemporary society, and though he did not produce a play until 1671, he admitted to his friends that he began writing dramatic compositions in the early sixties.

Young men and young noblemen who had gone to France in the wake of the King, or like Wycherley in order to find a schoolmaster suitable for patricians, now set the mode in the prodigal society of

[1] Cunningham, 2; Pepys, May 8; Pinto, 88–89.

Covent Garden. Of these repatriates, every one had
a hundred imitators, who were evolving into the
type called 'town-gallant,' fit stuff for vigilant tyros
in playwriting to ridicule. Whether they were
drinking laced coffee and sillibubs at Oxford Kate's,
or lounging in the perfumers' shops in the New Exchange, Wycherley could not avoid moving amidst
these pretenders, to a considerably greater degree
than he moved amidst his law books. A pamphlet of
the period sketched the kind, and as Wycherley
circulated around knots of them, this is what he saw,
heard, and turned over in his shaping intellect:

'A town-gallant is a bundle of vanity, composed
of ignorance and pride, folly and debauchery. . . .
A spawn of gentility, that inherits only the vices of
his ancestors. . . . His breeding was under the
wing of a too indulgent mother, who took a world
of pains to make him a fool. . . . He staid at the
University just long enough to commence drunkard
. . . for learning he says is pedantry, unbecoming a
gentleman. . . .

'His first care is his dress, and next his body, and
in the fitting these two together consists his soul and
all its faculties. . . . All his talk is rhodomontado
and bounce, calling a nobleman Jack as familiarly as
his foot-boy, and seldom naming a lord without
adding 'My cozen' . . . He confers titles of honour on all his shabby companions to create himself

the greater esteem with his landlady. . . . 'Twas he brought "I beg your diversion" into fashion, and may have a patent for the sole use of that noble compliment "Let me be damned, and my body be made a gridiron to broil my soul on, if I do not, madam, love you confoundedly."

'Till noon he lies abed, to digest his overnight's debauch, and then having dressed himself, and paid half an hour's adoration to his own sweet image in the looking-glass, he trails along the streets, observing who observes him, to the French ordinary. . . . After this, the coach is called to hurry him to the playhouse, where he advances into the middle of the pit, struts about a while, to render his good parts conspicuous, pulls out his comb, careens his wig, and kisses the orange wench. Then he gravely sits down and falls half asleep. . . .

'However, when the play is done he picks up a miss, and pinching her fingers, looks most abominably languishing and whispers, "Damn me, madam, if you were but sensible of the passion I have for you, and of the flames which your irresistible charms have kindled in my breast, you would be merciful and honour me with your angelical company to take a draught of love's posset at next tavern."

'When he and his fellow gallants vouchsafe to ramble homewards, about one or two o'clock in the morning, they set up the dreadful sa! fa! more

dangerous than an Indian running amuck. In these
heroick humours hath many a watchman had his
horns battered about his ears. . . . This is the bell-
wether of gallantry whom our younger fry of gentlemen admire for a hero. . . . Of himself he is a
painted butterfly.'[1]

It is difficult to think that Daniel Wycherley,
knowing his son to be surrounded by these 'apes and
echoes of men,' would lose an opportunity, if it
came, to remove William to a scene more suggestive
of work, and of a future more substantial. From the
'Memoirs of Ann Lady Fanshawe,' who at this
period twice mentions a 'Mr. Wycherly' on the staff
of her husband, Sir Richard Fanshawe, ambassador
of Charles II to the court of Spain, one is tempted
to believe that Daniel did push forward to such an
office a young man so eminently qualified for it as
the protégé of Julie d'Angennes.

Sir Richard and his party left London on January
31, 1664, for Madrid. The journey, which they
made overland, was so prolonged by accidents and
by diplomatic delays that the travellers did not arrive at their embassy until June 8. Ten days later,
when the ambassador and his suite went to present
themselves to King Philip IV for their first audience, Lady Fanshawe noted in her memoirs:

[1] Character of a Town-Gallant, 1680. But such 'gallants' were
notorious early in the reign of Charles II.

'My husband about 11 of the clock set forth out
of his lodgings thus: first went all those gentlemen
of the town and palace that came to accompany my
husband; then went twenty footmen all in new
liveries of the same colour we used to give, which
is a dark green cloth, with a frost upon green lace.
Then went all my husband's gentlemen, and next
before himself his camarados, two and two:

> 'Mr. Wycherly, Mr. Levine,
> Mr. Godolphin, Sir Edward Turnor,
> Sir Andrew King, Sir Benjamin Wright,
> Mr. Newport, Mr. Bertie.'

The next entry of importance by Lady Fanshawe
is that all of these members of the Ambassador's staff
except two, besides two others not previously named,
returned home in the following year:

'Upon Thursday the 19th of February (1665)
went from us to England Mr. Charles Bertie, Mr.
Francis Newport, Sir Andrew King, Sir Edward
Turnor, Mr. Francis Godolphin, Mr. Wycherly,
Mr. Hatton, Mr. Smythe, with all their servants.'

The evidence that 'Mr. Wycherly' was William
Wycherley of Clive Hall is negative rather than
positive: it can be said mainly that it is not known
that young Wycherley was elsewhere in the year
1664. There is not even a rumour or a legend that
he was then in England. Neither any relative, nor

any other family of the name (which seems confined to Shropshire) appears in the late seventeenth century of enough prominence to have been in the diplomatic service. But Will Wycherley had every qualification for a young attaché in Spain. French, a language much more useful in Spain than English, he spoke like one to the accent born. He had gained in France, in a locality not far from the Spanish frontier, five years of extraordinary training as a courtier. He was no stranger to Spanish statecraft, for he had lived long on the highway of Franco-Spanish intrigue. There were indeed few young Englishmen so fit for the post.

For more than three years Wycherley had been reading law, lightly, but enough to recommend him. Daniel would observe that his son was not yet supporting himself, but in an embassy would have both a salary and expenses paid. Daniel had been a steadfast Royalist; he deserved recognition and would not hesitate to ask for it. As for Will Wycherley himself, would not a young Templar of the time welcome as a holiday such a chance, go to the country offered, satisfy his curiosity, see no profit in remaining indefinitely, and in a few months return home precisely as most of the staff of Sir Richard Fanshawe did?[1]

[1] Most of these points were kindly suggested to me in one of my conversations with G. Thorn-Drury, Esq., K. C.

On the other hand one would think that if Wycherley passed a whole year in Spain some allusion at least to so memorable an event would have found record in the stories of his life.[1] But for that matter one might cite a dozen single years or half-years here and there in Wycherley's abundant and long career, years assuredly not void, in which there are no authentic incidents recorded. For example, Wycherley's visit to Holland went unregarded, and it is known only by his having written a poem in that country. Such happenings were simply forgotten, left untold by Wycherley himself, or neglected by his early biographers. In a later chapter I shall need to refer again to this question of Wycherley and Spain. It is a speculation which seems not altogether unreasonable.

Early in 1665 frequenters of the Piazza in Covent Garden were roundly entertained by a ballad 'To all you Ladies now at Land,'[2] written at sea during the winter by the Earl of Dorset,[3] when the British fleet was lying in wait for the Dutch and the name of the enemy admiral Opdam was on the lips of all English children as the supreme scourge of the world. Dorset's poem, voicing the laments of ama-

---

[1] However, for Wycherley's 'Song . . . of an English Lover to a Spanish Mistress,' see Summers, III, 228.

[2] Pepys, Jan. 2, 1665.

[3] It is simpler to refer to Buckhurst throughout as Dorset, though he did not succeed to that title until 1677.

teur sailor-gentlemen who had left their hearts behind, was continually sung in the taverns. From the
ships, said Dorset, the men sent in their tears, twice
a day by the tide, because the tide was speedier than
the post.

No argument could have been more persuasive in
gathering in recruits for the King's navy. It became
the fad for nobleman-rakes and gallants to join the
fleet. As Wycherley himself later wrote, 'All gentlemen must pack to sea,' even though they could not
tell a boom from a bowsprit. There were also other
reasons for the exodus: in April the plague broke
out in London; within a few days the theatres were
closed. These contingencies, one as dismal to the
rakes as the other, sent novices to the ships in droves.

The Duke of York sailed against the Dutch in
May. One would not have suspected sleepy-eyed
James the valiant commander of a fleet. His mane
of russet perruque made his face resemble an almond
blanched in its shell, and with his long hands, which
seemed always to dangle listlessly, he played a guitar, as doleful almond-faced men often do. But the
Duke was a man of action, methodical, courageous,
arrogant, and magnetic in his leadership when a
fight was in the wind. He drew to his following bold
gallants whose ignorance of seamanship was bliss.

Among them was Dorset, who, after a furlough,
sailed again with the Duke. Dorset was one of the

'confident young men' whom King Charles included
in the Circle of Wits he had assembled about him.[1]
Dorset was called 'the finest gentleman of the court.'
He was considered the best bred man of the age.
Even now, before he was thirty, he stood forth in
Whitehall as its ablest judge of painting, sculpture,
architecture, and acting. He was lazy and good-
natured, but phlegmatic until he was in wine; then
he sometimes looked as if about to roar with laughter. But he seldom did. He was a sort of moon-faced
Lucullus who grew fat from the colossal dinner parties he gave, where he alone was a guest because he
made all his guests feel themselves hosts. Some one
prescribed Nell Gwyn for his melancholy; he took
her to live in a cottage at Epsom with him. All asked
the judgment of Dorset, and all got his favours.

Another of the 'confident young men' who went
to sea with the Duke in May was the Earl of
Rochester, the man whom the Muses were 'fond to
inspire and ashamed to avow.'[2] Having taken his
M.A. at Wadham College, Oxford, when only
thirteen, Rochester had just put in four years in
France and Italy, and like Wycherley had returned
to England full of tremendous talk about perruques
and how to comb them. His talent was to sit close
and charm. He would raise his under-lids and tell
fibs so honey-laden that women begged for more,

[1] Pinto, 55; D. N. B. (Dorset).   [2] Grammont, 370.

though any woman seen three times begging Rochester quite lost her reputation. Greatest scholar of all the nobility, Rochester made it fashionable to write verse, but in his portrait,[1] to show what he thought of poets, he stood putting the laurel-crown on a monkey. As a sort of motto of the wits he wrote, 'Our sphere of action is life's happiness, And he who thinks beyond thinks like an ass.' And the King pardoned all in Rochester.[2]

Wycherley went to sea and fought against the Dutch, but in a poem which he wrote describing the battle he did not reveal the date. All well considered opinion of biographers[3] holds that it was the fight of 1665. Like Dorset, who had set the fashion of writing sentimental verses from sea to ladies at home, Wycherley in still another effort of his own wrote 'A Letter from Sea, to a Jilting Mistress Ashoar; in Answer to a Letter of Hers, which told Him, He wou'd forget Her at Sea; advising Him, Not to Pursue Danger there, but to return Home, to her Arms, to be safe.' Here again there is no date, but the title of the poem points to its being written on the eve of a battle, and its burden would put it in the same period as Dorset's. It is possible that

---

[1] National Portrait Gallery.   [2] Camb. Hist., VIII.
[3] Perromat, Leigh Hunt, Summers. M. Perromat has remarked to me that if Wycherley left Spain on February 19, and war against the Dutch began on the 22, he sees further reason for believing Wycherley went to this war, because of his connections at the time.

Wycherley at this time first met both Dorset and Rochester.

At any rate the adventurous young landsmen found action before they found their sea-legs. On June 3, off Harwich, the Duke of York engaged Opdam and blew him up. The Dutch admiral and his entire crew perished. Both Dorset and Rochester fought like demons; in the thick of the firing, Rochester carried a message in an open boat from his own ship, commanded by Sir Edward Spragge, to the Duke's.[1] The British destroyed fourteen Dutch frigates and led home captive eighteen more. John Dryden, now at thirty-four coming into national acclaim as a poet, celebrated this memorable day in his 'Annus Mirabilis.'

But the returning heroes did not find their haunts in London any too enlivening. The plague had fastened upon the town and was spreading apace. Whole streets had a Sunday look. Coffins lay stacked in crowded churchyards. Worst of all, for Wycherley and his friends, the playhouses remained shut up, and so they continued for over a year. Then, just as the pestilence seemed about to move on, came the Great Fire. London, mostly a city of wood and plaster, with streets so narrow that they allowed only those on horseback to pass, burned for a square mile, and when the flames had subsided, 89 churches and

[1] Johnson, Life of Rochester; Burnet, 6.

13,000 houses had been laid waste. Sir Christopher Wren was set to rebuild the town in brick.

At the other end of the city Charles resumed court merrily enough. Half the jobbing and half the flirting in London went on in Whitehall. This courtier got a frigate, that a company, this a pardon, that a lease of crown land.[1] Open house was held every day, and scores attended the levees while the King had his black wig combed and his cravat tied. Any one could then walk with him through the Park and feed the ducks. Parliament voted £70,000 for a monument to the King's father. Charles squandered the money on his mistresses, and when Parliament asked for an accounting Charles replied that he had looked everywhere but could not find his father's tomb.[2] Yet Old Rowley did have his moments of reserve: friends pressed him for favours on behalf of their own followers whom he did not like. 'It is strange,' countered Charles, 'that every one of my friends should keep a tame knave.'

Wycherley dawdled at the Inner Temple and wrote bad poems. Mistresses seem to have inspired most of his lines, but no mistress yet drew him very near to the Castalian spring. He drank at the Cock. Daniel Wycherley apparently wished his son to live with some show of elegance, and Daniel could well foot the expense, for out of the fleece of commis-

[1] Macaulay, History, III, *passim*.   [2] Cunningham, 91 ff.

sions he had clipped from selling the Winchester
lands he had bought in 1665 the Barony of Wem,
near Clive, together with the rich manor of Lop-
pington, and these purchases he celebrated by getting himself appointed Justice of the Peace for the
county of Salop.[1] This absorbing business took time.
Daniel, though he had enrolled at the Inner Temple
two years before the Restoration, was not yet called
to the bar, and he was thus hardly in a position
where he could with dignity (he was always reminding himself of his dignity) urge on his son to that
distinction. William for his part was in no hurry.

At the turn of the year 1667 the theatres in London reopened, and the town pulsated again almost as
if to the stimulus of a re-restoration. Wycherley in a
modest way appears to have remarked the new era.
His brother George, eleven years his junior, went up
to Queen's College on New Year's Day, where he
was duly entered as gentleman-commoner. Wycherley, as though memorising the event, donated on
January 4 to the Provost and Fellows a silver cup,
still to be seen amongst the treasures of the college,
and his name is inscribed in the White Book of
Benefactors of Queen's: 'Gulielmus Wicherley So-
cio Commensalis Cantharum Argenteum D. D.'[2]

Lord Rochester began the year (in February)
rather more showily. Finding himself poor in

---

[1] Shropshire Society, 338–9.   [2] Magrath, II, 40 ff.

pocket, but in tongue as rich as ever, he finally persuaded Elizabeth Mallett, the beautiful Somerset-
shire heiress to £2500 a year, to marry him. For two
years he had stormed her heart. Just before the victory over Opdam he had kidnapped her, at night, as
she was driving home with her grandfather from
Whitehall. Mrs. Mallett's two horses were no match
for the coach and six of Rochester, who dashed
alongside like a bandit and snatched away the fair
lady. For this the King sent the Earl to the Tower,
but soon pardoned him; Rochester's pardon from
the heiress, if somewhat delayed, was to him even
more welcome. This marriage,[1] perhaps not unnoticed by Wycherley, set an example to which
every gentleman-rake in London aspired.

Meetings of the wits at the Cock in Bow-street
were revived with all their old swagger. Another of
the 'confident young men,' an ingeniously outrageous Oxonian whom Dorset and Rochester often
drank with there, was Sir Charles Sedley, a dark
chinless little baronet with eyes like Puck and a
waterfall of lace between his black ringlets. To be
fashionable, 'little Sid,' as the rakes hailed him, also
put his wit into verses. They recalled the manner of
Tibullus. 'Too much so,' thought Rochester in
mock-seriousness, and he observed, 'Sedley, that can
with a resistless power impart The loosest wishes to

[1] Pepys, Feb. 4, 1667.

the chastest heart.[1] And a fourth member of the
Circle was 'Easy' Etherege, who had written a play,
but not for his bread, and was therefore welcome.
'Gentle George' like Rochester had married a lady
who could keep his purse full. He was a fair man;
with a great deal of hot rum he clouded his face
but cleared his wit.

One night after a party at Oxford Kate's—it was
long after midnight—Sedley and Dorset flung off
their clothes and ran up and down Bow-street naked,[2]
for an hour, shouting as if they were being chased
by devils. Every few minutes they stopped running
and upbraided timorous passers-by for keeping late
hours. Tiring of this, they beat the watchman, and
rather dented his lantern. A constable arrested them.
But they were friends of the King. They were released. And the Lord Chief Justice clapped the constable into gaol for annoying royal favourites.

'God will not damn a man,' King Charles had
said, 'for a little irregular pleasure.'[3]

In how much of this thumping and roistering did
Wycherley join? He was probably now on the fringe
of the circle of wits, if not quite within it, for like
Etherege, and like other 'confident young men' sea-
soned in France, he was a gentleman-writer, not
compelled to support himself by writing. He com-
fortably knew he was heir to an estate, and his am-

[1] Rochester, 41–2.   [2] Pepys, Oct. 23, 1668.   [3] Cunningham, 107.

bition was merely to live in the fashion of Drury
Lane, with hardly more thought of making his living as a practising barrister than had the Roman
Ovid, ignoring his father and blinking lawbooks in
order to write himself into the circle of Augustus
Cæsar. There is no certain light on the doings of
Wycherley in this year, 1668, except that he sat for
his portrait to Peter Lely, who as a rule painted men
of some standing. What may have drawn Wycherley
to Lely's studio was the news that the Duke of York
had requested this artist[1] to do portraits of all the
commanders in the sea-fight against Opdam. It was
a long task; more than a year went by and still Lely
did not have the heads done. Wycherley as a gentleman of the navy if not as a figure of prominence in
London may have followed the crowd to Lely's. The
likeness proved to be one of the court painter's finest
achievements; Wycherley with his auburn perruque
tumbling upon his shoulders, and his great all-seeing
eyes 'not unvain of his own handsomeness.' He wore
his Templar's gown, deep brown, which he took care
to make inconspicuous by a fancy cravat of light
blue. He was at once the perfect gallant of the age.

In February, Etherege had produced his second
play, 'She Would if She Could,' at the Duke's Theatre. It was not a pronounced success. At the opening,
Dorset and Sedley had sat with their dramatist

[1] Pepys, July 18, 1666.

57

friend in the pit, and 'little Sid' no doubt spared 'gentle George' the disparaging comments which it was his delight to make in 'Fop corner' at almost every play. There, where the exquisites and beau-critics foregathered, Sedley with agonised face and squirms would criticise aloud the words and enunciation of the actors, the dullness of the playwright, and the feebleness of the action. He did this always with copious wit and point, and not a few of the audience chose to sit near Sedley in order to beguile the tedium of the play.[1] Wycherley, noticing these fireworks in Fop corner to a nicety, came to hit off Sedley and Sedley's imitators in his writing with merciless accuracy:

'Gad, I go to a play as to a country treat,' says Sparkish, 'I carry my own wine to one and my own wit to t'other, or else I am sure I should not be merry at either. And the reason why we are so often louder than the players is because we think we speak more wit, and so become the poet's rivals in his audience: for to tell you the truth, we hate the silly rogues; nay, so much that we find fault even with their bawdy upon the stage, whilst we talk nothing else in the pit as loud.'

Later in the year Sedley, attempting to improve upon the flat plays he railed against, brought forth at the King's Theatre a comedy of his own, 'Mul-

[1] Pepys, Feb. 18, 1667; Pinto, 86, 106.

berry Garden,' with the scene laid in the rude and pretty wilderness now occupied by Buckingham Palace. The play flickered with a few Sedleyan epigrams, but there were not enough to please the King, though he had called Sedley 'Apollo's viceroy.'[1] The town went away unimpressed, all except Wycherley, perhaps. He profited by both Etherege[2] and Sedley, but in 'Mulberry Garden' he seemed to have taken note in particular of the setting, and he went back to his chambers and sat down to write. For the moment he pushed aside all tinkering with poems. He had found his work.

Wycherley called his first play 'Love in a Wood; or, St. James's Park.' It is not known how long he took to write, rewrite, and polish it. But he transcribed what his own eyes and ears had told him in his saunterings between the Inner Temple and Covent Garden and Pall Mall for ten years, making the play in five acts and twenty-one scenes, with only two scenes in the Park, though with the final one in Mulberry Garden. This ending was aptly turned, because after a play the audiences in great part always resorted to Mulberry Garden for cheesecakes and Rhenish. He dwelt on the theme that marriage and wit are incompatible, the doctrine in which he had been immersed when as little more than a boy he

[1] Pinto, 56.

[2] Wycherley's verses to Etherege (Summers, IV, 227) suggest this friendship, but do not reveal how early it began.

had sat under the spell of Julie d'Angennes and the Précieuses. The character 'Dapperwit,' 'a brisk, conceited, half-witted fellow of the town,' Wycherley put forth as a wit because the man objected to marriage, and later, to Dapperwit's confusion, as unfit for marriage because he was a wit.

Wycherley was fortunate in being able to assemble a lively and popular cast for his first bow in Drury Lane.[1] The company included two of the most gifted actors of the day, Charles Hart and Michael Mohun. Hart, first lover of Nell Gwyn, was the grand-nephew of Shakespeare, and rival of the great Betterton. He was perfect in 'gay gentleman' parts, which he rehearsed to the last syllable. Mohun, who played Dapperwit, was the foremost Iago in the Restoration theatre. There were also Lacy, the Tyrone Power of his time, and Wintershall, who had triumphed as Henry IV and Master Slender. But the one calculated to arouse the playgoers was Mrs. Knipp, as Lady Flippant, the 'merry jade' of Pepys, 'the most excellent mad-humoured thing, and sings the noblest that ever I hear in my life.' Wycherley wisely wrote her a song, 'A Spouse I do Hate,' for the end of the first act, a rather crucial juncture.

It is not difficult to call up the scene in the King's Theatre, Drury Lane, on a certain spring afternoon in 1671. By half-past two the pit, a great horseshoe

[1] Summers, I, 24 ff; Genest, I, 134; Doran, 69, 71, 100.

round the stage, must have begun to fill. Lesser gallants in buskins and laces were sauntering in, twitching their gloves off, and ignoring all lest they be ignored; here one chucked the chin of a girl selling oranges, there one arranged himself and his sword on the backless seats. The orchestra of 'nine or ten fiddles'[1] struck up a tepid ballad-tune. Then the beaux esprits, no doubt including Sedley and Dorset, Etherege and Rochester, perhaps the Duke of Buckingham and even the King himself, with their gay ladies whose acre of diamonds twinkled to the candles overhead, appeared in the first tier and took benches. Where was Wycherley? He was an unobtrusive man. One does not picture him thrusting himself in with the wits, to whom he was not yet familiar, but rather trying to lull his nerves in the shadows behind the last row, for at three o'clock his career as a dramatist, as a poet, as a sharer in renown, as anything, was in its birth-pangs.

What then of the first performance of 'Love in a Wood'? It won London.[2] The audience may well have surrendered to the satire in a swift scene of the third act, when Dapperwit, brazenly attempting to sell his mistress Lucy to Ranger, a young gallant of the town, was repudiated by both the rascally girl and her rascally mother:

MRS. CROSSBITE. What, have you mortgaged

[1] Pinto, 107.   [2] Perromat, 29.

my daughter to that gentleman; and now would offer me a snip to join in the security!

DAPPERWIT (*aside*). She overheard me talk of a bargain; 'twas unlucky. (*Aloud*) Your wrath is grounded upon a mistake: Miss Lucy herself shall be judge; call her out, pray . . .

(*Enter* LUCY, *holding down her head.*)

DAP. Your servant, dearest miss. . . . Can you have the heart to say you will nevermore break a cheesecake with me at New Spring Garden, the Neat-house, or Chelsea? nevermore sit in my lap at a new play? nevermore wear a suit of knots of my choice? and last of all, nevermore pass away an afternoon with me again in the Green Garret?—do not forget the Green Garret.

LUCY. I wish I had never seen the Green Garret! Damn the Green Garret!

DAP. Damn the Green Garret!—You are strangely altered!

LUCY. 'Tis you are altered.

DAP. You have refused Colby's Mulberry-garden, and the French houses, for the Green Garret; and a little something in the Green Garret pleased you more than the best treat the other places could yield; and you can of a sudden quit the Green Garret?

LUCY. Since you have a design to pawn me for the rent, 'tis time to remove my goods.

Dap. Thou art extremely mistaken.

Lucy. Besides I have heard strange things of you this morning.

Dap. What things?

Lucy. I blush to speak 'em.

Dap. I know my innocence, therefore take my charge as a favour. What have I done?

Lucy. Then know, vile wit, my mother has confessed just now thou wert false to me, to her too certain knowledge; and thou hast forced even her to be false to me too.

Dap. Faults in drink, Lucy, when we are not ourselves, should not condemn us.

Lucy. And now to let me out to hire, like a hackney!—I tell you my own dear mother shall bargain for me no more; there are as little as I can bargain for themselves nowadays, as well as properer women.

Mrs. Crossbite. Whispering all this while!—Beware of his snares again: come away, child.

Dap. Sweet, dear miss——

Lucy. Bargain for me!—you have reckoned without your hostess, as they say. Bargain for me! Bargain for me! (*exit.*)

Dap. I must return, then, to treat with you.

Mrs. Crossbite. Treat me no treatings, but take a word for all. You shall no more dishonour my daughter, nor molest my lodgings, as you have done at all hours. . . .

RANGER. Here, will you have my comb again, Dapperwit?

DAP. A pox! I think women take inconstancy from me worse than from any man breathing.

So Wycherley filtered a moral out of immorality.

And he raised on his gaff all the strange fish hatched by the Restoration, as when Lydia, the mistress of Ranger, asked Dapperwit to describe the varieties of town wits to her:

DAP. First, your court-wit is a fashionable, insinuating, flattering, cringing, grimacing fellow— and has wit enough to solicit a suit of love; and if he fail, he has malice enough to ruin the woman with a dull lampoon: but he rails still at the man who is absent, for you must know all wits rail; and his wit properly lies in combing perruques, matching ribbons, and being severe, as they call it, upon other people's clothes.

LYD. Now, what is the coffee-wit?

DAP. He is a lying, censorious, gossiping, quibbling wretch, and sets people together by the ears over that sober drink, coffee: for he is a wit, as he is a commentator, upon the *Gazette;* and he rails at the pirates of Algier, the Grand Signior of Constantinople, and the Christian Grand Signior.

LYD. What kind of man is your poll-wit?

DAP. He is a fidgeting, busy, dogmatical, hot-headed fop, that speaks always in sentences and proverbs (as other in similitudes), and he rails perpetually against the present government. His wit lies in projects and monopolies, and penning speeches for young parliament men.

LYD. But what is your chamber-wit, or scribble-wit?

DAP. He is a poring, melancholy, modest sot, ashamed of the world: he searches all the records of wit, to compile a breviate of them for the use of players, printers, booksellers, and sometimes cooks, tobacco-men; he employs his railing against the ignorance of the age, and all that have more money than he.

LYD. Now your last.

DAP. Your judge-wit, or critic, is all these together, and yet has the wit to be none of them: he can think, speak, write, as well as the rest, but scorns (himself a judge) to be judged by posterity: he rails at all the other classes of wits, and his wit lies in damning all but himself:—he is your true wit.

Gallants in the pit then knew that at last there had come amongst them a dramatist who had sailed into all the creeks and coves of their swampy hearts. They saw the play through.

By sundown Wycherley walked out of the King's
Theatre with the laurels of a satirist. A thousand
throbs were great within his bosom. Wits of the
Court sought him out. Wits of the town circled
round him. Rochester and Sedley gave him coast-
ing welcome to their band, while Dryden saw
Wycherley his rugged rival, and was glad of it.

News of the success of 'Love in a Wood' over-
spread London. To the King's box for one of the
first performances came a lady who caused a click
of lorgnettes. Her pearls, which she was in the habit
of wearing to the theatre, were worth forty thousand pounds, but what audiences thought of as their
glances congealed into stares was—her power. It
was incalculable. This lady, the most discussed
beauty in all England, was Barbara Villiers, Duchess
of Cleveland.

CHAPTER III

THE LADY OF THE CHARIOT

At Hampton Court, in the long gallery of the Court Beauties of the Restoration, hangs the portrait of a lady whose first child had three fathers: a fool, an Earl, and a King. The King acknowledged the child, the Earl was the image of it, and the fool claimed it. The fool was the husband: perfect, as fools go.

The portrait is of a tall sweeping willow of a woman, with a face in the classic cast, but with arms of a peasant's wife, arms that could push boulders aside. She has blue eyes, up at the corners, and the lower lids capable of instant scorn. Tangles of dark red hair reach down to her waist. She is in the costume of Bellona, the goddess of war, but like Homer's goddesses she is first of all a woman, for she is going to war in her big pearl earrings and with a curl on her forehead. Martial enough the rest: a rearing head-dress of ostrich feathers, a spear in one hand, and at the other a shield. The Amazons would have given her an immediate brigade. Impudent, positive, and vanquishing is this lady, as if she would elbow through triple doors of brass, as if she possessed such

midnight vigour as could light lamps to outburn
Canopus, as if she would cap the mockery in her
laugh with an oath like a bomb. Peter Lely has
painted her with motion and breeze, singing, fresh,
the very figurehead of an argosy breasting the waves.
Yet Barbara Villiers was more than a figurehead on
the ship of state of England.

She was the daughter of William, second Viscount Grandison, who when Barbara was three years
old died of a ball which struck him at the siege of
Bristol. She grew up in the country, poor, and as a
young girl came wide-eyed and open-mouthed to
London, in a plain ill-fitting country dress, to live
with her stepfather, the Earl of Anglesea.[1] In his
house, when she was sixteen, Barbara found her first
lover, Philip Stanhope, Earl of Chesterfield. He
was well-beloved. After three years, though Barbara had married a Mr. Palmer, Chesterfield was
still her lover. He did not give way until the eve of
the Restoration, when the King looked in and took
for himself the young woman with the red hair.
Chesterfield retreated with a bow, while Palmer was
soothed with the earldom of Castlemaine.

King Charles had a child by the Countess every
year for six years; three of the children were sons,
and for each their mother imperiously exacted a
dukedom.[2] Castlemaine had the first-born son bap-

[1] Boyer, 'History,' 112 ff. [2] Grammont, 443.

tized by a priest. Barbara, raging like a tigress, snatched the baby away to Hampton Court and re-christened him in the Church of England; then she promptly deserted her husband.[1] But in the following year the Countess herself became a Catholic. The conversion was due to no great upheaval of her soul.

The King then began to favour Frances Stewart, a captain's daughter, who was perhaps the prettiest of the ladies-in-waiting. Women said she was very pretty, fanned themselves, and looked the other way. She was tall and straight, wore her hair flat with thin curls in front, danced well, twittered better French than English, and dressed as one only can who learns how in France when young. But her face, like the face of a cinema star, was a painted desert. She was childish. She laughed at everything. She spent her time building card castles and playing blind man's buff.[2] In an evening gown she stood for her portrait holding a bow and arrow, in a forest, trying to look like a naughty girl caught poaching. Yet her leg was (and is) the model for Britannia on the reverse of the English penny, and the King loved her above all women. The Queen, Barbara, and Frances all insisted on being the first to ride in Hyde Park in a sumptuous French calash which had been presented to Charles. 'La Belle Stewart' prevailed. She had

[1] D. N. B. (Villiers).   [2] Grammont, 307 ff.

the strength of childlike guilelessness, and by means of it, for a time, she won.

The Countess of Castlemaine retaliated generously. She plunged into a whirl of amours, befriending successively Sir Charles Berkeley, Colonel James Hamilton, Lord Sandwich, Harry Jermyn of the large head and small legs, Jacob Hall the rope-dancer of Bartholomew Fair (to whom she gave a salary), and several footmen.[1] The King, annoyed, lessened the emphasis on Frances by receiving from his theatre Nell Gwyn. But Nell, whose merry laugh so flooded her face that one saw only the compressed lashes of her eyes,[2] came to Whitehall and mimicked the great Countess; whereupon Barbara matched the King's puppet by annexing to her own list the actor Charles Hart. And in the wind and tempest of her frown she looked about for more, allowing herself to be completely puffed away by the passion of the moment.

As the months wore on the King tried to tame the rampant Countess with gifts. He gave her Berkshire House, St. James's, to live in. By selling offices and exacting rents he swept together £30,000 for her.[3] Barbara took the money to the house of Hortense Mancini, niece of Cardinal Mazarin, who had come to England and set up a salon for gambling and lovemaking. It was a jolly inferno; without

[1] Brett, 275.   [2] Cunningham, 26.   [3] D. N. B. (Villiers).

groans, without fire: perdition made pleasant. Old
St. Evremond—who kept ducks in his bedroom because he said they reanimated his spirits—was at
home there and led the witty conversation. In one
night Barbara lost £25,000,[1] and the gamesters
called her 'Hilaria.'

In 1670 this master-mistress persuaded the King
to create her 'Baroness Nonsuch, of Nonsuch Park,
Surrey, Countess of Southampton and Duchess of
Cleveland in the Peerage of England.' This array
of titles Charles conferred 'in consideration of her
noble descent, her father's death in the service of
the Crown, and by reason of her own personal virtues.' Berkshire House the Duchess now sold, and
on a corner of the land she built Cleveland House.
The perquisites of her new title and property en-
abled her thenceforth to maintain on her pension
roll as many favourites as Charles himself had.

On the morning after she had seen the new play
'Love in a Wood' by the new author in Drury Lane,
and watched a lover of hers, Charles Hart, grace the
cast, the Duchess chanced to go driving in her coach-
and-eight. She took notoriety so easily that it was
her custom to lie back asleep with her mouth open
as she drove through Hyde Park.[2] But on this morning she was sitting up, fully aware of the world.
Her chariot, leaving St. James's, swung into Pall

[1] Grammont, 443.   [2] Leigh Hunt, xi.

Mall, and was spinning briskly along when suddenly
a coach driving in the opposite direction jostled it.[1]
The Duchess recognized the owner, whom someone
had pointed out to her before, as the author of the
new comedy she had just seen. Like a Jack-in-the-
box she thrust half her body out of her chariot and
cried aloud to him:

'You, Wycherley, you're a son of a whore!' At the
same time she burst into a peal of laughter, then
drove on.

The phrase which Barbara had called out was
fresh in her mind; Wycherley in his play had used
it twice in the same scene. But there was another
thing in 'Love in a Wood' which had touched her
to the depths: Mrs. Knipp's song, which was in
praise of harlots, had ended, 'Great wits and great
braves have always a Punk to their mother.' Barbara already saw her own children grown illustrious.

The surprised author also had driven rapidly
away. Should he have done that? To be spoken to
in any fashion by the Duchess of Cleveland was
good fortune.[2] Wycherley quickened to the chance.
His thoughts hit the roofs of palaces. He took it that
the Duchess had called him really a great wit and
a great brave; he resolved to make sure; he ordered
his coachman to drive back and overtake the lady.

[1] Cibber, III, 249.   [2] Leigh Hunt, xi.

As soon as he had drawn flush to the window of her chariot he said:

'Madam, you have been pleased to bestow on me a title which generally belongs to the fortunate. Will your Ladyship be at the play tonight?'

'Well,' replied the Duchess, 'what if I am there?'

'Why, then,' said Wycherley at the top of his gallantry, 'I will be there to wait on your Ladyship, though I disappoint a very fine woman who has made me an assignation.'

'So, you are sure to disappoint a woman who has favoured you, for one who has not?'

'Yes,' he replied swiftly, 'if she who has not favoured me is the finer woman of the two. But he who will be constant to your Ladyship till he can find a finer woman is sure to die your captive.'[1]

Barbara Villiers achieved a blush, not quite crimson, yet a blush. She was still only thirty—the same age as Wycherley—still in all her bloom, still the most sensational beauty known to England. She had heard herself not odiously compared to another woman, and the blandishment so ready on the lips of a brawny gentleman well-combed and well-gloved arrested her wandering emotions.

That night the Duchess went to the King's box in Drury Lane. She took a chair in the first row; in the darkness of the pit she made herself a planet

[1] Dennis, Familiar Letters, 215 ff.

amidst stars; Wycherley must not miss her. That
was the way of Barbara, a prodigy of experienced
innocence. With her, every new love was her first
love. Wycherley sauntered in, edged along to Fops'
Corner, and took a place on a bench directly beneath
the Duchess. Then began a balcony scene without a
ladder; a lowly man who led all his rivals in what
every woman seeks, good looks and wit, set the ear
of a lofty lady tingling with his spoken serenades.
Neither gave any heed to the stage. It was more absorbing for them to talk to each other, about each
other, and for the sake of each other. So Will
Wycherley entertained Barbara Villiers during the
whole course of the play; to her he alone was the
play.

On the next morning, alert to follow up this acquaintance alertly scraped, Wycherley called upon
the Duchess at Cleveland House. For ten years, ever
since the bright day of Julie d'Angennes, this man,
magnetic as he was, had not known the influence of
a woman to bear importantly upon what he said or
did. But at last a successor to Julie had come. A second woman had stepped into his fortunes: her life
and his had picturesquely collided—as lives do. This
morning Barbara and the poet conversed again. Barbara pulled at the latch-string of his affections,
Wycherley bowed her in, and over his slightly
abraded doorsill swept the Duchess, beautiful and

profane. There was no intimacy promised. It was commanded.

Wycherley soon took his place in the galaxy of declared lovers of the Duchess of Cleveland. And a high place it was. By means of it the young dramatist whose career was just spreading its petals was to gain the topmost favour in England. Barbara upon her side was enthralled by her new gallant. But at the moment she was actually simulating fidelity to Charles. How was she to see her new favourite at her pleasure? Where was she to find him without all Whitehall knowing her movements?

At about this time the Court had taken to the amusement of masquerading. The King and Queen and many of their train put on disguises, went into houses unknown, and danced and shouted,[1] rather to the annoyance of wry-necked citizens who had put aside their perruques for the night. Rochester, who was amazingly cunning at masking, was perhaps responsible for making the diversion popular. He had set up as an astrologer on Tower-hill, proclaiming that he tightened loose teeth and made forty-year women look fifteen. Miss Jennings and Miss Price, maids of honour to the Duchess of York, there visited him as orange-girls. Another masking incident was the appearance of the Queen and several duchesses in red petticoats and bodices

[1] Burnet, 168; Grammont, 370 ff.

at a fair in Audley-End. But they had overdressed;
a crowd collected, and the Queen, hastening to her
carriage, had to gallop home.[1]

Now that an occasion presented itself to Barbara,
it is said[2] that disguised as a country maid she went
time and again down Fleet Street to Wycherley's
chambers in the Temple. But unlike the Queen,
there was no overdressing about Barbara Villiers.
She well knew how to wear pattens and a straw hat,
how to tuck a box or a basket under her burly arm.
Not so very many years before she had soberly come
up from the provinces in almost the same costume.

The meetings of Wycherley and his amorous
Duchess could not go on indefinitely without being
remarked upon, for both were now too well known
in Drury Lane and the Mall. But the liaison might
have been kept quiet somewhat longer than it was
if the poet, ecstatic from the compliment paid him,
had not let his exalted spirits get the better of him.
In the autumn of 1671 he published 'Love in a
Wood' as a quarto, with a jibing line from his master, Horace, on the title-page: 'Democritus excludes
sane poets from Helicon,' and he dedicated the play
to the powerful and illustrious lady who had taken
him up, saying:

'. . . I cannot but publicly give your Grace my
humble acknowledgments for the favours I have

[1] Summers, I, 37.
[2] Leigh Hunt, quoting Voltaire (not verifiable).

76

received from you: this, I say, is the poet's gratitude, which, in plain English, is only pride and ambition; and that the world might know your Grace did me the honour to see my play twice together.

'Yet, perhaps, my enviers of your favour will suggest 'twas in Lent, and therefore for your mortification. Then, as a jealous author, I am concerned not to have your Grace's favours lessened, or rather my reputation; and to let them know you were pleased, after that, to command a copy from me of this play: the only way, without beauty and wit, to win a poor poet's heart. . . .

'Madam, take it from me, no man with papers in's hand is more dreadful than a poet; no, not a lawyer with his declarations. Your Grace sure did not consider well what ye did, in sending for my play: you little thought I would have had the confidence to send a dedication too. . . .

'I beseech your Grace have a care for the future . . . since your quiet is so much concerned, and since you have more reason than any to value yourself: for you have that perfection of beauty (without thinking it so) which others of your sex but think they have; that generosity in your actions which others of your quality have only in their promises; that spirit, wit, and judgment, and all other qualifications which fit heroes to command, and would make any but your Grace proud. . . .'

The disclosure of this friendship made a hubbub

in Whitehall.[1] Wycherley had revealed nothing of
the way in which he and the Duchess had met. What
else was in all these 'favours' she had been pleased to
bestow upon him? Courtiers from Covent Garden
to St. James's raised a sage eyebrow, and gave to the
printed words of Wycherley the last brimming measure of interpretation.

This crisis brought the startled young dramatist
across the path of the mighty Duke of Buckingham.
The second Duke, born twelve years before Wycherley, was the richest one of the three or four most
awesome nobles at Court.[2] He had been reared with
the children of Charles the First, had lived in Flor-
ence and Rome like a sovereign prince, and when he
saw fit to vote in the House of Lords he first stuffed
his pocket with twenty proxies. For his impudence
he had three times been flung into the Tower. Still
he was elected Chancellor of Cambridge University.
Though the Duke was a bit stoutish, to see him come
into a room was an event: from boyhood he had ridden so hard, fenced so fiercely, and danced so adroit-
ly that his walk was a miracle of ease and court-
liness.[3] He wore a perruque the colour of a panther,
and was himself as graceful as one. In conversation
he was as winning as Rochester; he was winning
even when he had no desire to win. But he did want

1 Dennis, Familiar Letters, 217.
2 D. N. B. (Buckingham).   3 D. N. B., ibid.

Mary Fairfax, mainly because Chesterfield did also; the Duke talked the lady away from the Earl and then got Cowley, his old classmate in Cambridge, to write his wedding song. Mary, a dowdy round little woman, grew fat; Buckingham then took as mistress the gentle Countess of Shrewsbury, who because she held the Duke's horse while he killed her husband in a duel found herself whispered about as a self-made widow. Saying he would rather be guilty of ill-breeding to a King than a beggar, Buckingham called Charles to his face 'father of his people,' and the King laughed till the walls of Whitehall boomed.[1]

Now the Duke had recently come home from Versailles, whither Charles had sent him to wheedle Louis XIV. Buckingham did. Word came to London that the King of France—in age ten years junior to his guest and in worldliness perhaps five—had been so charmed that he had exchanged pleasantries with the English diplomat twenty times a day.[2] Louis had given him a diamond-studded snuff-box worth a year's ducal income. So fell statecraft under a fusillade of anecdotes.[3] The Duke, again home, thus basked in the highest favour he had ever known— with all except one.

For months there had been smouldering in him

---

[1] Cunningham, 110. [2] D. N. B. (Buckingham).
[3] For a day in the life of Buckingham, see 'Peveril of the Peak,' chap. 28.

a passion for Barbara Villiers. Wherever she withdrew, Buckingham sought her out, entreated her, implored her. The Duchess repulsed him. Of all the nobles who might be called eligible for the favours of Barbara, the adventurous Duke, it appears, was the only one who could make no headway with her. She locked him out of her house. Buckingham was her cousin german, bore her own name, Villiers, and though he jeered at her protest that common blood should be a bar, to the Duchess, evidently, the idea of kinsman as lover was thoroughly distasteful. Barbara in any case had to be discreet. At this period she was trying to prevent knowledge of her love affairs from reaching the King, in whom she had begun to discern a faint neglect of herself, and Charles would discover at once, and denounce, any intrigue with a person of the rank and character of Buckingham.

The Duke fumed, stamped, swore, and raged. He insisted Barbara turned him away merely because she possessed lovers whom she thought superior to him in slimness of waist, in curve of the calf, in 'prettiness.' He resolved to ruin her. He set spies on her exits and her entrances. He would smoke out these rivals of his and dog them without mercy.[1]

A spy brought word that the Duchess was entertaining young Jack Churchill, a popinjay of a boy,

[1] Dennis, Familiar Letters, 217 ff.

who leanly strutted and glistened and tossed his youth about. This stripling by his insinuating reptilian charm and manner had even enticed Barbara into heaping money upon him: she gave him Harry Jermyn's pension and Jacob Hall's salary because she said he combined their graces. Buckingham contrived that the King should surprise Jack Churchill and the Duchess of Cleveland together. The King walked in upon them. It was a case of 'Jack be nimble, Jack be quick, Jack jump over the window-sill.' And he did. But the King merely called after the boy:

'I forgive you, for you do it for your bread.'[1]

Churchill, who was to become first Duke of Marlborough, founded the fortune of his family on this 'bread,' which was a little present of £5,000 from Barbara Villiers.

Still Buckingham went on, brewing venom, concocting blight for his roster of rivals. As soon as he knew who 'the blackguards' were he never let slip an opportunity to name them aloud to all the courtiers who happened to be round him, hoping by this blast to expose the obstinate Duchess. Among others, finally, he named 'handsome Wycherley, a writing fellow, who was not even a sprig from a titled family.[2]

This capsizing news soon came to Wycherley's

[1] D. N. B. (Villiers).   [2] Dennis, ibid., 217.

ear. He took alarm. Sense of the need for action
stung him like a whip. For the tide of his fortune
had started to roll in; it must not crash against the
breakwater of Buckingham. From the Court Wycherley had his expectations, his morsels of fame, his
stairway to independence, and to all the timeless
treasures greatness knows. What if this babble of the
Duke should reach the King?

Will Wycherley hurried to his friends, Rochester
and Sedley, who he knew were two of Buckingham's
intimates. These two gentlemen of the town had by
this time taken the young dramatist into bosom companionship. He was in their eye not solely a poet, but
like themselves was a 'gentleman-writer,' was not
dependent upon scribbling for a livelihood, and was
essential to the fellowship of rakes because in the
taproom at the Cock he was an absolute beam of
light.

Requesting them to remonstrate for him, Wycherley suggested to the Earl and Sir Charles that they
explain to Buckingham what a mischief the courtier
was about to do to one who had not the honour to be
known to him, and who had never offended him.

The noblemen went to the Duke forthwith.

'I do not blame Wycherley!' cried out Buckingham, interrupting them. 'I only accuse my Cousin.'

'Ay, but by rendering him suspected of such an
intrigue,' Rochester replied, 'you are about to ruin

him. That is, your Grace is about to ruin a man with whose conversation you would be pleased above all things.'

Rochester was a gallant to whom no one, however incensed, could help listening. And he was close to the heart of Buckingham. The two had often drawn on their drinking buskins and disappeared into the country for a harvest of fun; once they had rented an inn, posed as its landlords, and made free with the women guests.[1] 'Little Sid,' equally Buckingham's lieutenant of leisure, with his sudden wit and his odes to barmaids, was eloquent in the defense of his friend. Both of the rakes now so praised the manners of Wycherley, and so praised the spell his discursive talents cast, that the Duke—it must be said for him that he loved wit as vehemently as ever he loved women—smote the table with his brown fist and swore that Wycherley must be brought at once to sup with him. The persuasive harangue of the two intercessors drove out of his mind his lust for Barbara: the Duke was like a child whose clamour for sweets is stilled by giving him a jumping-jack.

Rochester and Sedley straightway arranged for the meeting, and it was no more than three nights later that they presented their poet-friend at the table of Buckingham. At this odd gathering of a duke, an earl, a baronet, and a commoner, brawny

[1] D. N. B.

Wycherley looked a nobleman every inch. There was little in the bearing of any of them to betray degrees of rank: it was a party of four swordsmen of France. After supper, Wycherley, knowing his future security might hinge upon his present conduct, gave free rein to all the vigour of his wit and fancy, and he drew this hardened audience to the edges of their chairs. The Duke was charmed, and cried out in a transport:

'By God! My cousin Cleveland is in the right of it!'[1]

From that moment Buckingham jettisoned rivalry, and made of Will Wycherley a friend. And the attachment was no loss to the Duke. Wycherley on his part was a king of friends, for such was his honourable temper that he charged to their defense if he heard them belittled, whether they were living or dead, whether they were right or wrong, whether their fortunes were prosperous or swept away.

Buckingham gave Wycherley early and substantial proofs of his affection and regard. Not long before their meeting the Duke had been made Master of Horse to the King. He appointed the poet one of his equerries. The Duke was also colonel of a regiment of foot. He made Wycherley a Captain-lieutenant in his own company,[2] and resigned to him at the same time his own pay as Captain and all other

[1] Dennis, Familiar Letters, 217 ff.   [2] Dalton, I, 120.

advantages derivable from the rank. Wycherley knew no more of soldiering than he could have learned on the stage in Drury Lane, but he was at least as much at ease on the drill-ground as aboard a battleship. Many of his companions in arms were equally awkward with guns and spurs. In the day of Charles II no one lost sleep over that.

The poet turned warrior aroused however some passing attention in London. 'I remember that about that time,' wrote John Dennis, 'I who was come up from the University to see my friends in town happened to be one night at the Fountain Tavern in the Strand with the late Dr. Duke, David Logger the painter, and Mr. Wilson, of whom Otway has made honourable mention in Tonson's first Miscellany, and that after supper we drank Mr. Wycherley's health by the name of Captain Wycherley.'[1]

Friends, as soon as town talk about 'Love in a Wood' began to wane, had urged the new dramatist to write another comedy. The excitement of the rather dizzy companionship of a Duchess, and then of a Duke, had interfered a little with further writing, but in the winter following his début at the King's Theatre Wycherley did resume work, on a second play. He finished it, and was on the point of putting it into rehearsal with the same company, headed by Charles Hart, when the theatre took fire.

[1] Familiar Letters, 220.

A news-letter (27 January 1672) thus reported the damage: 'A fire at the King's playhouse between 7 and 8 o'clock on Thursday evening last, which half burned down the house and all their scenes and wardrobe; and all the houses from the Rose Tavern in Russell Street on that side of the way of Drury Lane are burned and blown up, with many in Vinegar Yard; £20,000 damage. The fire began under the stairs where Orange Moll keeps her fruit. Bell the player was blown up.'[1]

Richard Bell, an actor from boyhood, had won prominence in Shakespearean parts, especially as Cæsar. And it more concerned Wycherley that Bell had ably created the character of Vincent, 'a young gentleman of the town,' in Wycherley's first play. It was reasonable to expect that Bell could have repeated his success in another Wycherley part; his death was a blow.

This loss of their theatre was a discouraging setback to the King's company. Their rivals, the Duke's players, only a few months before had moved into a new house, the Dorset Garden Theatre near Salisbury Court, and had opened brilliantly with Dryden's popular 'Sir Martin Mar-all.' The only chance now left for Hart and his fellow-players was to take the old theatre in Lincoln's Inn Fields which the Duke's company had vacated. But Hart's losses in

[1] Summers, I, 39.

costumes, settings, and properties were so heavy that he could not meet the expense of fitting out a new play; he could only go on in makeshift fashion with the old ones.

Wycherley had 'The Gentleman Dancing-Master' ready. Not wishing to wait indefinitely for Hart to recruit finances, though he preferred Hart as a leading actor, the poet gave his manuscript to the Dorset Garden company for spring production, 1672. It was the third play in the new house, which was under the direction of the widow of Sir William Davenant. Before the curtain, in a 'Prologue to the City,' Wycherley had an actor say that the author had deserted the other end of the town (Lincoln's Inn Fields) in order 'to throw himself on a substantial pit.'

But the pit which paid to see 'The Gentleman Dancing-Master' did not prove substantial enough to support such a comedy for more than six performances. Wycherley felt the shoots of his ambition rudely clipped off. Indifference, and nothing more, answered the exertions of the actors. Who cared that the author was the man who had written 'Love in a Wood'? Lady Davenant, a lady nothing if not firm, whisked the play aside to make room for other new ones.

Wycherley had been somewhat hurried in writing his second piece; he had made it more or less to

order, as Shakespeare wrote 'Merry Wives'; he had
made it in response to importuning of friends.[1] In
consequence, it lacked the trim and smart weavings
of plot which had stirred applause for 'Love in a
Wood.' But Wycherley hurried to advantage in one
respect: he wrote this time seven scenes instead of
twenty-one. The audience in Dorset Garden no
doubt liked the flavour of this simplicity, but what
they hungered for in a play was novelty. It was not
there. The town had still in mind a revival of Howard's comedy 'The English Mounsieur,' in which
the leading character was the same type as Monsieur
de Paris in the 'Dancing-Master.' Wycherley described him as 'a rich city heir newly returned from
Paris, and mightily affected with the French language and fashions.' But for all the author's accurate
knowledge of France, for all his expertness in drawing fops with Continental frills, the pit sat unre-
freshed.

In the cast were a father who had lived in Spain,
his daughter just out of a Hackney boarding-school,
his crabbed sister as watch-dog for the daughter, his
nephew (the man from Paris), two ladies of leisure,
and two town-gallants. One might say add spice and
slips of citron, stir, and you have a cake. A cake there
was, but it sank in the middle. The only develop-
ment in the pot was that the daughter refused the

[1] Summers, I, 39.

heir and married a gallant (who posed as the dancer), while the heir refused the daughter and married a light lady.

Nevertheless in such ordinary situations the audience often saw through a looking-glass. The play was true. For example: as has been intimated, Wycherley could hardly fail to have experienced something during this winter of the London fad of masquerading. In the 'Dancing-Master' he once more used his own adventures, his eye squarely upon what was happening round him both in the theatre and after the play:

'I am for going into the throng of temptations,' said Hippolita, the daughter, . . . 'to tattle to your men under a vizard in the playhouses, and meet 'em at night in masquerade.'

'There I do believe you again,' objected her aunt. 'I know you would be masquerading: but worse would come on't, as it has done to others who have been in a masquerade, and are now virgins but in masquerade, and will not be their own women again as long as they live. The children of this age must be wise children indeed if they know their fathers, since their mothers themselves cannot inform 'em! O, the fatal liberty of this masquerading age! When I was a young woman——'

'Come, come,' interrupted Hippolita, 'do not blaspheme this masquerading age, like an ill-bred

city dame whose husband has been turned out of the
Temple or Lincoln's Inn upon a masquerading
night. By what I've heard 'tis a pleasant, well-bred,
complaisant, free, frolic, good-natured age: and if
you do not like it, leave it to us that do.'

For this play Wycherley borrowed from Calde-
ron's 'El Maestro de Danzar' only three incidents,[1]
which touched merely upon the dancing lessons
which the young gallant gave to Hippolita. Why did
he need no more? If he did live a year in Spain with
the British Ambassador he naturally then learned
far more of the Spanish people and mannerisms than
the reading of any number of Spanish plays would
have given him. When he came to characterise
Spaniards he wrote like one who perhaps from actual
contact had known the Spanish people. Don Diego,
the father, assisted by his blackamoor lackey, tried
to give dancing lessons to his nephew, and said:

'Be a Spaniard like me, and ne'er think people
laugh at you: there never was a Spaniard that
thought any one laughed at him. But what! Do you
laugh at a golilla, baggage?—Come, sirrah black,
now do you teach him to walk with the verdadero
gesto, gracia, and gravidad of a true Castilian.'

And the Blackamoor: What! a Spaniard, and
laugh aloud! No, if you laugh, thus only—so—
Now your salutation in the street, as you pass by your

---

[1] Perromat, 147, examines these borrowings in detail.

acquaintance; look you, thus—if to a woman, thus
—putting your hand upon your heart; if to a man,
thus, with a nod—so—but frown a little more,
frown!—but if to a woman you would be very
ceremonious to, thus—so—your neck nearer your
shoulder—so— Now, if you would speak contemp-
tibly of any man, or thing, do thus with your hand
—so—and shrug up your shoulders till they hide
your ears.'

'The Gentleman Dancing-Master' could hardly
have failed because of ill acting if Genest, in his account of the English stage, supposes correctly that
the parts of Don Diego and Monsieur de Paris were
taken by Edward Angel and James Nokes. These
men were two of the drollest comic actors of the day.
Nokes in particular was an astonishing mimic of the
French, and only a few months before had put the
King 'to excessive laughter'[1] in the same sort of part:
Sir Arthur Addle in Caryl's 'Sir Salomon.' 'The ridiculous solemnity of his features was enough,' says
Doran,[2] 'to have set a whole bench of bishops into a
titter . . . when he debated any matter by himself
he would shut up his mouth with a dumb studious
pout, and roll his full eye . . . the moment he
spoke, the settled seriousness of his features was utterly discharged, and a dry, drawling, or laughing
levity took full possession of him.' Monsieur de

[1] Summers, I, 45.   [2] p. 76.

Paris, in a scene with Hippolita, hit off both Angel
and Nokes by name as the men who gave the best
lessons in foolery in England. These bits would have
been rather pointless unless Nokes and Angel were
themselves acting in the play.

At the end of the year Wycherley published his
second comedy without a dedication, but again with
a Horatian line, from the Satires, on the title-page:
''Tis not sufficient to make the hearer laugh aloud,
although there is a certain merit even in this.' The
line seemed to carry a suggestion that Wycherley
chose it as an epitaph for the play, marking an end,
as he may have feared, to the stage life of the 'Dancing-Master.'

While Wycherley was making a name with men
of froth, his father moved ahead with men of sub-
stance. Relations between father and son at this time
appear to have been rather torpid. Daniel could not
be expected to approve Will Wycherley's neglect of
gainful law for profitless playwriting; unlike docile
George, the second son, who had plodded through
Queen's College to a degree in divinity and in this
year 1672 subsided into a vicarage in Wem,[1] William
was a rebel, steeped in the sins of London. The lord
of the manor of Clive, whatever his feelings were
towards his heir, possibly was now too busy collecting lawsuits to express concern. After twelve years

[1] Shropshire Society, 340.

of membership in the Inner Temple—Daniel believed that all things came to those who waited—he had been called to the bar. And now he manœuvred himself into an appointment as teller in the King's Exchequer;[1] his many years of manipulating the funds of the Marquess of Winchester had taught him the ways of finance. Outside his hours devoted to counting up pounds sterling, Daniel sailed the raging seas of litigation. His sense of the dramatic, which he transmitted so cogently to his son, found its theatre in the courtroom.

Still happy in the good graces of Barbara Villiers, Wycherley allowed neither the indifference of his father nor the ill fate of his new play to interfere with his saunterings in and out of the taverns of Covent Garden. He lived without pretence on the plane of the nobility because his life in France had addressed him to it. The Duchess of Cleveland did not relinquish her fondness for him. No woman could. No woman could readily forego a man whose wit was so robustly graceful and whose person was so gracefully robust. And Wycherley had the honest chill of candour combined with the warmth of masculine assertiveness: he could quench a dispute with a jest which made every one laugh away a frown.

Barbara, an anxious and heartsick woman for all her spinning ribaldry, could depend upon such a man

[1] Perromat, 17.

for sincerity of companionship. At Court she could depend upon nobody. There was a time when visits to Whitehall had thrilled her. Will Chiffinch, keeper of the backstairs, used then to admit her, Chiffinch, 'that exquisite critic in beauty and blanc mange,' old maid in face and procuress in mind, holding a lank finger to his lank lips. Then had Barbara tasted the sweets of mystery and supremacy. Now she came insipidly through the front door, and she was free, unhindered, admired; she missed not the romance of the other way, but the strife of it.

But Barbara kept on being covetous with her right hand and prodigal with her left, lavish to her friends and miserly to every one else. As she intrigued incessantly for her children, so she schemed for the advancement of her favourites. She shuddered from the suspicion that her word was being balked, but her name throughout this year, 1672, remained on the list of bedchamber women in Whitehall.[1] Charles was no longer jealous of her lovers: he was now too engrossed with an attachment of his own, Louise de Querouaille, whom he had made Duchess of Portsmouth, and he might well wish Barbara to do as she liked in order that he might avoid her reproaches. The presentation of Wycherley, a poet and a gallant of such persuasive charm, would be certain to raise Barbara Villiers, not

[1] D. N. B. (Villiers).

lower her, in the King's liking. Wycherley in any case was her protégé. She boldly brought him to the notice of the Court.[1]

The success of Wycherley with his sovereign was almost as as immediate as it was with Buckingham. The King, not only witty in himself but on occasion the cause that wit was in other men, offered a spark to which Wycherley responded with a flame. As Lord Lansdowne wrote long after, to a friend to whom he wished to introduce Wycherley, 'Horatian wit will not be wanting when you two meet,' so it was with the King and the poet-lover of Barbara Villiers: the spirit of Augustus and Horace enkindled their conversation. Before many days Wycherley was coming to the private parties of his King.[2]

All who had been properly introduced at Court could go without an express invitation and see Charles dine, sup, dance, gamble, and hear him tell stories; if D'Urfey the song-writer was there, they might see the King leaning on D'Urfey's shoulder and humming songs in doubtful harmony.[3] Or they could go to Inigo Jones' great banqueting-house in the palace, where Tiberio Fiorelli, the renowned 'Scaramouche' to whom Wycherley had paid tribute in his 'Dancing-Master,' was acting with his com-

---

[1] Dalton, Introduction; Gaetschenberger, III, 63; Perromat, 35.
[2] Lansdowne, Verse and Prose, II, 108; Granger, I, 238.
[3] Cunningham, 83.

pany of Italian comedians from Hotel de Bour-
gogne.

Promenaders whom Charles recognised in the
galleries came in for a courteous word. These galleries at a time of political excitement were like a
modern club-room. Predictions were drawn from
the tone the King spoke in; foreign news was gos-
siped aloud, domestic news was whispered. But
Charles himself was not a listener. He found out the
secrets of foreign diplomats by talking to them,
talking like a child given to telling everything he
knew. The ambassadors thought the King rather
brainless, but they, having to say something, fell into a way of making disclosures to the King. Even
Louise de Querouaille, who looked like a mealy-
winged moth but was known to be a spy of Louis
XIV, did not altogether succeed in raising the
French tricolour over Whitehall. The witless wit of
Charles proved to be sounder kingcraft than either
his father or his grandfather had displayed.

Very often the King chose Wycherley for a companion in his hours of leisure. From time to time he
gave the poet a hundred pounds,[1] as if in payment
for a hundred bubbles of merriment. It was not too
much. Unlike so many contemporary dramatists who
were dependent upon the receipts of the third-night
performance of their plays for a livelihood, Wych-

[1] Spence, 17.

erley regardless of his father's help began to feel a certain measure of security. What had a man to fear, why had a man to labour, when the bounty of Whitehall upheld him?

In this Court of perfumed gloves and apricot paste, this Court of glass buttons laced with thread of gold, this Court where twenty-four violinists played at dinner[1] as they had played for the wedding of Julie d'Angennes, Wycherley found old friends, new friends, and friends of his future. Buckingham was there. More than ever, all eyes followed the leonine grace of his walk. For almost at the moment that Wycherley had published his second play the Duke had produced a play of his own, 'The Rehearsal.' It really owed its wit to his chaplain, the lively Mr. Sprat, who himself went to Dorset for criticism of his writings; and it also profited from the aid of Samuel Butler the satirist.[2] But the Duke was admitted to the glorious company of the dramatists. Dorset was there. Dorset, moon-faced and melancholy arbiter of elegance, Petronius to the King, had pronounced Buckingham's play good. The Court accepted his fiat, as always, and scampered to the theatre. Then the town aped the Court. The Duke of York was there. The Duke thrummed his guitar. Between ditties he indulged his favourite diversion of selecting mistresses. Most of them were

[1] Cunningham, 83.   [2] D. N. B.

so ill-looking that the King insisted priests had given them to his brother for penance. James did not argue; if he was seldom delighted, he was never chagrined. The Duke favoured tyranny, but Charles, mindful of his father, exclaimed:

'Ods fish, brother! I am too old to go again to my travels. You may, if you choose it.'

Wycherley, packing away observations for his next comedy, may have noticed in Whitehall that the straight lines on the furniture had all been softened into curves.

CHAPTER IV

GOLDEN OPINIONS

HAVING written himself into fame as a dramatist, Wycherley resolved to move himself out of obscurity as a barrister. The living in the Temple was rather gray. Temple walls seemed sedate without beauty, friendly without warmth, toilsome without recompense. Lodgings for flint-faced men of law were not lodgings for a courtier and a poet admitted to the favour of Charles II. Will Wycherley wanted to live in the very streets he wrote of, to live every day in the breathing world of the strollers in the piazzas and the wits in the wine-houses. He moved to the modish Covent Garden quarter.

The rooms he took were in the house of the Widow Hilton, who kept lodgings for gentlemen of fashion in Bow-street, on the west side, the left going towards Longacre. In that day houses bore no numbers, for many people could read neither numbers nor letters. Wycherley's address, late in the reign of William, was described as 'three doors beyond Doctor John Radcliffe and over against the Cock.'[1] The poet in time came to find it highly convenient to be living near both.

Had Wycherley settled in chambers next the King's Theatre itself he could not have chosen a

[1] Wheatley, I, 229.

99

more congenial milieu. He had only to walk a minute from his door back to Russell-street, whence at night he could turn left into Drury Lane; in the morning, right, into Covent Garden. In Russell-street near the theatre stood Ben Long's Rose Tavern, rival of the Cock as a meeting-place of the wits. Poets and gallants, critics and lordling rakes, strolled in at the Rose after the theatre. The Wits' Room there usually provided a comedy more diverting than any in the playhouses. One massive round table with straight leather-back chairs nearly filled the floor, except a corner for a harpist and a man with a doleful cornet. Portraits of Roman emperors from Augustus to Vespasian, not strictly in order, hung almost touching the ceiling. That was well. Ben Long knew if he hung them lower he might look in one evening and see Nero dashed over the head of Rochester. Old Romans in a tavern suggested revelry, not classic reserve. There was also a grimy wall-map of the world, in Latin; that too must have raised disputes rather than settled them. Over the table dangled a bell-pull to call the waiters. The rope was strong. Poet-rakes often dined in the Wits' Room as prelude to a spree, and each had a pewter plate—happily unbreakable—engraved with his name and the words, 'At the Rose Tavern, Drury Lane.'

As Shakespeare paused at Mermaid Tavern in the

course of his walk home of an evening from the Bankside to his lodgings at Christopher Mountjoy's, so Wycherley on his way from the theatre to Widow Hilton's tarried at the Rose. He won friends of two sorts. Truest son of the age, Wycherley was first a fine gentleman; after that, a congenial man of letters. Thus his earliest important acquaintanceships between the Rose and the Cock were made with the boisterous 'confident young men' of the nobility. But there was also in these taverns a fireside-and-Burgundy[1] circle, men distinguished above all for their writings, whom Wycherley was now coming to know better. In the early sixteen-seventies he was devoted to the company of such authors as Dryden and Samuel Butler.

Butler was now over sixty, a lumpish choleric old man with sorrel hair, who let his satiric humours run free in his conversation and made enemies. But for ten years his 'Hudibras' had been the toast of the Restoration, and all London from Court to commoners had rolled in mirth over its procession of very dignified characters saying and doing very undignified things. Butler saw how the people felt, freed from the clamp of the Puritans, and he exalted the Royalist spirit. Dorset the critic took the 'Hudibras' to Whitehall: the King was delighted: he

---

[1] A mention of Burgundy in 'Love in a Wood,' Act V, Sc. 1, is said to be the first use of this word in English literature.—D. I. Nichol.

walked about with the book for months and read from it aloud. Astonished courtiers had not known before that Charles had ever read a book. Butler, like Etherege and Rochester, had married a wealthy widow, and then let his pen rust and his ink thicken. In 1670, in the diplomatic train of Buckingham, Butler had gone to France as one of the amazing troop of cronies whom the Duke took along: Dorset and Dr. Sprat, Sedley and Joe Haynes.[1] When the Duke became Chancellor of Cambridge in the next year, Butler is said to have served him as secretary, and in 1672 to have helped him in writing 'The Rehearsal.'

Wycherley and Butler were neighbours, but it is not known how they met. Buckingham may have introduced them. The old poet lived round the corner from Widow Hilton's, in Rose-street, Covent Garden.[2] At all events one of the remarkable friendships of the decade, probably struck up some time after Buckingham's play was produced, was that between the scowling old satirist and the young comedy-writer half his age. For the satirical mantle of Butler was soon to drape the shoulders of Wycherley himself.

During a great part of the year 1673 Wycherley was busy fashioning his third comedy, 'The Country Wife.' He had taken rather to heart the ordeal of his

[1] Pinto, 114.   [2] Biog. Brit., 1075.

second play, and with this deepened experience tied to his native energy and ambition he worked on a new idea. It should combine his knowledge of country types with those he had found in town. And as a guide in playmaking he resorted to another combination: his Latin studies and his observations in France. Abandoning the disapproved Spanish theatre he took a hint from Terence's 'Eunuchus,' and wove into it a character and two incidents from the master hand of the author he had no doubt first heard of in Angoumois: Molière. As a wise bird makes its nest of a variety of twigs, so Wycherley sought still farther: he looked into the Court as he wrote, and served up to the public the spiced intimacies of Whitehall.

At thirty-three this poet was growing up. He let go some of his impertinence and sufficiency and shaped his pen to character in the drama. In his prologue he apologised for his shortcomings as 'the late so baffled scribbler'; the verses reflected his true humility, but also the bruised knuckles of a courageous man.

For a season the rebuilt Theatre Royal in Drury Lane had now been open, and Wycherley gave his play to the returned company who had done so well with 'Love in a Wood.' Charles Hart, the actor who 'might teach any king on earth how to comport himself,' played Horner, a man who pretended to be an

eunuch in order to outwit husbands and flirt with
wives. Mohun had the part of Pinchwife, one time
a rake, who brought his country bride to London
and tried to keep her in a pumpkin-shell. The rôle
of Margery Pinchwife (prototype of Congreve's
Miss Prue and Van Brugh's Hoyden) was created
by lovely Mrs. Boutell, while that of Lady Fidget,
eager for the arms of any man except her husband,
fell to the incomparable Knipp.

But one of the resounding successes of the first performance, which took place at the turn of the new
year, was the character of Sparkish. Wycherley
wrote it for his old friend from Queen's College—
Joe Haynes. Haynes had developed astounding
talent as a comic, and he was almost equally brilliant
as a dancer. In Sparkish he found something new,
the part of an excruciating coxcomb who hung about
men of sense in order to be regarded a wit. The type
was only too familiar in Drury Lane. Haynes played
it with incredible mimicry and sent the pit into an
uproar. Wycherley had drawn some of his characters from his own friends,[1] such as Dorset and
Rochester, who well served for the parts of Dorilant
and Harcourt, two rakes only slightly less impudent
than Horner. But Sparkish he could hardly make
out of a friend; Sparkish was the embodiment of
a town pest.

[1] Perromat, 346.

The author skilfully worked up a dramatic entrance for Joe Haynes by a dialogue between the gallants. When Sparkish was announced below stairs Harcourt said:

'What, my dear friend! A rogue that is fond of me only, I think, for abusing him.'

'No,' observed Dorilant, 'he can no more think the men laugh at him than that women jilt him; his opinion of himself is so good.'

'. . . You know 'tis a very hard thing to be rid of him,' Horner added, 'for he's one of those nauseous offerers at wit who, like the worst fiddlers, run themselves into all companies.'

'. . . The rogue will not let us enjoy one another,' said Harcourt, 'but ravishes our conversation.' . . .

Then DORILANT. 'And to pass for a wit in town shows himself a fool every night to us, that are guilty of the plot.'

They agreed with Harcourt that most men are the contraries to that they would seem:

DORILANT. The usurer is a poor rogue possessed of mouldy bonds and mortgages; and we they call spendthrifts are only wealthy, who lay out his money upon daily new purchases of pleasure.

HORNER. Ay, your arrantest cheat is your trustee or executor; your jealous man the greatest cuckold; your churchman the greatest atheist; and your noisy pert rogue of a wit the greatest fop, dullest ass, and worst company . . . as you shall see, for here he comes.

SPARKISH. How is't, sparks? How is't? . . . Come, come, sparks, but where do we dine? I have left at Whitehall an earl, to dine with you.

DORILANT. Why, I thought thou hadst loved a man with a title better than a suit with a French trimming to't. . . .

SPARKISH. No, sir! A wit to me is the greatest title in the world.

HORNER. But go dine with your earl, sir; he may be exceptious. We are your friends, and will not take it ill to be left. . . .

DORILANT. We'll thrust you out if you won't. What! Disappoint anybody for us?

SPARKISH. Nay, dear gentlemen, hear me. . . . Why, dear rogues. . . .

All three gallants then got up and pushed the wretch bodily out of the room. But he came back, pleading:

'But sparks, hear me. What, d'ye think I'll eat then with gay shallow fops and silent coxcombs? I think wit as necessary at dinner as a glass of good wine; and that's the reason I never have any stomach when I eat alone. . . . Come, but where do we dine?'

'Even where you will,' said Horner wearily.

'At Chatelin's? . . . Or at the Cock? . . . Or
at the Dog and Partridge?'

'Ay, if you have a mind to it,' Horner stopped
him, with quiet impudence, 'for we shall dine at
neither.'

SPARKISH: Pshaw! With your fooling we shall
lose the new play; and I would no more miss seeing
a new play the first day than I would miss sitting in
the wits' row. Therefore, I'll go fetch my mistress,
and away.'

And so throughout 'The Country Wife' Sparkish
cackled of his wit, until he lost his mistress and
fiancée to Harcourt. Even at the last he said he
would never be a husband, because he 'refused to
disparage his parts.' As a character, Sparkish at the
fall of the curtain bore precisely the same traits, in
the same degree, as he showed when he first came
on—the insufferable bound up with the incorrigible.
Haynes himself was by nature incorrigible: he had
only to half-act in order to be Sparkish to the letter.
He was. On this first evening both Court and town
left the King's Theatre re-enacting over and again
in drawing-room and coffee-house the antics of Joe
Haynes. He made the play and the play made
Wycherley.

The author was supposed to have taken the characters of Mr. and Mrs. Pinchwife from a Mr. and
Mrs. Smith, of North Tedworth, Wilts, 'in which

family he was very conversant.'[1] The manner of his
meeting with such a country couple is conceivable:
Daniel Wycherley must have taken his son occasionally, perhaps when William was beginning to read
law in the Inner Temple, to the estates of the Marquess of Winchester in the neighbourhood of Basing
House, Hants. Their jaunts round the lands could
easily have brought them from time to time through
North Tedworth, only a few miles away in the adjacent county. It is not likely that Wycherley visited
in Wiltshire otherwise. He detested the country. He
found it unbearably tiresome even to go down to his
own home in Shropshire, and when he did appear
in his father's house he went to Daniel delicately,
to speak of money:

'I am only down here to rob the countryside,'
he once wrote from Clive Hall to a friend in London, 'and get out again as fast as I can.'

From Drury Lane, the provinces and everything
in them were in these years regarded with a shudder.
Dames of London rejected wealthy countrymen
with scorn; town husbands punished wilful wives by
rustication. Wycherley in his new play thus amused
the pit on the subject of banishment:

'Jealousy in a husband,' said Alithea, the sister of
Pinchwife, 'begets a thousand plagues to a poor woman, the loss . . . of her life, and what's as bad

[1] Summers, I, 48.

almost, the loss of this town; that is, she is sent into the country, which is the last ill-usage of a husband to a wife, I think.'

'The country is as terrible, I find,' said Lucy, the maid, 'to our young English ladies as a monastery to those abroad; and on my virginity, I think they would rather marry a London jailer than a high sheriff of a county, since neither can stir from his employment. Formerly, women of wit married fools for a great estate, a fine seat, or the like; but now 'tis for a pretty seat only in Lincoln's Inn Fields, St. James's Fields, or the Pall-Mall.'

Many London mothers, themselves amorous as Lady Fidget, actually vowed that their sons should never set foot in Italy, lest they bring back the infamous Italian custom of laying restraint on their wives.[1] It was a day when cuckoldry was the badge of fashion and infidelity the boon of marriage. Margery Pinchwife, though up from the country, naturally refused to remain stifled in a pumpkin-shell. She was discovered sitting alone at a writing-table, leaning on her elbow, and sighing:

'Well, 'tis e'en so, I have got the London disease they call love; I am sick of my husband, and for my gallant. I have heard this distemper called a fever, but methinks 'tis like an ague; for when I think of my husband I tremble, and am in a cold

[1] Grammont, 186.

sweat . . . but when I think of my gallant, dear
Mr. Horner, my hot fit comes, and I am all in a
fever indeed; and, as in other fevers, my own chamber is tedious to me, and I would fain be removed to
his, and then methinks I should be well. Ah, poor
Mr. Horner!'

Wycherley in his epilogue implied that in the
character of the husband, Pinchwife, he was simply
warning the 'Falstaff of fifty,' who while boasting
his achievement of a young wife was by the very
act inviting his friends to steal her away, then to
laugh at him. The author showed that surrender to
vice was to be forestalled only by ridicule. Since
Wycherley had returned from France, Molière had
captured Paris with his later comedies, and studying
these plays closely, Wycherley found Pinchwife in
the 'Ecole des Femmes'; from the 'Ecole des Maris'
he took two ruses by which the wife (Margery) got
her husband to deliver her with his own hands to her
lover (Horner). For the rest, Wycherley merely
took walks from Covent Garden to Whitehall, not
forgetting the bucolic types he knew quite as well
as Shakespeare did.

London from King to candlemaker enjoyed hearing the inflexible truth about itself. The town dis-
cerned that Wycherley had diagnosed the ailment
of the age: it possessed no love. Cupid was locked up
in a foundling asylum and the town gallants had

pocketed the keys. Now acknowledged as a favoured son of the Muse of Comedy, Wycherley was hailed as 'the Thalian bard'; the Court proclaimed it and the taverns affirmed it. The sort of enthronement which London accorded the poet after he had produced 'The Country Wife' is suggested in a minor writer's[1] later apostrophe to Comedy:

> 'She strait pull'd off her Sattin cap, and Band:
> Bade Wycherley be bold in her Defence,
> With pointed Wit, and Energy of Sense:
> Etherege and Sedley join'd him in her cause,
> And all deserved, and all received Applause.'

Wycherley had not only overtaken 'easy Etherege' and 'little Sid'; he had passed them. Judging his talent, his staunch friend Rochester wrote: 'He frequently excels, and . . . makes fewer faults than any of the best.' Though Wycherley was yet to do his finest work, Lord Lansdowne has told how London regarded the dramatist in this period: 'He was universally admired, and reckoned in the first rank of comic poets, and next excellent to Ben Jonson.'

In particular, Wycherley now emerged as a maker of characters: Sparkish and Margery Pinchwife had carried Drury Lane quite away; compared to them,

---

[1] E. Fenton, Poems, 1717.

the types in his two previous plays were half-moons. But there was something still more noticeable, one readily imagines, in town talk: Wycherley had now loomed forth as a figure in himself. He was being admired for his dialogue of epigrams, for his incisive similes, for his acuteness in putting life on exhibit. It was Wycherley—who could bother to remember which character of his?—it was *Wycherley* who said:

'A man drinks often with a fool only to keep his hand in use.'

And it was that line of Wycherley's: 'A beauty masked, like the sun in eclipse, gathers together more gazers than if it shined out.'

The wits at the Rose perhaps greeted their friends with: 'Though I have known thee a great while,' as Wycherley says, 'never go if I do not love thee as well as a new acquaintance.'

And gallants no doubt reminded one another of what 'Wycherley said' about town-ladies: 'Mistresses are like books. If you pore upon them too much, they doze you, and make you unfit for company; but if used discreetly, you are the fitter for conversation by 'em.'

As for the women of London, they could be sure 'Wycherley understood them' when he said: 'There are quacks in love as well as physic, who get but the fewer and worse patients for their boasting; a good

name is seldom got by giving it one's self; and women, no more than honour, are compassed by brag-
ging.'

Wycherley, looking not at all the poet, trod the
marble galleries of Whitehall and brushed against
life. The palace was a museum of hypocrisy. It had
on view every sort of flatterer England had ever
known, together with a new collection of exotics,
hybrids, and funguses. The King, dispassionately,
as he might watch toy race-horses, watched his four
most-favoured mistresses strive and strain to be in
the lead. They were a bawd's daughter, a cardinal's
niece, a spy of a rival monarch, and a voracious lady
who clasped either a duke or a valet with the same
ardency. Barbara Villiers was certainly yielding
ground to the others. Louise de Querouaille was
profiting by the mistakes of all. Hortense Mancini
and Nell Gwyn were sowing the least effort and
reaping the most security. Nell called baby-face
Louise 'the Weeping Willow,' but this emissary of
the French king was stealing close to Charles by way
of her gentleness and her manners. She went in for
the arts and good taste. There was of course in
Whitehall a man—Dorset—who did that, but there
was no other woman. The King was drawn to her.
Louise seated beside Barbara was like 'a dainty rogue
in porcelain' next a beautiful china pitcher that was
cracked, with the cracks turned a bit brown. The

Duchess of Portsmouth was twenty-four, the Duchess of Cleveland was thirty-three. And Louise glanced at the King as if to say, 'What judgment would step from this to this?'

Barbara Villiers was not of the spirit which beseeches nor of the temperament which droops. Her hair was very, very red. She had shrewdly foreseen the day when Charles would tire of her, and she had anticipated it by wresting her duchy from him. This concession freed the King, and he turned more and more to the baby-faced Breton. He had given to Barbara, with her title, Nonsuch Great Park, in the parishes of Cheam and Malden, Surrey, and this place now began to see more of the Duchess. Whereupon Whitehall saw less, and consequently Wycherley, who was being entertained by the King with increased frequency as a kind of dramatist-laureate, drifted out of touch with the tempestuous Medea whose friendship had bought him golden opinions from all sorts of people.

These opinions Wycherley was now wearing in their brightest gloss. He did not let them tarnish. For he was now turning over in his mind the great character which was to be the deepest of his adventures into authorship. In 'The Country Wife' he had taken manners of the day and built his characters upon familiar situations which were studies in contrasts. In 'The Plain Dealer,' a phrase from a popu-

lar game of cards called 'Plain Dealing,' he decided
to project a type he had known for twenty years, a
type he had observed in the circle of his friends
both in France and in England. The character
of Manly, a misanthropist, Wycherley had first
noticed in Angoumois as a boy: it was the Marquis de Montausier. And he had watched the behaviour of that man for nearly five years. Returning
to England, Wycherley had found again misan-
thropy rather marked in the Earl of Dorset, and for
a period of from five to ten years he had either
known or known of him, perhaps even more com-
prehensively than he knew the Marquis.

But while Dorset was mildly a poseur, a really
modest, jovial, and generous man who tried to think
he was a misanthropist because he was by nature
choleric and fastidious (common qualities in a good
critic), Montausier was the absolute: an honest man
but habitually disagreeable. Molière had made his
famous Alceste out of Montausier, wholly and without adulteration. The dour Marquis, after the days
of his governorship in Angoumois, lived mainly in
Paris as companion and tutor to the Dauphin. He
never knew that Molière stood by and threaded him
into a play, for he had greased his mind with books
until knowledge of men, including himself, slipped
from it. Montausier went to a performance of 'Le
Misanthrope,' so the story goes, sat through it and

never winced, then left the theatre saying, 'I should desire nothing better than to resemble so noble a figure as Alceste.'[1]

Wycherley of course examined the play of Molière, Anglicized some of its lesser characters and followed some of its structure, but since he knew Montausier personally almost as well as Molière did he had no need to make Manly a copy of Alceste. Memory came to aid his imagination, and his own experience with English types supported his inventive powers.

Again Wycherley called upon the King's actors: Charles Hart, the ever reliable, was given the part of Manly. The next most important rôle, the Widow Blackacre—a creation completely original—was played by Mrs. Cory, who had been so applauded in the character of Mrs. Joyner, the matchmaker, in 'Love in a Wood.' Mrs. Boutell again appeared, as Fidelia, a character probably suggested by Shakespeare's Viola. And once more Wycherley wrote a part for Joe Haynes: Lord Plausible, a shell of a man not unlike Sparkish. Then, in order to provide the audience with a double measure of foppishness, the author added as a foil for Lord Plausible another character of the Sparkish type: Novel. Freeman, Manly's true friend; Vernish, his false friend; and Olivia, his false mistress, were the other important

[1] Summers, I, 13.

parts, all of which strengthened Manly as protag-
onist.

The public were somewhat taken aback by 'The
Plain Dealer.' Drury Lane at first did not understand the complexity of the character of Manly.[1]
Wycherley had struck deep. But Dorset was interested, among other reasons because Manly was a
sea-captain and the Earl himself, perhaps with
Wycherley at his side, had been an officer in the sea-
fight against Opdam. A further reason no doubt
was the common traits of character which Manly
and Dorset possessed: Dorset was really as sympathetic with Manly, in his own way, as Montausier
had been with Alceste. At Whitehall, the Earl and
a few other courtiers of critical sense distributed
their opinion that 'The Plain Dealer' was an epochal
play.[2] The town, which until then had rather held
aloof, rushed to see Manly as if the theatre were a
side-show exhibiting an outlandish creature.

'The Country Wife' had been partly a diary of
Wycherley's own life—a loveless escapade. And as
persons who write their own lives sometimes evolve
into essayists, so Wycherley undertook an essay. In
'The Plain Dealer' he wrote on the subject of
friendship, the monstrous rarity of it in the London
of the Restoration. He had been pondering long on
the truth about people he knew. The City was like a

[1] Perromat, 235.   [2] Ibid.

field of clover: three-leaved friendliness everywhere, but four-leaved friendship dishearteningly
elusive. So many persons appeared from a little distance to have four aspects to their character, but
they usually reduced to an unsymmetrical three:
length, small breadth, and depth only too trans-
parent.

Wycherley in his prologue brawnily defied poets,
wits, gallants, and critics, denounced plays written
with sugared ink, and in good set terms warned the
audience that they were to be scourged with honesty:

> 'But the coarse dauber of the coming scenes
> To follow life and nature only means,
> Displays you as you are, makes his fine woman
> A mercentary jilt, and true to no man. . . .
> He draws a friend only to custom just,
> And makes him naturally break his trust.'

In Drury Lane the audiences seeing 'The Country Wife' had comprehended and quite agreed that
in their London love had gone begging. But when
with 'The Plain Dealer' Wycherley almost roared
that even friends were as little to be trusted as wives
or husbands, the pit blenched. For as the author told
them, they were all getting new friends, like new
mistresses, by disparaging old ones.

'Friends!' exclaimed Manly, a scant three minutes after the curtain rose, 'I have but one . . . for

a true heart admits but of one friendship, as of one love. But in having that friend, I have a thousand; for he has the courage of men in despair, yet the diffidency and caution of cowards; the secrecy of the revengeful, and the constancy of martyrs; one fit to advise, to keep a secret, to fight and die for his friend. Such I think him; for I have trusted him with my mistress in my absence: and the trust of beauty is sure the greatest we can show.'

But in the course of the next act the author divulged that this remarkable friend had stolen Manly's jewels and married his mistress. The audience grew uneasy, began knotting their fingers.

Wycherley had described in Manly his own character, perhaps without thinking so at the moment; but friendship seemed to him so fragile a thing, so rare a thing, so much a thing of trust, that he always tried to guard and cherish it, and he could not keep himself out of his play:

'. . . What d'ye think of me for a friend?' asked Freeman, lieutenant to Captain Manly.

'Of thee!' cried Manly. 'Why . . . thou art indeed like your Lord Plausible, the pink of courtesy, therefore hast no friendship . . .'

'. . . What, you observed me in the galleries at Whitehall, doing the business of the place? Pshaw! . . . could you think I was a friend to all those I hugged, kissed, flattered, bowed to? . . .'

'You told 'em so, and swore it, too; I heard you.'

'. . . But, sir, pray believe the friendship I promise you real . . . try me, at least.'

'Why, what would you do for me?'

'I would fight for you.'

'That you would do for your own honour. But what else?'

'I would lend you money, if I had it.'

'To borrow more of me another time . . . But what other piece of friendship?'

'I would speak well of you to your enemies.'

'To encourage others to be your friends . . . But what else?'

'Nay, I would not hear you ill spoken of behind your back by my friend.'

'Nay, then,' said Manly, 'thou'rt a friend indeed.'

Richardson Pack, who used to frequent the coffee-houses of Covent Garden in the company of Wycherley, said of the poet: 'He was certainly a good-natured man, and I reckon it as one great mark of such dispositions that he was as impatient to hear his friends calumniated as some other people would be to find themselves defamed. I have more than once been a witness of that honourable tenderness in his temper.'[1]

After Manly had discovered the callous treachery of his mistress (Olivia), he brooded upon his un-

[1] Introduction, 9 ff.

happiness. Freeman tried to cheer him by reminding the Captain of his own words: that he had done with love.

MANLY. I was only wondering why fools, rascals, and desertless wretches should still have the better of men of merit with all women, as much as with their own common mistress, Fortune.

FREEMAN. Because most women, like Fortune, are blind, seem to do all things in jest, and take pleasure in extravagant actions. Their love deserves neither thanks nor blame, for they cannot help it: 'tis all sympathy; therefore the noisy, the finical, the talkative, the cowardly, and effeminate, have the better of the brave, the reasonable, and men of honour; for they have no more reason in their love, or kindness, than Fortune herself.

MANLY. Yes, they have their reason. First, honour in a man they fear too much to love; and sense in a lover upbraids their want of it; and they hate anything that disturbs their admiration of themselves; but they are of that vain number who had rather show their false generosity in giving away profusely to worthless flatterers than in paying just debts. And in short, all women, like fortune (as you say) and rewards, are lost by too much meriting.

This was acid talk for followers of the King's actors to withstand. Even from the beginning the playgoers had appeared a bit afraid of Manly. Was there to be no relief? Women in the pit, like Hamlet's mother, began to feel their eyes turned upon black and grained spots in their own souls. But Wycherley, writing at the top of his genius, offset his misanthrope with a character dizzily comic: the Widow Blackacre.

The Widow was a walking brief-case of squabbles in court. It was said that in sketching the part Wycherley had attained to such startling truth by putting his father in skirts.[1] The career of Daniel Wycherley, Teller of the King's Exchequer (a title alarming to opponents), was now known to others than his son to be a perpetual lawsuit. At this very moment of the production of 'The Plain Dealer' Daniel in his Shropshire fastness was entering a fight to exhaustion with the copyholders of Wem, demanding that their fines be increased, and at fifty-seven his hair had gone white from fear that he might lose a case. But Will Wycherley enriched the portraiture of his characters, as he had done before, from his own searching view of London life, and though Daniel was probably the original of the Widow, his son's observations as an Inner Templar were patently her overlardings. Thus spoke Mrs. Blackacre to her lawyers:

'Go, save thy breath for the cause; talk at the Bar,

[1] Summers, I, 9.

Mr. Quaint: you are so copiously fluent you can
weary any one's ears sooner than your own tongue.
Go, weary our adversaries' counsel, and the court;
go, thou art a fine-spoken person: adad, I shall make
thy wife jealous of me if you can but court the court
into a decree for us. Go, get you gone, and remember
. . . (*whispers*). (*Exit Quaint.*)

'Come, Mr. Blunder, pray bawl soundly for me at
the King's bench; bluster, sputter, question, cavil;
but be sure your judgment is intricate enough to con-
found the court; and then you do my business. Talk
what you will, but be sure your tongue never stand
still, for your own noise will secure your sense from
censure: 'tis like coughing or hemming when one has
got the bellyache, which stifles the unmannerly
noise. Go, dear rogue, and succeed; and I'll invite
thee, ere it be long, to more soused venison.'

This old skinflint quite counterpoised Manly.
Together they were the two most living persons in
the play. London had come to 'The Plain Dealer'
expecting to find the usual comedy of manners, but
London had been struck in the face by Charles Hart
and Mrs. Cory in strangely new dress. When London recovered its balance it knew that this play just
come to town was a brutal exposure of character.
Brawny Wycherley had 'led forth his Muse as to a
battle, he had charged in iron,'[1] piled Pelion on Ossa,

[1] Lansdowne, Memoirs.

123

and when the discomfited pit came to reflect upon what had happened it knew itself lashed with the whip of morals for having laughed at manners that were outrageous.

In three weeks' time Wycherley had written a play[1] which was to endure in popular repertory for three generations. However long the poet may have contemplated the character of Manly before he started to write, the wit behind his pen during actual composition drove him furiously on. Rochester, between bumpers of wine at the Cock paying tribute in verse to his companion, said Wycherley had touched on true comedy, was painstaking, hard-working, and supreme in judgment. To such compliments Wycherley entered no objections, but he did not let pass Rochester's saying also that he was slow:

'For that slowness my Lord Rochester taxed him with,' Wycherley's friend Lord Lansdowne has recorded, 'he absolutely denied his due, notwithstanding his correctness. 'Tis certain he writ not so many comedies as Shadwell, but then it must be considered he writ not for profit, and that the third day was the least consideration that set him to work.'

Wycherley had never been the sort of author who took up his pen every morning whether he had anything to say or not. But he thought long, and (for his two greater plays) read Molière long, before he be-

[1] Spence, 200.

gan; a great deal of his plotting and writing he obviously did only in his head, with the manual transcription still far off. Then, once started, he could write with torrential gusto. As Lord Lansdowne further observed:

'Those who would form their judgment from Mr. Wycherley's writings without any personal acquaintance with him might indeed be apt to conclude that such a diversity of images and characters, such strict enquiries into nature, such close observations of the several humours, manners and affectations of all ranks and degrees of men, and, as it were, so true and perfect a dissection of human kind, deliver'd with so much pointed wit and force of expression, could be no other than the work of extraordinary diligence, labour, and application.

'But in truth we owe the pleasure and advantage of having been so well entertained and instructed by him to his facility of doing it. If it had been a trouble to him to write, I am much mistaken if he would not have spared himself that trouble. What he has performed would have been difficult for another, but the club which a man of ordinary size could not lift was but a walking-staff for Hercules.'

Wycherley now stopped writing for the moment, and surveyed London in its enthusiasm for 'The Plain Dealer.' He had withheld publication of 'The Country Wife,' but on the crest of the demand for his later play in the theatre he set about putting 'The Country Wife' in shape for the printer. In May, 1675, it appeared on the bookstalls without dedication, but as usual with a quotation from Horace, expressing the sentiments of the author, under the title: 'I am out of patience when anything is blamed, not because it is thought coarsely and inelegantly composed, but because it is new: when for the ancients not indulgence, but honour and rewards are demanded.' With that line Wycherley disposed of the opposition—it was not tremendous—to the affair of Horner and Margery Pinchwife.

While Dorset under the banner of his critical sanction led the City to the theatre and established 'The Plain Dealer' as an actable and a profitable play, it remained for a greater man, a man who had now been poet-laureate for five years, to recommend it as literature. John Dryden had won the laureateship on the fame of his poem in which he celebrated the memorable victory over Admiral Opdam. He was now in his middle forties, a short, stout, florid little man with a sleepy eye and a bloated face. The wits called him 'Poet Squab,' and he looked the more like a squab for his beakish nose. On his right cheek he had a mole nearly the size of a halfpenny, which when he talked moved up slightly together with a soaring right eyebrow. Dryden was more tavern-haunting than home-keeping. He lived in Soho, in

Gerrard-street (the house still stands, number 43,
four stories of time-blackened brick, now given over
to squalid shops), where in the front room on the
street-floor the laureate would work of a morning,
and at mid-day dine with his family.[1] He then hastened off to the coffee-houses, to escape the rather
dull but socially superior friends of his wife, the
Lady Elizabeth Howard.[2] She was the sister of an
Earl; Dryden was 'merely a grandson of a Baronet.'
Even with his short little legs taking short little
steps the poet could walk in a quarter of an hour to
the Rose or the Cock. There he could unbend, and
find talk worthy of his wit.

The friendship of Wycherley and Dryden, probably begun not long after the production of 'Love in
a Wood,' was now becoming something akin to
brotherly affection. Wycherley as an embryonic author had kept to the society of men who wrote by
living; now developed, he rather sought out the men
who lived by writing. His growing intimacy with
Dryden (and Butler) marked this passage. Whenever opportunity arose for the laureate to commend
Wycherley he took it. In 1675 Dryden published his
'State of Innocence,' and said in the preface:

'Comedy is both excellently instructive and extremely pleasant: satire lashes vice into reformation,
and humour represents folly so as to render it ridicu-

[1] Timbs, 272.   [2] D. N. B. (Dryden).

lous. Many of our present writers are eminent in both these kinds, and particularly the author of 'The Plain Dealer,' whom I am proud to call my friend. He has obliged all honest and virtuous men and enriched our stage by one of the most bold, most general, and most useful satires which has ever been presented on the English theatre.'

Dryden looked upon Wycherley as a vigorous reformer, and the greater part of thinking London accepted this penetrating estimate.

It was about this time that Wycherley again sat to Peter Lely for his portrait.[1] His face had filled out, his mouth had grown more firm, and his luminous eye, if less questioning, a little heavy from rollicking nights in the palace of the King. Compared to his demeanour when he was alertly twenty-eight his whole countenance showed the difference between a man surfeited with fame and a man determined to win it. In the earlier picture Wycherley was carefully cheerful, almost gravely so, as if with a desire to appear the correct gallant and a candidate for prominence. Now in his middle thirties, he had given full play to his prevailing passion of humour, and he wore a reminiscence of a smile and was very self-possessed. Perhaps he smiled too because he was

---

[1] This picture, in the National Portrait Gallery, is listed in their catalogue as by Lely. It is not dated. The Assistant to the Director tells me that "it appears to agree, in everything but age," with the engraving after the early Lely portrait.

posing—and posing a little flagrantly—again in his
Templar's gown; that might mollify the lord of the
manor of Clive. Wycherley's first sitting to Lely
had been an achievement, the achievement of an unknown young man merely good-looking and ambitious; but he came the second time as the satirist from
Whitehall, as the poet admired by all London, as the
lover for whom mistresses of great men played false
and their lords forgave them the holiday, and to
have Lely do a new picture now was for Will Wycherley as much a matter of course as to order a new
auburn perruque from Paris.

It was probably during this period also that
Wycherley, when his influence was weightiest with
those in high place, besought Buckingham to inter-
cede with the King on behalf of their friend Samuel
Butler. The old poet, bent with years, was poor, and
in want. His wife's estate had vanished in the maw
of speculation and the talons of lawyers. Butler was
also unfortunate in his friendships: from childhood
he had made sardonic observations on what every
one said or did: his friends were few and he could
not keep those he had. Preferments were offered
him, but he felt superior to any but the best; and
now he had no offers. He may have offended the
Duke; since the production of 'The Rehearsal' their
companionship had withered. In three or four years'
time many a friend forgets a friend.

But Wycherley at all events thought it a reproach

to the Court that a man of Butler's loyalty and wit
should have to dress in tatters and be unable to pay
his scot in the coffee-houses, especially when Butler
with no little truth could once write of the King,
'He never ate nor drank nor slept, But Hudibras still
near him kept.' Clearly, some recognition from
Whitehall was not undeserved.

Buckingham seemed sympathetic, and he assured
Wycherley of his willingness to speak to Charles
about the old satirist. But in unselfish matters the
Duke, unlike the man who importuned him, was
ever slow to get started. Wycherley, with the per-
sistence characteristic of his almost embarrassing
fidelity to his friends, kept prodding his noble admirer every time the chance offered, until at length
Buckingham consented to talk things over with the
destitute author, in Wycherley's presence, and himself named a day and hour. The place agreed on was
the Roebuck, a tavern favoured by the rakes for
midnight carousing.

Butler, ponderous old frog of a bygone generation
though he was, came with Wycherley and sat ready
to renew his comradeship by force of his own pleasantries, which he knew the Duke relished since the
day they had disported in France. Soon Buckingham
joined them, and took a seat near an open door of
the room. Except for the gravity of Butler's neediness, the scene might have been out of 'Twelfth

Night'; two humourists and a buffoon at their cakes
and ale. Butler, poor in funds though rich in wit,
was prepared with Wycherley at his side to speak
without rancour, and all boded well.

Suddenly a panderly knight known to the Duke
skipped by the door, on his way to an inner room,
with a giggling young woman on either arm. Fiddles began to squeak; and the lure was too much for
Buckingham. He went. Both poets then knew that
any charitable impulse they might have stirred in
the Duke would that evening benefit none but the
ladies. Wycherley had done perhaps as much as he
could. And Butler made his heavy way back to his
lodgings in Rose-street, brooding on the mockery of
hope.[1]

Wycherley was now engaged in preparing 'The
Plain Dealer' for the reading public. The play had
taken a fixed place in Drury Lane as the most popular of his comedies, and in the months immediately
after its first performance Charles Hart and his
company found it moreover one of the most dependable in their whole repertory. In 1676 they
produced 'The Plain Dealer' for the Christmas season, and the King, not quite so outspoken as Dryden
with regard to the power of the embroglio between
Manly and Olivia to inspire reform, but liking a
good play, went twice to see it, on the 11 and 13 of

[1] Pack, Miscellanies; Macaulay, Comic Dramatists, xxx-xxxi.

December.[1] Such enthusiasm from royalty drew all Covent Garden in the wake of Charles. Wycherley, though he was accustomed to take more time to revise and amplify a play for the printer than he took to write his whole original acting version, probably saw fit to make hay while the sun of majesty shone thus upon him, for within the next month booksellers had copies of 'The Plain Dealer' on their tables.

During the long interval between production and publication Wycherley had amused himself by writing for this play a jeu d'esprit of some 2,500 words as a mock dedication, which he gravely addressed 'To My Lady Bennet.' Mother Bennet was the most adept procuress in London. Wycherley did not know her, but with graceful irony he praised her industry and benevolence, and calling her 'great and noble patroness of rejected and bashful men,' said:

'This play claims naturally your protection, since it has lost its reputation with the ladies of stricter lives in the playhouse; and, you know, when men's endeavours are discountenanced and refused by the nice coy women of honour, they come to you. . . .

'Madam, you would not be one of those who ravish a poet's innocent words, and make 'em guilty of their own naughtiness (as 'tis termed) in spite of his teeth. . . . You, madam, have too much modesty to pretend to't, though you have as much to say

[1] Summers, II, 93.

132

for your modesty as many a nicer she: for you were
never seen at this play, no, not the first day; and 'tis
no matter what people's lives have been, they are un-
questionably modest who frequent not this play. . . .

'It must be the doubtful obscenity of my play
alone they take exceptions at, because it is too bashful for 'em . . . some there are who say " 'Tis the
plain-dealing of the play, not the obscenity; 'tis taking off the ladies' masks, not offering at their petticoats, which offends 'em"—and generally they are
not the handsomest, or most innocent, who are the
most angry at being discovered: "Nihil est audacius
illis deprensis; iram atque animos a crimine sumunt."[1]
Pardon, madam, the quotation; for a dedication can
no more be without ends of Latin, than flattery. . . .

'Your house has been the house of the people;
your sleep still disturbed for the public; and when
you arose, 'twas that others might lie down, and you
waked that others might rest; the good you have
done is unspeakable. How many young inexperi-
enced heirs have you kept from rash foolish marriages, and from being jilted for their lives by the
worst of jilts, wives! How many unbewitched
widowers' children have you preserved from the
tyranny of stepmothers! How many old doters from
cuckoldage, and keeping other men's wenches and

[1] Nothing is bolder than they who are detected. They assume anger
and spirit because of their infamy.—Juvenal, Satires, 283-4.

children! . . . "Nimirum propter continentiam, incontinentia Necessaria est, incendium ignibus exstinguitur."[1] There's Latin for you again, madam: I protest to you, as I am an author, I cannot help it: nay, I can hardly keep myself from quoting Aristotle and Horace, and talking to you of the rules of writing (like the French authors), to show you and my reader I understand 'em, in my epistle, lest neither of you should find it out by this play. . . .

'But, madam, that this may prove to the end a true epistle dedicatory, I'd have you to know 'tis not without a design upon you, which is in behalf of the fraternity of Parnassus; that songs and sonnets may go at your houses, and in your liberties, for guineas and half-guineas; and that wit, at least with you, as of old, may be the price of beauty, and so you will prove a true encourager of poetry, for love is a better help to it than wine; and poets, like painters, draw better after the life than by fancy. . . .

'You, in fine, madam, are no more a hypocrite than I am when I praise you; therefore I doubt not will be thought (even by yours and the play's enemies, the nicest ladies) to be the fittest patroness for, Madam,

'Your ladyship's most obedient, faithful, humble servant, and   THE PLAIN DEALER.'

[1] Incontinence really is necessary for continence; fire is put out by fire.—Tertullian, De Pudicitia, Ch. I.

When he had finished this frolic in raillery, the author turned to his Horace. He opened it at the Satires, and copied out a line to be printed under the title of his play:

'Ridicule commonly decides great matters more forcefully than severity.'

So Wycherley declared the purpose he wrote for.

CHAPTER V

THE LADY OF THE PARADE

THE Duke of Buckingham, so often a Court Fool in all but bells, was finding life in the midwinter of 1676–77 insupportably drab, for there was nothing more on the befogged horizon of London to amuse him. He was forty-nine. He had capered long to the lascivious pleasing of a lute. Now he was as fearsome as the ogre in the ancient tale who defied all who came near to make him smile, and as each man failed, devoured him.

'He has studied the whole body of vice,' said Samuel Butler, indeed as only a man who had been secretary to the Duke might say. 'He does not dwell in his house, but haunts it like an evil spirit. He loses time as men do their ways in the dark. He endures pleasures with less patience than other men do pains.'[1]

In a fit of remorse not long before, the Duke had taken to going to church with his wife. That was a reckless departure. The shock of unaccustomed righteousness jarred his nerves, Buckingham fled from his round ball of a Duchess, and he was now almost suffering remorse because of his remorse.

[1] Grammont, 370 ff.

136

At long last came opportunity for recreation: Parliament convened in February, for the first time in over a twelvemonth. To the slight abashment of lesser peers, the Duke with dramatic tardiness sauntered into the House of Lords. Was he turning over in his mind what he should do to introduce a small hurricane into the chamber? His last exploit there had been to pull off the Marquess of Dorchester's periwig.

The King opened the session. Buckingham was on his feet as soon as procedure permitted, and raised the question whether Parliament, having failed to assemble once in the year, according to an Act of Edward III, should not be summarily dissolved.

This was an occasion on which Charles II did not come off his throne and stand by the fire. He adjudged Buckingham guilty of contempt. The act invoked had in any case been long obsolete, and that in the opinion of the sovereign made the offense more gross. The King on the next day committed Buckingham to the Tower for his fourth imprisonment, together with certain of his supporters—Shaftesbury, Wharton, and Salisbury.[1]

News of this latest predicament of the beloved blackguard set all heads in London wagging. When Wycherley heard it he rallied to the side of the Duke, whose punishment, the poet believed, out-

[1] D. N. B. (Buckingham); Macaulay, Hist., III; Leigh Hunt, ix.

weighed the crime which had provoked it. This sentiment he felt impelled to publish. Yet why should he risk the displeasure of a Court which had so favoured and elevated him? From the King, certainly a more powerful friend than Buckingham, a friend who had already done much more for him, he might still expect to win bounties. From Buckingham, now declining in wealth and influence, he could count on nothing, not even help for Samuel Butler in distress. But Wycherley was a friend to both accuser and accused, and he impartially considered the obligations of friendship due as much to a Duke as to a King. He concluded that he must decide against what he thought to be unjust, and he wrote and circulated a poem of some seventy-five lines: 'To the Duke of B——, Imprisoned in the Tower by a Court-Faction,' and containing the bold verses:

> 'Your late disgrace is but the Court's disgrace,
> As its false accusation, but your praise. . . .
> Scorning Court-pity, pity more the Court,
> Which now has parted with its best support. . . .'

Wycherley's protest may or may not have fallen under relenting eyes, but in July the Duke was released, on parole, for a month.[1] To be released on a string was not altogether a happy condition for

[1] Summers, IV, 259.

Buckingham. Who could help him? Ten years before, when he had been put into the Tower for treasonable practices, Barbara Villiers called the King a fool to inflict such penalty. But neither through Wycherley nor any other friend could the Duke now appeal to Barbara, for she had marched off to France. The King, as if tossing the Duchess a toy to quiet her, had made her stewardess of Hampton Court. Suburban composure, however, in addition to that afforded by her house in Surrey, was not quite the circle of life for a lady still under forty and who had regarded herself as 'mistress of the world.' Having played out the conquest of London, Barbara cocked an eye at Paris, selected one of her daughters as companion, and crossed the channel.[1] It was not only Buckingham who was thus deprived of any aid the Duchess might have given; Wycherley as well lost the backing of the most devoted, most generous, most influential woman he had ever known. At the moment, very likely, he thought nothing of her departure.

Then who could help Buckingham?

No other than Nell Gwyn, it is said, was the one persuaded to step close to the King's ear to plead for untethering the Duke.[2] Mistress Nelly was doubtless the favourite to whom Charles would now accede most readily. She was at the top of her power

[1] D. N. B. (Villiers).   [2] Summers, IV, 259.

and she used it. Her house, 'the first good house on the left hand of St. James's Square, as one entered from Pall-Mall,' where the King had established her and where she lived with her old mother, very fat and fond of brandy, was as full of intrigue as a Government bureau. Its back room on the ground floor was a rendezvous, with walls and ceiling entirely of mirrors; in this room Nell probably kept her basset-table, at which one night she lost 1400 guineas to the Duchess of Mazarin. Yet she did not lose her laugh. And there were enormous-looking glasses in carved frames elsewhere in the house: they also encircled her bedroom, where Nell arrayed herself in red satin nightgowns and scarlet slippers laced in silver. But there, one looked first and last at her bed: it was bedecked with silver crowns and eagles, silver Cupids and slaves, the head of King Charles in silver, and a statuette of Jacob Hall, silver-muscled, dancing on a silver rope.[1] Nell in her harvest year of 1677 could have what she wanted, and if she wanted complete freedom for Buckingham she got that. After certain official delays the Duke was set permanently at liberty.

'Wycherley wrote as if he only lived in the Rose Tavern,' said Horace Walpole to a friend. 'But then the Court lived in Drury Lane too, and Lady Dorchester and Nell Gwyn were equally good com-

[1] Cunningham, 118 ff.

pany.'[1] Walpole indicates the milieu in which the
Plain Dealer was now moving, for to all appear-
ances Wycherley in the course of his saunterings
between Drury Lane and Whitehall knew both of
these young women well. He could hardly have
avoided Nell; she was the bosom friend of Mary
Knipp, for whom Wycherley had written two of his
brightest character parts, Lady Flippant and Lady
Fidget. The Countess of Dorchester (Katherine
Sedley) was the daughter of his old friend 'little
Sid.' She was a bony girl, and like her father rather
the colour of bran, but she won admirers by the dis-
concerting fascination of her repartee. Before she
was twenty (1678), Katherine found herself one
of the bizarre group of mistresses in the collection
of the Duke of York. 'We are none of us handsome,'
said Lady Dorchester, 'and if we had wit, he has
not enough to discover it.'[2] James smiled wanly at his
'Dorinda,' and thought her ravishing.

But there was at least one other tavern (probably
the Beare, at the Bridge-Foot, whence the Duke of
Richmond eloped with Frances Stewart, twittering
and very well dressed)[3] that was frequented in the
same years by Wycherley and the circle of wits.
Gallants made a point—as they did not so much at
the Rose and the Cock—of taking their mistresses
with them to this tavern.

[1] Letters, Vol. XVI, 3.   [2] Pinto, 137.   [3] Pepys, April 3, 1667.

'I cannot forbear to mention (just for the oddness of the thing,)' said Major Pack, 'one piece of gallantry, among many others, that Mr. Wycherley was once telling me they had in these days. It was this: there was an house at the Bridge-Foot, where persons of better condition used to resort for pleasure and privacy. The liquor the ladies and their lovers used to drink at these meetings was Canary; and among other compliments the gentlemen paid their mistresses, this it seems was always one, to take hold of the bottom of their smocks, and pouring the wine through that filtre, feast their imaginations with the thought of what gave the zesto, and so drink a health to the toast.'

Dryden made himself familiar with the prank, and in March, 1678, alluded to it in a play:[1] 'Before George, I grew tory-rory, as they say, and strained a brimmer through the lily-white smock, i' faith.'

Their revels now were ended—for a time. In this very year a blight seemed visited upon gatherings of the Society of Wits. Rochester collapsed upon a sick-bed, nearly dead from countless brandied nights. Dorset fell in love with his own wife, and stayed home. Etherege vanished abroad darkly upon diplomatic errands. Buckingham, himself now a 'Falstaff of fifty,' after a half-year in prison was more inclined to babble o' green fields than to drink through

[1] The Kind Keeper, Act I.

the smock of Doll Tearsheet. Sedley gave over his
nights-out, and dwindled into constancy for the sake
of his fair but firm Ann Ayscough. And Will
Wycherley, though the King at this juncture is said
to have asked the poet to be tutor to the young Duke
of Richmond,[1] found it needful, rather, to drive
down to Tunbridge Wells for the cure.

The Plain Dealer would take to the waters for
his health, but he would also amuse himself with the
Londoners there on holiday. It was full summer.
The water-drinking season had well begun. Knots
of visitors were crammed into rustic cottages on the
heath and against the brown hills. A fair was being
held near the fountain, and shrill-voiced farmers'
girls could be heard crying up their cheeses, rasp-
berries, and quails. Town gallants were tossing
glances over their shoulder at the promenaders, at
anyone from a maid of honour to an orange-wench
astray. Hawkers from Cheapside were selling gew-
gaws under trees, while gamblers, fiddlers, and mor-
ris-dancers enlivened the fields.[2]

Those who went to Tunbridge for carnival always outnumbered those who went for cure.[2] Together they made rather a crowd, but not an objec-
tionable crowd. Thankfulness for just being alive so
possessed the sojourners who strolled between the
line of trees and the line of shops on the historic

[1] Dennis, Familiar Letters, 222.   [2] Macaulay, Hist., III, 345.
[3] Grammont, chap. XII, *passim*.

143

Parade that the whole day seemed given to hand-
shakings and well-wishings. Constraint was forgotten. Two who by chance drank at the same moment
at the fountain saw enough excuse for arm-in-arm
confidences. Lords idled gracefully. Ladies lounged
elaborately. And commoners attained at least to the
nobility of holding a tin dipper with a grand air.

Wycherley, a few days after he had come down,
happened to fall in with a friend of his, Robert
Fairbeard, a fellow Templar, though from Gray's
Inn. They had not a little in common, by way of
gossip of barristers and courts; it was inevitable
that they should see something of each other while
they stayed at the Wells. One morning they were
doing the usual promenade along the Parade. As
they came up to the stalls of a bookseller they
paused. Almost at the same instant a youngish woman of rather remarkable beauty drew near, approached the bookseller, who stood by, and inquired
for 'The Plain Dealer.'

'Madam,' spoke up Fairbeard, overhearing her,
'since *you* are for the Plain Dealer, there he is for
you.'

And he pushed Wycherley towards the lady.

Will Wycherley's presence of gallantry, no whit
diminished since the day he met Barbara, swept to
his aid, and he added, 'Yes, this lady can bear plain
dealing, for she appears to be so accomplished that

144

what would be compliment said to others, spoke to her would be plain dealing.'

'No, truly, sir,' said she, half avoidance, half encouragement, 'I am not without my faults any more than the rest of my sex, and yet, notwithstanding my faults, I love plain dealing, and never am more fond of it than when it tells me of my faults.'

'Then, madam,' put in Fairbeard, 'you and the Plain Dealer seem designed by heaven for each other.'[1]

And Fairbeard made his adieux. That was the code of Tunbridge.

Wycherley strolled away with his Lady of the Parade. She had told him she loved plain dealing. Then she would talk. Wycherley walked like a King, and listened. She told him she was the Countess of Drogheda. And what more? What of her husband, the Earl, who had not come to Tunbridge with her?

Will Wycherley was ever the sort of man to whom women did tell things. They told straight into his wells of eyes all they had to tell, though sometimes it may have been rather more about others than about themselves. And Wycherley always knew what to say—chapters of it. He had said it to a slighted wife like Julie d'Angennes, he had said it to a jealous mistress like Barbara Villiers, and he could say it again to a Countess, fair to look upon,

[1] Dennis, Original Letters, 222 ff.

145

and alone, like Laetitia Moore. They all wanted to be consoled by the 'understanding' third person, who somehow seems ever to be thought endowed with divine perception.

Wycherley walked with the Countess clear to her lodgings.[1] She was charmed by the wit that interlaced his courtesy. She showed the unconcealable desire which a woman does show when she wishes to know a man better, and Wycherley, measuring his own eagerness, bowed the perfect bow of a Buckingham.

Impetuously soon the Plain Dealer was calling every day to see Lady Drogheda in her chambers at Tunbridge. What had his friend Fairbeard wrought? Wycherley came to find out that the noble lady— like no few other water-sprites in Tunbridge—had once been a maid of honour at the Court of his benefactor, King Charles.[2] They must have talked about Whitehall: she feared it, he laughed at it. But the conversation would have a way of returning to the subject of themselves. Something about this acquaintance, as it ripened, probably made the poet surmise that though he found himself in the usual Tunbridge flirtation—a maid of honour and a gallant—his own adventure was to be rather less fleeting.

Perhaps the Countess, for her part, did not tell

[1] Dennis, ibid.   [2] Grammont, 301.

her captivating caller too much of herself. The Lady
Laetitia Isabella Robartes was the daughter of a
Cornishman, John Robartes of Truro, first Earl of
Radnor, a man said to be 'sullen, morose, intolerably
proud.'[1] Laetitia as a girl had been in Ireland with
her father. He at that time was Lord Lieutenant
there. It was inevitable that the young woman
should meet the Moores, of Moore Abbey, seat of
the Earl of Drogheda. The Abbey, in Monasterevan,
County Kildare, was only about twenty-five miles
southeast of Dublin. And it came to pass that Charles
Moore, heir to Henry, first Earl of Drogheda,
courted and won Laetitia Robartes. In 1669—it
was now nine years since—they were married.

Almost from the start they led a life of turmoil.
The Viscount was a mild man, inwardly, but the
Lady Laetitia revealed a splitting temper, and between quarrels her own relatives put in an oar which
condoned rather than checked her thunderbolts. She
bore two children, but both were daughters, and they
died in infancy.[2] These mishaps by no means helped
to silence the domestic battlefield.

The old first Earl of Drogheda died in 1675.
Lady Laetitia's husband as the new Earl must then
have found himself little more than a thing for the
Robartes daws to peck at. He appears to have fallen
into poor health. It was probably to suit the whim

[1] D. N. B. (Robartes).   [2] Drogheda, period 1665-75.

of his wife that, leaving the cheerless Abbey, the Earl went away with her to live in London. At all events they took lodgings with a Mrs. Gibbons, in Bow-street. In January, 1678, the Countess there engaged a waiting-woman, Sarah Barnaby.[1]

Departure from Monasterevan naturally laid the Earl open all the more to torment by the Robartes family. The Cornish phalanx did not stop short of cruelty to him.[2] He appears to have been unable either to help himself or to get help, to have run short of money in London, and in June of this year, his health seemingly broken, he returned alone to Ireland 'upon some sudden and urgent occasions,' the news of which he no doubt received with more relief than alarm.

The Countess waited for funds to be sent from the Abbey; none came. She was extravagant, and she had now to live on credit. But the invalid Earl, if he had promised to remit money to his wife during these months, possibly had an excuse: at about this time he is said to have been suffering, perhaps not too painfully, from loss of memory.[3] The landlady who kept the house in which the Countess lodged, soon aware of the shortage which embarrassed her noble guest, was at first forbearing. Lady Drogheda, however, as the summer advanced and still no help came from the Earl in Ireland, apparently finding

---

[1] *Chancery.* Proceedings C 5. 454/72.   [2] Drogheda, 1675-80.   [3] Ibid.

life in London little more than a concatenation of
duns, drove off to Tunbridge Wells. At this turn her
husband seems to have roused himself a bit: he
agreed to allow her £20 a week while she was away.[1]

But the luxurious life of a watering-place was too
tempting for a Countess to evade. Lord Drogheda
may not have kept up his remittances; in any case
his wife began to borrow. She is said to have borrowed £100 from a Mr. Kindon, and she pawned
the Drogheda plate, to the amount of £50 received,
with a London goldsmith called Fowles.[2] By such
means was the Lady Laetitia keeping up appear-
ances, then, in Tunbridge, when she involved herself in the giddy affair with that most winning of
men of the world, Will Wycherley, to whose tales
of the taverns and theatres she could only respond
with a recital of her abandonment in London, or
with the complaint of her ostracism beside an Irish
lake. If they talked of their future, together, as
sometimes happens tête-à-tête, the Countess may
have had reason to conjecture that her enfeebled
husband could not long survive.

The end of this lark came soon enough. A hundred and fifty pounds was not sufficient to keep Lady
Drogheda indefinitely at the Wells; Wycherley as
usual had nothing. The Countess departed for Co-
vent-Garden once more, and in the same coach to

---

[1] *Chancery*. Proceedings C 5. 454/72.   [2] Ibid.

town Wycherley is said to have booked a seat beside her.

In London the poet continued his assiduous attentions, calling at the Drogheda lodgings almost as often as he had waited upon the Countess at Tunbridge.[1] And Lady Drogheda, though she may now have risen to the heights in love—for Wycherley appears to have become her lover[2]—unfortunately sank towards the depths in debt. She borrowed more. She raised £40 more at Fowles' by pawning more of the family plate, with the aid of her waiting-woman Barnaby. The Countess was determined to keep up her position in fashionable London, and this money 'was paid at the White Horse Inn in Covent Garden for the standing and keeping of the Countess' horses.'[2]

But the prolonging of this affair seems to have proved too much for the well-being of Beau Wycherley. It was as if he had thrown away his chance to recuperate at Tunbridge Wells, and had come back really more unsteady than he was when he went away. He was seized with a fever, probably before the summer was past, and lay stricken in his lodgings at the Widow Hilton's. Buckingham, Rochester, Dorset, Sedley, Etherege, and now Wycherley— all had disappeared from the taverns. It was a lean year at Adam Locket's and Oxford Kate's.

[1] Dennis, 222 ff. [2] Ibid., 223. [3] *Chancery*. Proceedings C 5. 454/72.

Weeks wore through into months, while Wycherley grew hollow-eyed, wearily gazing at one picture on one wall, then at another on another wall, until his hot head saw nothing in either. He was so enfeebled that he could not hold a pen. His hair began to turn gray.[1] But the last line of the prologue of his last play had been: 'Some friends at Court let the Plain Dealer find.' The appeal had not been unfruitful. Nor indeed had his verses in defence of Buckingham seemed to damage the poet's favour in Whitehall.

Word came to the King that Will Wycherley, the blithe spirit, the Horace of his jovial hours, was not getting well. Charles himself lost no time driving to Bow-street one morning, and with his train of courtiers in buff leather coats and high buskins worked with Persian silver he climbed the stairs at the Widow's to the chambers of his favourite. The King found the poet pallid and despondent. He sat down by the side of the high bed.[2] He at once urged Wycherley to try drier air, to go as soon as strength allowed to the south of France, and to stay away until he was beyond a doubt well. 'I shall have five hundred pounds sent you,' said Charles, 'for the expenses of your journey.'

The exchequer accounts were low. But Charles the Second always seemed able to conjure up money

[1] Summers, I, 53.   [2] Perromat, 37; Tinsley, 235.

to give to men whom he admired. Early in the autumn Wycherley found himself fit enough to leave London. He decided upon Montpellier for his cure, and supplied with the King's funds, and taking leave of Lady Drogheda, he set out upon another visit to France.

Montpellier since the year of the Restoration had enjoyed among Englishmen the social preference held to-day by Cannes and Grasse. Its air was thought to be a sovereign remedy for chronic coughs and lingering fevers. But the old archives of the city say, a little placidly: 'The English come to Montpellier to cure spleen, listlessness, and melancholy, which they contract at home.'[1]

Half way up a dry slope between sea and mountain stood the town, and in the heart of it the University, whose faculty of medicine, even then nine centuries old, was the most learned and the most skilled in France. Montpellier came into view as a citadel of four bastions, with ramparts engirdling the houses, which from the mountain looked like dominoes and chessmen wedged about two taller chessmen—a clock-tower and a church. The streets were so narrow that the carriages of Louis XIV, en route to Spain for his wedding twenty years before, had to go round the walls, Julie d'Angennes and the other ladies in the party being borne through the city

[1] Tome IV, 6.

in chairs.[1] These crannied highways, built as protection against the sun in summer and the wind in winter, of themselves suggested nothing regal. But sheer upon them stood stone mansions with lofty porte-cochères, windows as large as doors, and within, one found magnificent palatial staircases—Montpellier was ever known for staircases and marble balustrades—leading to rooms of state whose balconies gave upon courts white with narcissus and gardenias. For Montpellier was a seat of the Treasurers of France. In its House of Kings, Rue des Trésoriers-de-France, Charles IX had lodged, Richelieu and Louis XIII, and Le Roi Soleil himself, lately, several times. The city was rich too in memories of Petrarch, of Rabelais, of Molière, who had made long sojourns in the homes of its princes.[2]

Will Wycherley came happily to Montpellier in a year of festival. In October, when he arrived, Louis XIV had proclaimed peace with Holland. Cardinal de Bonzy, to celebrate the peace, in the same month gave at his home the first opera seen in Montpellier, with words by a native poet and music by Sablieres.[3] And it was a time for charities. Charles de Pradel, bishop of the diocese, took this lead and had just established a general hospital. And there was a palace to be admired. Only a month before, the Court had moved from the old castle to the

[1] M. Thomas (Montpellier).　[2] Vialles, 247 ff.　[3] d'Aigrefeuille, 178.

Palais-Neuf, which had taken fifty years to build and was now in the blazon of its grand opening.[1]

The dramatist from London, though he may have expected to keep somewhat to the English colony in Montpellier, was thrown as a courtier and a polished man of the world once more into that French society which had burnished him as a boy. A panegyrist of this period has recorded that 'The education of the leading men of Montpellier, as elevated as their birth, seems to have been perfected in the palace of our kings. The women seem to acquire sweetness of manner from the suavity of the very air they breathe.'[2] It was true that when Molière had played in Montpellier in 1654 he thought its salons cluttered with literary ladies rather hyper-æsthetic, whom amongst others he satirised, as some critics thought, in 'Les Précieuses Ridicules' five years later. Whether a short generation since then had wrought new affectations or not, Wycherley in this town was to feel fully as much at ease as in Angoulême. For there is more explicit information of the noble dames of Languedoc: another panegyrist of the age, M. de Rosset, had published 'Portraits of the Most Beautiful Women of Montpellier.' His ecstasies centred upon 'Madame la Marquise de Castres, with her laughing black eyes, imperious heart, and the liveliest conversation; Madame la

---

[1] Vialles, ibid.   [2] Garronne, 43.

President de la Roche, a sweet and sociable spirit, the mirror of beauty, never melancholy, with a little flame-coloured mouth and her neck full white; Madame la Baronne de Lozieres, with thick blonde hair and languorous eyes, a temperament cold and good, appearing outwardly like the pictures of Virtue and Victory by painters.' With such ladies, or their daughters, perhaps, could a wanderer from Whitehall, who in his romantic past had been reared by the bonafide Précieuses, find entertainment after his own heart, especially if he had no heart. Wycherley doubtless very soon began to feel no older than he was: thirty-eight.

In his absence from home, however, the poet could not have altogether forgotten Lady Drogheda. There can hardly be any question that they corresponded; the Countess at least knew where to reach Wycherley, for she planned during the winter to send him a ring, as a present.[1] It never arrived. She gave her woman Barnaby 'a gold ring sett with small diamonds' to take to Montpellier, together with ten pounds for expenses on the journey. But Barnaby, 'lookeing upon it as a thing that might reflect upon her Ladye's honour and that it was onely the effect of her present passion which on second thoughts she might repent of,' pawned the ring and stayed hidden away with kinsmen in London. All of the money she

[1] *Chancery.* C 5. 454/72; C 5. 583/78.

used, it must be said, to discharge a debt of the Countess's for 'ffaggetts Butter Eggs Soape herbes and severall other things.'[1] But the Countess believed that Barnaby had gone abroad.[2] The waiting-woman conceivably was afflicted less with righteousness than with fright at the idea of trekking across France.

This episode must have occurred not long before Wycherley was well enough to come home. However he was in Montpellier in January, when peace with Spain also was proclaimed. He could not have avoided seeing the celebration, which alone would have given fresh life to an invalid. It was on the thirtieth of the month. The night was so fair and clear that it was like noon. Every townsman built a fire before his house, put lights in his windows and hung up paper lanterns, while in front of the Hôtel de Ville young men stacked a towering bonfire. There was a grand parade, with horsemen in red and silver, hautboys, heralds, trumpeters, a band of violins, finally two hundred youths in cavalcade wearing blue plumes and holding high the arms of the king and the city embroidered in gold. Fireworks and pistols cheered the procession up one street and down another. It was such a night as Montpellier had not seen since the Kings of Majorca were driven out.[2]

Change of scene and society, in addition to the

[1] *Chancery*. C 5. 454/72.   [2] Ibid.   [3] Delort, II, 8 ff.

balmy air and winter sun of the Midi, infused Wycherley with his brawny vigour once again. If he thought now of flower-girls huddled round the clean column in Covent Garden, he thought too of poor rogues in Whitehall, sloshing in the quagmire of Court news. That was home, and he wanted to go back. There was delightful company in Montpellier, but there was in London a Countess, in whom he was at least interested.

In the early spring of 1679 he set out upon his return. He seems to have travelled by way of Holland, and stopped at Nimeguen (Nijmwegen on the Rhine), where the general European peace treaties had been signed on February 7. There he saw a little town of tiles and wooden shoes, a very little town now bristling with pride that great nations had named it the spot upon which to forswear guns and drums and wounds. Wycherley, perhaps because of recollections still fresh of the jubilee in Montpellier, perhaps the more because wherever he had roamed abroad he had always met with a herald and a hautboy on each hand, saw and pondered on the meaning of this newest peace. What was the meaning of it? Louis XIV had now paused after the mightiest sweep of his power, and peace decreed by him should mean peace to a continent. Whereupon Wycherley, more soberly convalescent than divinely inspired, before he journeyed on set down some verses: 'To the King of France, at the Treaty of Nimeguen, written there':

> 'You by your sword long since have given us law,
> And kept the European world in awe;
> While still you did your conquering forces send
> A foe to vanquish, or protect a friend;
> But, yielding now that warlike sword to sheath,
> Your triumph's greater than in giving death. . . .
> Monarchs by war can vanquish earth alone,
> But by their mercy they make heaven their own. . . .'

Wycherley arrived in London with a stout heart but a slender purse. How well his renewed spirits stood by him when he again took up his friendship with Lady Drogheda is not quite so certain. For full nine months the Earl had rusticated in Ireland. For full nine months he had given no indication of returning. So much was well enough. But there was little money forthcoming. The Countess, no less overjoyed, had a picture made of Wycherley;[1] she went to the goldsmith's, bought a silver cup, and had Wycherley's name engraved on it. But as her passion rose her credit fell, and in early springtime she perforce determined 'to go after her Lord into Ireland.'[2]

There was of course no ready money for the journey. Barnaby shrewdly got an agent, acting for her, to advance £79 to Lady Drogheda. As the Countess

[1] *Chancery.* C 5. 454/72.   [2] Ibid.

then made ready to leave London, however, another obstacle arose: her landlady seized all the Drogheda effects for rent in arrears. It was not until Laetitia Isabella had pawned her coach and horses for £75 (a new coach, possibly purchased in celebration of Wycherley's return home) and turned the money over to the woman at the lodgings, that this creditor was willing to unfold her arms and stand aside. Towards the end of March (1679) the Countess and Barnaby finally managed to get started, setting out by way of Reading for the west coast,[1] to take ship to Dublin, and the love affair of the Plain Dealer came to a pause.

Lady Drogheda had not been the only one to welcome Wycherley back to England. Whitehall received the poet ardently. It was difficult to tell which was the more glad at his homecoming: Wycherley or the King. Charles now made clear his project of appointing the poet as tutor to the new Duke of Richmond, seven-year-old son to the King by Louise de Querouaille. The salary was to be £1,500, and a pension payable as soon as the boy should no longer require his preceptor's time. This pension was stated as being to the end that 'Mr. Wycherley would thenceforth be placed beyond the malice of the world and the inconstancy of fortune.'[2]

The young Duke, according to Evelyn, was 'a

[1] *Chancery*. Ibid.   [2] Spence, 44.

very pretty boy, well shaped, with a black complexion much like King Charles.' It seemed that Wycherley could look forward to a delightful occupation, and later in life be as carefree as a cricket. Otway, his distinguished fellow dramatist, had been under the protection of a Prince; but Wycherley was to be more than that—he was to be companion and teacher, Chiron to Achilles. No higher recognition of scholarly merit could be granted; Wycherley stood poised for a moment upon the summit of his fortunes. Then, almost before he knew what his next move was to be, came news from Ireland that the Earl of Drogheda was dead. And Wycherley rather lost his poise.

As soon as the Countess had arrived at Moore Abbey she made certain of the reason, outstanding among others, why her husband had sent her so little word during their separation. He was not well enough to bear a sense of responsibility. It appears that his Lætitia Isabella found him not altogether bed-ridden, but it appears also that, abetted by some of her own relatives who evidently were within call in Ireland, she did not take any heroic steps to keep him on his feet.[1] Young though he was, the Earl with his strength sapped and his memory gone was in no fit state to withstand a renewed assault of his wife's kin. He collapsed. And this seizure, it was plain,

[1] Drogheda, 1675-80.

would prove mortal. Finally the Countess and her associate demons compelled him to make a will leaving all the Drogheda estates to them, instead of to his brother Henry, who would succeed to the title.[1] The dying Earl, not refusing, not consenting, could only stare at his persecutors, and repeat after them what they told him, as if he were learning his catechism. His will still exists, signed in a hand jagged and trembling,[2] on June 18, 1679. On that same day he gave up the ghost.[3]

It did not take the Countess long to transmit these details—all of them—to Wycherley in London. Certainly the funeral baked meats had hardly disappeared from the boards in Moore Abbey before the conquering widow began to envisage her second wedding breakfast. What thought Wycherley now? Both in his plays and in his own life he had flouted marriage as something heterodox. He had forsworn it since his earliest days in France with the Précieuses, who had shaped his career. Yet had he altogether disapproved the ambition of gentlemen in Covent Garden to marry young heiresses who were noble, beautiful, and rich? His friends had done it —Butler, Etherege, Rochester. Why not? Butler had slid into disaster, true, but Wycherley, the Plain Dealer, would not make Butler's mistakes, would not speculate with the fortune now willed to his

[1] Drogheda, 1675–80.   [2] Ibid.   [3] Ibid.; Summers, I, 55.

Countess. He evaded the impending trust arranged
for him by the King; such a tutorship at all events
probably was not tenable by a married man. To be
the husband of Lady Drogheda was all in all a prospect more inviting than the task of drumming the
rules for the ablative absolute into the dubious mind
of a child of seven.

Still it seems that Wycherley did not feel too sure
of the wisdom of this step, for he went so far as to
get in touch with his father, and to discuss the project with him. Now Daniel Wycherley, in all his
white-haired pomposity, was at sixty-two priding
himself more than ever upon his shrewdness. He
knew that his scamp of a son was financially inse-
cure; that it was the King, not this Plain Dealer,
who had paid for Will Wycherley's season of idleness over in France somewhere; and above all Daniel
knew that his own lacerating lawsuit against the
copyholders of Wem, now six years in process and
loaded with expense, needed all the money he could
scrape together. In short, he longed to get William
off his hands. Always a money-headed man in true
Widow Blackacre fashion, the father not only favoured the match with the Countess but insisted upon
it.[1]

A curious weakness of William Wycherley, one
of the most brilliant minds and the greatest drama-

[1] Dennis, 222 ff.

162

tist then living, seems to have been that he was unable, after writing for six years on every phase of the subject of matrimony, to decide at the critical moment whether it was a good thing for himself. If he knew that meanwhile Henry, third Earl of Drogheda, was on the point of taking proceedings in Parliament to contest the will of his late brother and bring about restitution of the family property,[1] would such a man as Wycherley have retreated? If the Countess herself knew it, would she have told the man, the one man in the world who infatuated her? Lady Drogheda in any case would scoff at the Drogheda opposition. Wycherley no doubt was unenlightened.

For him there was only one difficulty: the King. But Daniel, in his avaricious way, desired his son to eat the cake and have it too. And the end of the discussion between father and son seems to have been that, giving way to parental chicanery, Will Wycherley allowed Daniel to prevail upon him not to tell the King, for 'it was reasonably supposed,' as John Dennis relates, 'that the lady having a great independent estate, and noble and powerful relations, the acquainting the King with the intended marriage might be the likeliest way to prevent it.' Counselled further, it is said, by his father, Wycherley agreed to persuade the Countess to keep the wedding

[1] Drogheda, 1675-80.

secret, with a view not to displease the King and lose his good graces. Whitehall, both before the fact and after the fact, was to be hors de combat.

Lady Drogheda, remaining through the summer at Monasterevan and trying to settle the estate of the late Earl, was finding it no less difficult to raise funds as a widow than as a wife. It was as if her husband were crying out from his grave against the will which the Robartes persecutors had forced out of him. Yet she continued to make herself answerable for money which she did not possess. On August 16 she gave Barnaby a bond for £100, 'for guift money'[1] —indicating no small elation over her coming espousal of Wycherley. In a suit in Chancery later, Barnaby testified that 'some tyme after the said Earl's death there was a treaty of marryage to be had between the said Countess and Wm. Wycherley Esqr. . . . and the said Countess about Michas (Michaelmas) formed an intention to come over to England in order to consumate said marryage.'[2]

Again there was no money for travelling. The waiting-woman loaned the Lady Lætitia £113 more for this journey (Barnaby seems to have practised money-lending from her savings), and taking Jane Buckston, a chambermaid, as a third member of the

---

[1] *Common Pleas*, Docket Book for 1680; King's Bench, Docket Book for 1684.
[2] Proceedings, C 5. 454/72—complaint and answer.

party, the Countess pointed for London. At West-
chester she despatched Thomas, Buckston's husband,
to town, to request Wycherley to meet her en route
at Northampton. The three women followed by way
of the Great North Road, probably passing through
Wycherley's own Shrewsbury, then on into War-
wickshire and Coventry. At Coventry the Countess,
importuned by her servant, gave bonds for the whole
amount which she owed to Barnaby. The waiting-
woman, perhaps nervously overwrought, was taken
ill. Whereupon Lady Drogheda, keeping hold of the
papers, said, 'Barnaby, I will lay upp the bonds for
you till Morneing.'[1]

The lovers were to meet on the road in secret, because the Countess feared intervention from her own
family. The old Earl of Radnor, Laetitia's father,
would of course be opposed to such a hasty marriage
by his widowed daughter, in particular to a commoner, a play-writer from Drury Lane, but he was
chiefly concerned in not letting the property extorted
from Drogheda pass out of the Robartes control. As
the Countess and her women proceeded from one inn
to another along the way, the Countess grew ever
more apprehensive that they might miss her fiancé;
but Barnaby, who had had something to do with
arranging the appointment through Thomas Buck-

[1] *Chancery*. Town Depositions C 24. 1053–10 and 1061–48; six clerks'
Depositions C 22; Proceedings, C 5. 454/72.

ston, insisted that Wycherley would be waiting at Northampton. He was not. Lady Drogheda then 'fell into a great passion, and bawled and roared as if she had been stuck with a knife.'[1] She promptly suspected that Barnaby had thwarted the meeting, possibly had intrigued with her father against her. And she burned the bonds on the spot.

Northampton was three-quarters of the distance into town. Perhaps for the first time since her husband had died Laetitia began to droop under the pall of widowhood. The perplexity, the uncertainty, as they thumped along the highway, must have seemed drawn out unbearably. Ten miles outside London, in the toe of Hertfordshire, they pulled up at the old coaching-station of Barnet.[2] It was where the decisive battle in the Wars of the Roses had been fought, two centuries before. And there stood brawny Wycherley. The joy of the Countess was so exceeding that she apologised to her servant for the scene at Northampton. That was the way of Laetitia Isabella.

In all haste, the poet and the heiress on reaching London were married. It was Michaelmas. Wycherley took his bride in October to live with him in his old chambers in Bow-street, which was still the fashionable end of town. Conforming to the subterfuge which Daniel Wycherley had urged his son to

[1] Town Depositions, ibid.   [2] Ibid.

assent to, the Plain Dealer attempted to pass as a bachelor. For a time he succeeded. Before the marriage he had not been seen in town with the Lady Laetitia so long, he thought, that an occasional sight of him now with her would provide any gossip for the curious.

But the love-stricken Countess could not find it in her heart to allow her husband to go out alone. It came to pass that wherever Wycherley went his lady followed him, like a vexing young sister determined to join in all of her brother's games. The Countess showed a tendency to believe that a handsome gallant who had vanquished the belles of Drury Lane for twenty years might still be led into the wine-shops by that very species of town women whom he had put in his plays. The Countess would see about that. She made herself not unnoticeable. So it happened that news of Wycherley's marriage, as well as the preposterous effort to hide it, was soon tattled round Covent Garden, and naturally winged its way thence to Whitehall; the very endeavours made to suppress it only accelerated its breaking out.

The King objected. Not only did he resent the methods Wycherley had taken to keep the wedding dark, but he thought he perceived in such conduct the poet's discarding of the royal offers. It was one thing for Wycherley to denounce his sovereign's punishment of Buckingham; it was quite another for him to hold lightly the King's solicitude for Wycherley himself. Charles remembered that he had granted to Wycherley marks of favour perhaps beyond what any English ruler had ever before shown to an author not of the nobility.[1] The King and the Plain Dealer had been confidential friends: now Wycherley had wavered and not held to that confidence. There was no more discussion in Whitehall of the poet's £1,500 appointment in the household of Louise de Querouaille.

But Charles was tender to excess, and upon Wycherley's return to him he might in time have bridged the gap. The temperamental Lady Laetitia however, waxing militant, stepped in and doomed any bridge-building of the sort. Having by experience her own opinion of the esteem in which fidelity of husband to wife was held in Whitehall, she would not permit the brawny man whom she loved with the fierceness of a Latin to return to Court. She became a stamping yellow fury of jealousy—there was language in her eye, her elbow, even in her foot. Within the gray and green loneliness of an Irish castle the Countess could feed her temper only with cruelty; now, in London, she found Wycherley too hard a stone to grind thin by being cruel to him; she must swing the sledge of jealousy and crack him in two.

The King waited in Whitehall; the Horace of his

[1] Cibber, III, 252.

leisure hours did not come. Such indifference in a man like Wycherley was incomprehensible. Could his mind be affected from the strain of his long fever? This silence appeared at best to be ingratitude. Slowly the Court began to forget the most feasted dramatist of the day, who was not even being prudent enough to keep his friendships in repair.

If the Countess and the poet stood at variance upon proper procedure in this instance, they found within six months after their marriage another matter needing discussion which must have made them bury the family hatchet and act together. Sarah Barnaby, having been turned out of service by Wycherley, caused the Plain Dealer and his wife to be subpœnaed on March 16, 1680, to the end that her loan of £200 to the Countess might be recovered.[1] The Lady Laetitia made her answer in May, citing as one defence that she had as yet received nothing from her former husband's estate. (The new Earl was defying the Robartes family with a vengeance.) But Mrs. Barnaby, upon this reply of the Countess, petitioned for a 'ne Exeat Regno' against the defendants, inasmuch as she had heard that to evade her, they were planning to leave England. Wycherley and his wife, after a month of manœuvring, managed to get this writ set

---

[1] Decrees and Orders Entry Book for 1680; C 33. 253.

aside on June 22.[1] They then are reported to have slipped away to Ireland for a time.

However, this suit lodged by a dismissed servant was, thus far, of minor consequence in the Bow-street life of Wycherley and the Countess. If the Plain Dealer crossed the Irish Sea he no doubt found living in and about Dublin with the vigilant Laetitia less tiresome than when he remained in the midst of his friends. At the Widow Hilton's he was literally house-bound. The irony of it: Wycherley could now see the Countess dressed in the character of his own stamping and fuming Mr. Pinchwife, whilst he himself was by way of enacting a leashed and ken-neled Margery. The Lady Laetitia could not endure that her husband should be one moment out of her sight.[2] Directly across Bow-street from their lodg-ings stood the Cock Tavern: it had been Wycher-ley's school of life, his stage-box, his wine-cup and his midnight song. But now, if he so much as peeped into the Cock with one or two jocund companions to greet Oxford Kate, the poet had to take his wine as if beneath a lorgnette. Wycherley must open the tavern windows, so that the beady eyes of the Coun-tess, straining down from the Widow Hilton's house

[1] Before bringing suit, Barnaby went to Wycherley at Epsom to de-mand payment of him. Wycherley drove her from the house, 'all bloody and much beat on.' The landlady is said to have feared Wycherley would murder Barnaby.—Proceedings C 5. 454/72; Town Deposition C 24. 1053–10.

[2] Cibber, III, 254.

opposite, could see that he was not holding some Moll Davis on his knee.[1] By an oversight, merely, the curtains of these windows at one time or another remained drawn. Then the Lady Laetitia raved and shrieked like Xantippe, pounded upon her floor, pushed over the furniture and rocked the house in her fury.

As Wycherley in 'The Plain Dealer' had harped upon the identity of cowardice with bullying, so in his own life, that of a chivalrous gentleman, he practised the other extreme and identified fortitude with good-nature. He was so good-natured that he thought he had to humour the passions of his volcanic lady. To his surprise, perhaps, the Countess loved him as a husband with the same explosive violence she had ultimately shown towards him as a lover.[2] That was hardly the etiquette of the Restoration. But Wycherley considered furthermore that he could not be too indulgent to a woman who had bestowed upon him both her person and her fortune. For all his deep study of Horace he seemed to have overlooked the phrase 'aurea mediocritas.' And what he did not consider so much as his indulgence to his wife was that while he was acquiescing to her whimsies and her petulance he was day by day letting himself grow so resistless as to impair the fibre of his independence.

The more Wycherley yielded to the Countess, by

[1] Dennis, 223 ff.   [2] Dennis, ibid.

avoiding whatever her jealousy foresaw, the more
unreasonable and turbulent she became. Looking upon her husband, Laetitia could not, or would not 'in
his each feature truth and candour trace, and read
plain-dealing written in his face.'[1] Wycherley had
been an idol of the ladies. The Countess shattered at
least that idolatry. Wycherley had been sought after
by the men for the vivacity of his genius. The Countess grew jealous even of men, and she strangled her
husband's old friendships. What was there left for
him?

It was bad enough to be shut off from a friend,
from time to time, but it was worse to hear of that
friend's death before one could enjoy his company
again. Forlorn as he might have felt in his own
house, Wycherley must have heard with acute distress of the death of the eldest of his old friends,
Butler, and of the youngest of his old friends,
Rochester, both in the last half of this year, 1680.
Butler, a genius, thrown in a corner like a cast-off
coat, forgotten by a nation whose literature he had
honoured and enriched, slowly succumbed to starvation. Yet one must say that he died rather more disappointed than disregarded. He had scorned as unworthy of him certain modest livelihoods once
offered by the Government.[2] Rochester, the only
writer of the age at once a nobleman and a genius,

[1] Ward, A. W., Hist., II, 578.   [2] Aubrey, passim.

lay dead at thirty-two because his friends had kept
him drunk for five years in order to hear his saint-
seducing ribaldry.[1] Quite aware of this, Rochester
still could say, in a letter, when he was sick and peni-
tent, 'If there be a real good upon earth, 'tis in the
name of friend, without which all others are fan-
tastical.'[2] He had named these friends. Starting with
Horace's 'Odi profanum vulgus,' the Earl had listed
his favourites, in the famous lines:

> 'I loathe the rabble, 'tis enough for me,
> If Sedley, Shadwell, Sheppard, Wycherley,
> Godolphin, Butler, Buckhurst, Buckingham,
> Approve my sense; I count their censure fame.'

There was only one Rochester. Old rakes may
have recalled the speech he was said to have made
when disguised as a quack-doctor on Tower Hill: 'I
am the famed Paracelsus of the age, by name Signior
Doloso Euprontorio, son of that wonder-working
Chymist lately deceased in Alsatia and famed
through all Europe, Asia, Africa, and America . . .
who . . . has by the prayers . . . of divers Kings,
Emperors, Princes, Lords, Ladies . . . been prevailed with to oblige the world with notice to . . .
young and old, lame and blind, that they may know
where to repair for . . . all Cephalgies, Orantal-
gies, Paralytical Paroxysms, Rheumatisms, Gout,

[1] Camb. Hist., VIII.   [2] Letter to Henry Savile.

Fevers, Fractures, Dislocations, and all other Distempers incident to the human body. . . . My medicines are the quintessence of Pharmaceutical Energy. . . . I have an excellent hypnotical, captical, odoriferous, carminative, renovative, stiptical, corroboratory Balsam of Balsams, made of Dead Men's Fat, Rosin, and Goose-Grease. It is the true Pharmacopoeia of Hermes Trismegistus, the true Pentemagagon of the triple kingdom, which works seven several ways and is seven years preparing, which being exactly completed Secundum Artem by Fermentations, Solutions, Sublimations, Putrefactions, Rectifications, and Quidlibelifications in Balnea Mariae in the Crucible, becomes Nature's Palladium, Health's Magazine, one drachm of which is worth a bushel of March Dust. . . .'[1]

Rochester was missed, even by Dryden, who could not pronounce malediction, though he had perhaps most reason. Rochester had suspected that Dryden was going to publish 'An Essay Upon Satyr,' an anonymous pamphlet, already somewhat known in the coffee-houses, which daubed the nobleman rakes with pitch.

'If he falls upon me with the blunt,' said Rochester, 'which is his very good weapon in wit, I will forgive him, if you please, and leave the repartee to Black Will with a cudgel.'[2]

---

[1] Wootton, II, 204–205.   [2] Scott, note to "Peveril of the Peak."

'Black Will' was a ruffian hired by noblemen to beat commoners who offended them, the noblemen themselves declining to fight with those beneath their own rank. When the pamphlet appeared on the bookstalls it was attributed to Dryden. One night as he was walking home through Rose Alley, Strand, after leaving a coffee-house, Black Will waylaid and thrashed him.

The libel was actually written by the Earl of Mulgrave,[1] rather a hanger-on than a member of the group of wits, rather a 'Lord Plausible,' or even occasionally a 'Sparkish,' though he had gone to sea and fought against Opdam as bravely as the rest. He sought revenge for his repulses by the wits in the taverns. But the poet-laureate was the one to suffer. And now, almost before Dryden's black and blue marks were gone, Rochester was dead.

'I shall not disturb his ashes,' said Poet Squab, quietly.

Towards the end of this year, an 'interesting event' in the family of George Wycherley, the dramatist's clergyman brother, was the occasion of paying compliment to the Countess, if it was any comfort to her. On November 28, George had a daughter born to him in his vicarage at Wem, and in the week before Christmas he baptised her Laetitia Isabella.[2] The country Wycherleys were seemingly

[1] Pinto, 144.   [2] Shropshire Society, 357.

impressed by their noble sister-in-law. They had not lived with her. It is possible that the Countess, en route to Holyhead about this time, even stopped at Wem to see her namesake, for in December Wycherley and his wife are said to have 'gone over into the Kingdom of Ireland.'[1]

The pertinacious Sarah Barnaby continued to haunt the courts, harassing Wycherley and demanding her two hundred pounds. In January, 1681, the poet resorted to the defence of bringing a cross-suit against the woman.[2] Between a wrangling servant itching for money and a wrangling wife whose inheritance was frozen, life in Bow-street for a poor man with a rich but miserly father was not altogether a bed of ease. Wycherley was unable to return to the writing of comedies. His rearing Countess would not tolerate his rambling in Covent Garden to gather the berries of comedy material; and that had been Wycherley's way. A full third of the scenes in his plays—in the French House, the New Exchange, St. James's, the Cock, Pall Mall, Westminster Hall, the Piazza—were scenes instantly out of his own free walks and free talks. Perhaps he feared himself incapable of writing again up to the strength of 'The Plain Dealer.' He would not risk again being a 'baffled scribbler' in the theatre. Un-

---

[1] *Chancery*. Decrees and Orders Entry Book for 1680, C 33. 253.
[2] Ibid., 1681, C 33, 255; *Common Pleas*, Docket Book, 1681.

doubtedly he saw, like Molière, abundant comedy
in his own rôle of husband, but the siege of fever
which had worn him down might well leave any
man less inclined to humorous writing. If Wycherley now locked his ears against the vituperation of
Laetitia and took up his pen, it was only to produce
some of his undated verse. Yet his partial eclipse did
not dim his popularity as a dramatist in Drury Lane.
Because of the resounding plaudits upon his masterpiece, the phrase 'The Plain Dealer' had become
a household word, and in this year James Magnes,
Wycherley's grasping publisher, printed still another edition of that play.[1] Wycherley piled up debts
and piled up duns and disregarded both. He thought
money from the Drogheda estates would eventually
end all difficulties.

The Barnaby case was not heard until the end
of the year—December 7. Neither Wycherley nor
the Countess was present,[2] and the defence was ar-
gued only by lawyers. Mrs. Barnaby won, possibly
on the testimony of the burning of the bonds. The
Court ordered the defendants to pay £200 with interest, the costs, and the costs of the cross-suit
brought by Wycherley, which had been dismissed.[3]

[1] Perromat, 300.
[2] They had gone down to Farringham, Surrey, where they were
lodging with a Christopher Steward.—Decrees and Orders, 1682, C 33.
257.
[3] *Chancery*. Proceedings C 5. 583/78; Decrees and Orders, 1681,
C 5. 33. 255.

Following hard after this confusion visited upon the fugitives of Bow-street came still more. Wycherley seemed beset. His fiery Countess, who had grown so warm in his house, suddenly lay cold in her coffin. She died at forty, having been married to her second husband a scant two years. Her fury utterly spent itself, crashed, against the good-natured hardiness of Wycherley that, for all his outward wavering, was deeply ingrained in him at birth. It was almost as if Laetitia Isabella had tried to pluck up a cedar by the spurs. If at the end she felt any contrition for her marital outrages she no doubt believed she atoned for them not only by dying blessedly early, but by leaving to Will Wycherley the whole of her fortune. This amounted to a jointure of four thousand pounds on the St. Mary's Abbey estate of the Drogheda family.[1]

But while Wycherley waited for his legacy, his creditors, marshalled perhaps by Barnaby, declined to possess themselves with patience. On February 23, 1682, Barnaby reported to the court that Wycherley had 'absconded himself.[2] She girded up her skirts and pursued him.

[1] Drogheda, 1680–85.   [2] Decrees and Orders, 1682, C 33. 257.

CHAPTER VI

THREE PRISONS

UNHAPPILY for the still-vexed widower, his Countess without any warning had bequeathed to him not a legacy, but a lawsuit. It was not even a simple lawsuit, man to man, but a suit whose very existence seemed to depend upon the outcome of another lawsuit. For the first time in his life, perhaps, the Plain Dealer wished himself in the shoes of Daniel Wycherley. And the Barnaby case, now, seemed small indeed.

The Earl of Drogheda, while Will Wycherley was in the throes of domesticity, had begun in Parliament his proceedings against the Robartes family. Viscount Bodmin, son to the Earl of Radnor and brother to Laetitia, was now fighting the Drogheda attack on the deathbed will of Charles Moore. Laetitia's banded relatives had succeeded in appropriating the Drogheda estates, the solidest wealth they had known, and they were standing by like hungry lions.

Who was this Wycherley, this man who had got the daughter of Lord Radnor to marry him, then put in a claim for her fortune? The Earl and his son, attacked now on both right and left, did not know but their family might even have to relinquish to Lord Drogheda that jointure which Laetitia had willed away to a play-writer.

But the Drogheda-Radnor suit was no concern of Wycherley's. Intent upon collecting what he regarded his rightful inheritance, he prosecuted his demands on his wife's relatives with as much energy as he had shown in courting the Countess. Into the hands of his lawyers he put all the money he could sweep together.

He had not thought, a few years before, that he should one day have to eat his own satire, that a chance flirtation at Tunbridge would within three years force him to play the parts of both Margery Pinchwife and Mrs. Blackacre. The very puppets he had created and laughed at had risen to enjoin that he in turn appear in their rôles for themselves to see. Wycherley knew now, if ever he had doubted, that two of the plays he had written were 'real life.'

The three-cornered suit dragged on, a hound snapping at either flank of the Radnor stag. While the Earl of Drogheda never had to slacken, Wycherley began to descry over his own shoulder the gathering clouds of debt. It was costing him more to besiege than it was costing his opponents to defend. In February, 1682, Laetitia's brother, Viscount Bodmin, died. The old first Earl, the father, was now seventy-six, and unable to engage in legal combats, but Bodmin's heir, Charles Robartes, had just attained his majority and was thirsting to enter the dispute.[1] He had married Elizabeth Cutler, daughter of Sir John Cutler, a miser worth £300,-000. This patch of a man had pulled tight the strings of his money-bags and refused to give the bride a penny of dowry. Whereupon the young Viscount now found all the more reason not only to defy Lord Drogheda, but in particular to resist the less formidable claim of Wycherley: as his wife had brought him nothing he shrank from giving up what his aunt had left. He resolved to attack with every technicality the will of the onetime Countess of Drogheda. Her jointure should be his at least as long as the courts allowed him to keep the Drogheda estates.

Wycherley took occasion to address a poem, 'The Praise of Avarice,' to old Cutler. Verses from the most generous of men to the most miserly could have been given only one interpretation by the public: ridicule. At all events Wycherley exhorted Sir John to keep on hoarding, saying, 'the fox thrives ever best by being curst.' The poet may have wished to brighten his own chances by inducing Cutler to settle a dowry, or he may have wished only to gibe at the Radnor dilemma. But he said:

'The man that does possess a glitt'ring store,
   And uses not the treasure in his power,
   Is not a slave to luxury or pride,

[1] Summers, I, 56.

But must contemn the wealth he strives to hide:
And to contemn what vulgar spirits prize
Is, sure, to be most temperate and wise. . . .'

However, to rail against Sir John Cutler, satisfaction though it might be to a poet's feelings, was
not to produce any very sudden miracle of finance.
Debt began to engulf the improvident Plain Dealer,
who had swum into the current of law only to have
it draw him towards a whirlpool, and he had now to
cast about for a spar to keep him afloat.[1] Too late he
saw what the loss of the friendship and patronage of
Charles II was going to mean: the King was indif-
ferent to the poet's struggle. Barbara Villiers, who
might gladly have tided him over if he could appeal
in person to her, was still living in France, inaccess-
ible. What old friends remained? Buckingham was
now depleted in wealth and power alike. Dryden
had barely enough for himself to live on. Sedley,
the year after Wycherley married, had nearly died
from a fractured skull when the roof of a tennis-
court in the Haymarket fell on him, and he was not
even now, after a prolonged and critical illness, a
fit man to approach. Where was Dorset, that philan-
thropist to poets? He too had gone to Paris, with

[1] Miss Boswell has found in the Docket Books (Courts of King's
Bench and Common Pleas) that Wycherley was sued, 1680–85, on
no less than ten actions for debt.

Fleetwood Sheppard, to stay with the British Ambassador.[1] And Rochester—was dead.

Will Wycherley, so little time ago the lion of Pall Mall and a beau in Whitehall, now alone in his lodgings, ignored, debt-ridden, almost forsaken by hope itself, began to know the bleakness of one in trouble when no friend comes. After days of anxiety, one nobleman, no close friend but a wholehearted admirer, rather as Sparkish admired Horner, did extend some assistance—five hundred pounds, to be loaned on bond. The Earl of Mulgrave, of all men, possibly in memory of a historic acquaintanceship at sea with Wycherley when the British blew up Opdam, possibly as a gesture that he now harboured no grudge against the wits for their rebuffs to him in the coffee-houses, was the Dorset of the hour. But one reason of course was that Wycherley, unlike Rochester or Buckingham or Butler, had never excited hostility from those he knew.

Still believing in his chances to triumph over the Robartes family, Wycherley left all his debts unheeded except some of his lawyers' fees, and plunged again into the Prerogative Court, with Mulgrave's money. It vanished like a leaf in a gale.

The poet was forced now to bury his reluctance and appeal to his father, who after all had been his abettor in forwarding his marriage to the misleading

[1] D. N. B. (Sheppard).

Countess. Bills unpaid now amounted to seven hundred pounds.[1] Creditors were slinking about Bow-
street, keeping watch at the Widow Hilton's. Unfortunately, it was not a propitious moment to
approach Daniel Wycherley on the subject of funds.
He had just emerged defeated from an expensive
lawsuit against his arch-enemy, one George Tyler;
he had been required to pay (perhaps as the price of
social ambition) rather amazing college bills for his
youngest son, Henry, who had gone up to Oxford,
not to Queen's where the living was sober, but to
Christ Church[2] where the spirit of Wolsey ran red;
and most burdensome of all, he was now in the ninth
year of his epic of litigation against the stubborn
copyholders of Wem. Daniel had once borrowed
thirty thousand pounds for the Marquess of Winchester, but now he could not borrow seven hundred
pounds for his son. The poet might as well have
asked his own Widow Blackacre for it. It was a
solemn day for the heir to Clive Hall.

Then came a moment of the most pressing necessity, when not one wolf but a pack of them pawed
and snarled at Wycherley's door. As a last resort
the beset man went to Magnes, his publisher, who
according to Major Pack had got almost as much
money from the sale of Wycherley's plays as the
author had gained reputation. In order to have a

[1] Dennis, Familiar Letters, 221.   [2] Summers, I, 5.

little more time in which to make still further efforts, Wycherley asked the man for twenty pounds. Magnes turned his back.

In 1682, anyone who recalled that Will Wycherley had once been the protégé of Julie d'Angennes may have observed how strangely parallel, during critical years and at critical moments, the lives of the Princess and the poet had run. Both had grown up in a salon of wits. Both had remained single, mining the silver of experience, until they were about forty. Both had married scolds. Both had won immense favour from the mistresses of Kings. Both were named preceptors to the sons of Kings.[1] Both knew everything there was to know about love except the full possession of it.

There was now no longer a double track in the sand—one had branched off, gone. The shadow of the Marquise across Wycherley's life vanished, if what would seem the whim of fortune can so be called a shadow. But perhaps it vanished only because Wycherley had ceased to stand in the sun, and where there was no sun, no radiance, there was nothing of Julie d'Angennes.

The creditors of the Plain Dealer were now peremptory; they had lost faith in the chances of a mere poet against a noble family. The debt of £700,

[1] Julie became a favourite of Mme. de Montespan, and was Gouvernante to the Dauphin.

which to-day would be the equivalent of £3,000, seemed mountainous, nowhere to be borrowed, never to be earned. Wycherley was notified one morning that he was to be taken to Newgate.[1]

Almost before he knew what had happened he was standing in custody before the black, gray-black, soot-clotted walls of the prison, and hearing the deep shudder of the bell at the gate—a gate which mocked a statue of Liberty overhead. The door was of iron six inches thick; at the screech of a lock as broad as an atlas it swung inward. Before one saw any living creature one became aware of rasping cries and growls as if from a jungle, bursts of loud obstreperous laughter, sobbing, mewing, whining, blaspheming, and perhaps as an overtone, the curses of a woman answered by roars from a man, the woman's thick gasp, a steamy gasp, and the end of that. Above all this tumult the clanking of chains sounded accompaniment, and momently it bore the hideous suggestion of applause. The air was as poisoned as the air of a swamp where adders nest. It was as acrid to breathe as gas, and almost seemed to scorch internally one who had just entered the prison gates. And within the cold stone court, where ragged debtors were playing handball and pitch-and-toss, looking down upon this lethal uproar stood the statues of Justice, Mercy, and Truth.[2]

[1] Gildon, 7.   [2] Griffiths, 144.

Newgate at this period was a den of coiners, pick-pockets, highwaymen, kidnappers, murderers, and prostitutes. It was a county gaol for debtors as well as for malefactors and criminals, all of whom were so densely packed in quarters so illy ventilated that the place was a nursery of epidemics. Prisoners in good health when they arrived soon gave way to gaol distemper. Whenever these wretches were arraigned, the floors of the Court of Justice had to be strewn with herbs, in order to prevent infection spreading amongst the judges and barristers.

All men taken into Newgate were heavily weighted until they bought 'easement' from the gaoler; the usual shackles were a strap round the waist, and from it two chains of wrist-size links to the arms, then two leg-irons like Brobdingnagian safety-pins reaching to the ankles. Wycherley no doubt had reserved enough 'garnish' to purchase easement and other gaol privileges described as comforts. The prices of lighter chains, all exhibited on the hospitable wall of the anteroom, ranged from one guinea up.[1]

'Ten guineas, sir,' chuckled the greasy Captain of the Gaol, 'if you wish to die like a gentleman.'

Wycherley could see down a black corridor of cells, where lived the human relics who had not paid. Over each cell-door hung a skull and cross-

[1] Ibid., 149.

bones. Inside, a dingy lantern on a nail revealed a suggestion of a chair, a table carved with names and appeals to God, and a pile of matted burlap for a bed. Rats the size of rabbits crept damply over the men lying in these vestibules to death.[1] From cell to cell passed a turnkey with a hammer, striking the fetters on every prisoner, to see if any had been filed in the night. Nearby was the 'press room,' to induce those who refused to plead, and thus delay sentence, to change their minds. The engine of inducement was a sort of gigantic nut-cracker; even the thickest-shelled villains usually gave in to its persuasion. And execution was swift, swifter than the disposal of those executed. Quartered bodies of felons lay about for days in the yard, while the hangman boiled the heads in his big kettle with bay-salt and cummin-seed in order to keep fowls from pecking at them when he set them up on pikes.[2]

But the Plain Dealer would not die so sanguinarily beneath his station. He probably avoided being lodged very close to the worst of this shambles by paying his admission to the Master Debtors' Side of the prison. Here he could associate with gentlemen much deeper in debt than himself, as well as with a number of the more prominent murderers. There was a room twenty-five feet long and fifteen wide, with a window nearly as large as a double

[1] Pitt, 22.　　　　　　　　　　[2] Griffiths, 156.

door. It had a fireplace with a sea-coal fire always kept in. It had wooden benches and a common table. Round the room ran a gallery, with beds between partitions in it, and under this gallery the prisoners took their exercise. A bed cost half a crown a week, and sheets two shillings a month. The newest member of this 'club'—though he were Wycherley himself—had to be chambermaid, or pay twopence daily to have that work done.[1] Club-room, tavern, dining-hall and bedroom in one, these quarters were fairly tolerable, except for the pandemonium that raged round outside. The Master Debtors at certain hours were almost like men holding a stockade in an African jungle, with wild animals prowling and roaring near enough to be rather a nuisance.

After eight o'clock at night the din and the bellowing rose to madness. Piercing voices shrieked imprecations. Choruses of gutturals sounded like wolves tearing at bones. Cackle echoed cackle, crazily, down damp vaulted passageways. The women, always worse than the men, screamed revilings at one another that would make Satan hold his ears.[2] Perhaps Sunday night—the night before executions —was the most harrowing of all: then the more hardened criminals had the habit of clanking their chains like fiends, to defy the booming of St. Sepulchre's bell: it swung to the swish of the bell-rope,

[1] Ibid., 150 ff.   [2] Ibid., 156.

the clapper fell with a thump, and the air shook
to the toll of the bell for a hanging to come at
dawn.

In this first scene of his confinement Wycherley's
dry humour did not forsake him, for writing in a
letter a description of Newgate and his conversation
with criminals there, he said 'that of those good and
honest friends and companions, every sessions he was
deprived of one or more, who taking the air to Pad-
dington (the place of execution) seldom lived to
come back.'[1] The poet must have observed with
amusement many phases of human character new to
him. He may have beguiled some of his time by
attending the trials in the gaol at which the prisoners tried one another; 'thieves condemned their ac-
complices,'[2] and by the outcome of such a trial the
defendants judged whether they in reality were
likely to be acquitted or condemned.

Wycherley, like Defoe after him, probably found
not a few murderers distinctly more intelligent than
poetasters of the coffee-houses. But it was annoying
to befriend a jolly good felon only to have him taken
off the next day to be hanged. The gruesome atmosphere of Newgate appeared after several sessions to
touch the nerves of the Plain Dealer. He took out a
writ of habeas corpus,[3] which permitted a debtor to
choose his own gaol, had himself brought up before

[1] Gildon, 7.   [2] Letter to Pope, April 1, 1710.   [3] Gildon, 7.

a magistrate, and managed at length to get himself transferred to Fleet Prison.[1]

The Fleet, on the east side of the Ditch, between Ludgate Hill and Fleet Lane, extended east to Cock Alley and north to the Old Bailey. It had been re-built after the Great Fire, was now only about fifteen years old in its new trimmings, and because of its pleasantness, its gardens, and the larger leniency of its rules, it was preferred before most other prisons. Many gave money to have themselves turned over to the Fleet from gaols which were more dismal and somewhat less sanitary.[2]

The prisoners there, too, were quieter: the Fleet was only for debtors, bankrupts, and those charged with contempt. It was an aristocracy of culprits. Lodgings of ease were provided for men accustomed to ease. Whereas in Newgate 'ease' referred mainly to the degree of hindrance in one's manacles, in the Fleet it bore rather more upon beds and outdoor privileges. The bribe for this ease—the gaoler was as black a rogue as his colleague of Newgate—ranged from ten to thirty shillings weekly. Two gentlemen could occupy a bed free, but if a prisoner wished to sleep alone he had to pay.[3]

[1] Fleet Prison Commitment Book 1a reports the date of Wycherley's commitment to the Fleet as June 7, 1685. Probably 1685 was the date of a re-commitment. No date for an earlier commitment of Wycherley is extant. Books were not kept at the Fleet until 1685.
[2] Hatton, 247 ff.   [3] Ashton, 260.

There was a tap-room, a coffee-room, and a billiard table with reasonable remnants of its cover still left, while the garden afforded space to play at skittles and tennis. These conveniences, prison luxuries, were all allotted to the Master Debtors, whom the warden of the Fleet flattered, then preyed on. Men who died were always in debt to him; he would hold the dead bodies from eight to twelve days, until he had extorted all the money he could from weeping relatives at the gates of the gaol, whilst all the prisoners walked about holding their noses. If the warden was pressed for money he sometimes did not wait for a man to die: a short time before Wycherley arrived in the Fleet the warden amused himself by shutting two hostile prisoners in a cell until one murdered the other.[1]

To say that Wycherley, now free at least from Newgate, was mingling in exclusive gaolbird society is not to say that he found any great number of his new acquaintances overburdened with honour. Few prisoners brought to the Fleet for debt ever paid that debt in full. The place was sanctuary to cheats and villains, who as soon as they arrived entered into conspiracy with the gaolers to defraud their creditors, and this end they often accomplished by bribing and feasting the prison officials. There were men of considerable estate who rather than satisfy

[1] Hatton, 247.

their creditors lived in the Fleet and spent their money on debauchery. Such men turned 'night into day and day into night by drinking, dycing, roaring, cursing.'[1] It was hardly a restful retreat.

On the other hand, conspicuous in the crowd at this time were several hapless clergymen. Some died, wretchedly. They were then spoken of as having 'left for some other preferment.' Among them, one woful morning, came Wycherley's brother George, who had fallen on ill times in his parish of Wem. Daniel Wycherley was George's creditor, had cast his own son into prison,[2] and the poet of course could do nothing but offer congratulations that George had missed Newgate. Another odd group were the Puritans. No prison in London after the Restoration was quite up to the mark in vengeance unless it housed a few of the desperadoes who had interfered with the monarchy. But they were said to be in gaol 'for conscience sake.' The Puritans were one of the less popular horrors of the Fleet. 'In their prayers,' said a writer of the time, 'one speaketh, and the rest do groan and sob and sigh as if they could wring out tears.'[3]

Fortunate it was for the poet that in these desolate days, however much he suffered from bad food, health impaired, and sleep broken by death-watch spiders, he could always divert himself with pen and

[1] Pitt, 22.   [2] Garbet, 156.   [3] Hatton, 247.

paper. He was able by very force of his habit or
writing to take a philosophical view of his confinement, if not a cheerful one. Wycherley insulated
himself in gaol, like Bunyan, his Puritan contemporary, and spun a cocoon of rhymes round him to
ward off loneliness. In his verses 'In Praise of a
Prison, called by its Prisoners their College; and
written there,' the Plain Dealer made his habitation
sound like both a sanitarium and refuge for husbands:

'. . . Thus, we have sense, peace, quiet, safety here;
He who has nothing, nothing has to fear.
Within thy walls, so hospitable Fleet!
A man is safe from all arrests i' the street. . . .
A prison is from marriage a reprieve,
To keep men from hanging themselves alive. . . .
A prison so may for a convent go . . .
A college, in which fools may wiser grow;
Where poor men well-read in adversity,
From fickle fate learn sense and constancy. . . .'

Wycherley began to prefer the hazards of friendship to serious experiments in love, and he wrote
about a hundred lines of verse on the subject to confirm his preference.[1]

Whilst the poet once so well-gloved lay stoically
dishevelled in prison, playgoers continued to enjoy

---

[1] For this poem see Summers, III, 43.

his comedies as if Wycherley were still a beau in Drury Lane, still the observed of all fair dames in the theatre as when he attended his own first nights. Yet none thought of him now. And he was paid no royalties from occasional performances of his plays. There was a special production of 'The Country Wife' in 1683, cast from members of both the King's and the Duke's companies, who had united during the year before.[1] New upon the scene was the famous actor Mountfort, who according to Cibber 'could at once throw off the Man of Sense for the brisk, vain, rude, and lively Coxcomb, the false, flashy Pretender to Wit, and the Dupe of his own Sufficiency: of this he gave a delightful instance in the character of Sparkish . . .' But Wycherley in prison heard nothing of it. In November of the same year, Alexander Davenant and the rest of the sharers in the Duke's Theatre put on 'The Plain Dealer.' What might seem to have made this performance still more a reproach to those aware of the author's distress was that it was done in a setting peculiarly Wycherley's own: the Hall of the Inner Temple. The General Account Book of the Temple shows that '£20 was on November 1 disbursed to Alex. Davenant for the use of himself and the rest of the players.'[2] But there was not a penny of relief for Wycherley in his confinement.

[1] Summers, II, 5. [2] Inderwick, III, lxxii ff.

Not all was well this year outside the prisons, as a matter of fact, with some of Wycherley's oldest friends. Dryden was in as much distress as if he were being ground down in gaol with Wycherley. 'It is enough for one age,' complained the poet-laureate, 'to have neglected Mr. Cowley and starved Mr. Butler.'[1] Dorset is said to have overheard this plea, and acted upon its justice. Another event touched the theatre: Charles Hart, last kin to Shakespeare on the stage, the Garrick of the Restoration, the Ranger, the Horner, the Manly of Wycherley's finest character satires, died, and with him died something of Wycherley that could never reappear. With Hart gone, it may well have seemed to Wycherley that there was no one left to write a comedy for.

But those who had known the dramatist himself up and down the merry patchwork of avenues round Covent Garden appeared simply to have let him fade out of their consciences. Did they know, or had they forgotten, that their Wycherley was beleaguered in prison? They did know that he had married, and they did know, sourly enough from mishaps at the Cock, that his raging wife had kept the poet away from them over two years. After that, having grown used to conversation without him, perhaps they had left off enquiring. Wycherley was like caviar under embargo: resignedly done without.

[1] D. N. B. (Dryden).

So the poet in prison had to endure from his friends as well as from his own relatives, even from his 'new acquaintances,' the sum of that baseness and indifference, that pretense and sham, against which Manly had with so much warmth inveighed. Wycherley in a play of his own making had forecast the torment of his own future:

'You see now,' Manly had said to his lieutenant Freeman, 'what the mighty friendship of the world is; what all ceremony, embraces, and plentiful professions come to! You are no more to believe a professing friend than a threatening enemy; and as no man hurts you that tells you he'll do you a mischief, no man, you see, is your servant who says he is so. Why the devil, then, should a man be troubled with the flattery of knaves if he be not a fool or a cully; or with the fondness of fools, if he be not a knave or a cheat? . . .

'Those you have obliged most, most certainly avoid you when you can oblige 'em no longer; and they take your visits like so many duns. Friends, like mistresses, are avoided for obligations past . . . relations have so much honour as to think poverty taints the blood, and disown their wanting kindred; believing, I suppose, that as riches at first make a gentleman, the want of 'em degrades him. . . .

'You who know all the town, and call all you know friends . . . find ingratitude too. For how many lords' families (though descended from black-smiths or tinkers) hast thou called great and illustrious? how many ill tables called good eating? how many noisy coxcombs wits? how many pert cocking cowards stout? how many tawdry affected rogues well-dressed? how many perukes admired? and how many ill verses applauded? and yet canst not borrow a shilling. Dost thou expect I, who always spoke truth, should?'

Critics had said with reason, that is to say with wincing, that 'The Plain Dealer' had too much wit. It can be understood why Wycherley, having in the back of his mind this play, this diatribe on friendship, and now feeling its sting, was prompted in his acid humour to allude to the felons in Newgate as 'those good and honest friends and companions.'

But the winter of 1684-85 held in store a change for him, a moving of events hardly to be perceived at first, almost unheard, like the first morning robin, then swelling into a chittering indescribable. The pragmatical Duke of York in 1684 was restored High Admiral. Sobered and docile after two years of enforced holiday in Belgium and Scotland—Fleet Prison to him—because of his meddling in Catholicism, James was back in the full gayety of Whitehall. And never before had the Court of Charles seen a more riotous season.

Barbara Villiers, still bewitching and regal at forty-five, had returned from her seven years of Paris to recapture a swaggering share of her old favour. Ladies at the French Court, when the Duchess had first arrived amidst them, cut her. That amused Barbara. When had she ever been interested in ladies? She started an intrigue with the British Ambassador, Montague, who after a little showed himself no diplomat, by transferring his affections to Barbara's daughter. The Duchess thought it tiresome that her country should be represented by so ungracious an envoy, and had Montague recalled.[1] And now she was back, just looking in on Whitehall.

There were two others at the King's elbow: Louise de Querouaille, baby face and kinky hair still winning, sat complacently reticent, knowing she could still boast of nature's gifts as the roses boast. And Hortense Mancini was there, her voice the rise and fall of music in a spirited song, one arm round her French page and the other, as ever, sweeping in her winnings at the gaming-table. It was quite a restaging of old times: these two and Barbara, the three sultanas together again, each with enough beauty left to quicken the sparkle in the bright and amiable eye of Charles.

On the night of February first, 1685, twenty

[1] D. N. B. (Villiers).

courtiers wagering hillocks of gold sat at play round the King.[1] Of the ladies, three, the sultanas, were being talked to; the ones unregarded were mistresses of the Duke of York. But for the clink of coins, the vast salon was oddly quiet. There was no orchestra. Lackeys moved soundlessly to and from the island of play. Charles, silent in his chair, seemed intent upon baize and gold alone, and but for the tip of his long nose his profile was hardly visible, because with his chin against his cravat his black ringlets fell so far forward. Of a sudden, before anyone at all knew what was astir, the King had lurched over in a paroxysm.

Six days later Charles II lay dying[2]—no one knew of what, though physicians had bled, purged, and cauterised him for almost every disease in the canon. The King had his arm upon Louise, close by,[3] but his thoughts upon Barbara, who was not there. 'Be kind to Barbara,' he said to the Duke. Louise was younger. Until the last she had received Charles of a morning in her peach-coloured peignoir. Kindness was still hers to command, for she possessed a lingering girlishness not to be evaded.

So died Charles Stuart, the King who had ever worn his heart upon his sleeve, but that he changed his sleeve so often.

A certain Dr. Walcot long afterwards made a

[1] Evelyn, III, 145.   [2] Ibid., III, 145 ff.   [3] Tinsley, 240.

rhyme which echoed the affection of many a crannied wine-house round the town:

'As for John Dryden's Charles, I own that King
Was never any very mighty thing,
And yet he was a devilish honest fellow,
Enjoyed his friend and bottle, and got mellow.'

James II ascended the throne on February 16.

'And now, sir,' wrote John Dennis later to Major Pack, 'is it not matter of wonder that one of Mr. Wycherley's extraordinary merit, who was esteemed by all the most deserving persons of the Court of King Charles II, and in high favour with the King himself, should in a little time after he had received these gracious offers which seem to have made and fixed his fortune, be thrown into prison for bare £700, and be suffered to languish there during the last four years of that monarch's reign,[1] forsaken by all his friends at Court and quite abandoned by the King? 'Tis no easie matter, sir, to find a more extraordinary instance of the vicissitude of human affairs . . .'

But Will Wycherley's friends, even his friends at Court, had not all passed him by like Levites. Perhaps they had been expecting the uncompromising

[1] This testimony (and Gildon's, that Wycherley went first to Newgate) would indicate that Wycherley was in prison long before June, 1685. Yet he had evidently got out temporarily, because the writ for his arrest was directed to the Sheriff of Hertfordshire; Barnaby was not a creditor.

Charles to die. When he did, and when the new
reign had swung fairly into being, they set about
seeking the help of King James. The opportunity
came by the way of entertainments given in Whitehall for amusement of the new Court. During the
autumn and winter (1685-6) plays were produced.
Colonel Brett, a profligate and good-natured favourite of the King, happened also to be a friend of
Wycherley, whose absurd imprisonment he had
borne in mind. The Colonel suggested a performance of 'The Plain Dealer' for Whitehall.[1]

The play was acted before the King and Queen
on December 14. The mere fact that it had been
judged diverting enough to offer at Court made the
King attentive. But he was moreover in good humour this night, for he was anticipating the celebration of the first Christmastide of his reign. He applauded the comedy. Like Montausier, the King
believed that the character of Manly expressed precisely his own rigid stand for truth and plain dealing, though none of the courtiers to whom James
confided this impression had quite noticed the re-
semblance before. He asked who the author was.
When Colonel Brett told him, the King remembered
Wycherley in the poet's brawny heyday ten years
earlier, and remarked that he had not seen him in a
long time.[2]

[1] Perromat, 43.   [2] Tinsley, 240 ff.

This gave Brett his chance. He told the King the story of Wycherley's misfortune, his distress, his health failing in the wretchedness of Fleet Prison. James, probably reminded also that the poet had fought gallantly aboard a royal frigate against the Dutch, and had commemorated the action in verse, gave immediate orders for his release from gaol. He directed that the full account of Wycherley's debts be paid. To this he added a pension of two hundred pounds as long as Wycherley chose to live in England.[1]

In the wake of Colonel Brett, the Earl of Mulgrave, for the second time, now sped to the Plain Dealer's assistance. Mulgrave may have been merely a 'hanger-on' of the circle of wits, but King James thought him competent enough to appoint him Lord Chamberlain. And the King commissioned the Earl to ascertain the total of Wycherley's liabilities.[2] Mulgrave hastened to the Fleet. He found the poet weakened from ague, his broad frame shrunken, and his eyes, once so alive to the moment, now eloquent of doubt and wonder, though indeed with a glimmer still left of that humour which once had quickened all Covent Garden. The Earl told him what the King had commanded. Wycherley was nearly overcome. Too modest to reveal the full amount of his obligations, and showing 'childlike unworldliness in

[1] Pack; Spence; Biog. Dramat.   [2] Summers, I, 56.

a man of the world,[1] he told the Lord Chamberlain that the sum was only £500. Payment of that much, he thought, would set him at liberty.

Mulgrave went away, and sent the money requested. But it did not release the debtor. In despair, Wycherley, not having the assurance to bother the Court further over his mistake, turned once more to his father. This time Daniel Wycherley seemed willing to help—as his second son George was still in the Fleet the family showing did not look any too well—and he paid the remaining two hundred pounds.[2] The delay prolonged Wycherley's confinement several months, but by the spring of 1686 he appears to have been set free.

One may picture Wycherley as he again sought his old haunts in Bow-street, again put his hand, not too steadily, across the banister at the Widow Hilton's. His hair had begun to turn gray before his imprisonment; it must have been now full gray. His face was lined with anxiety, and his brawny step, once so graceful and positive, was shorter, slower, measured, the step of one who had paced rather than sauntered. But his mouth had lost none of its determination. And he could still stand proudly, even though not quite erect; erectness would come back, with the burden of gaol lifted. The Fleet had seemed to curtail his middle age; free now, and

[1] Leigh Hunt, xiii.   [2] Spence, 45.

204

free for all time, Wycherley must set about casting off the years upon him which he had not yet lived.

He looked round the taverns. He might find someone he knew, and good cheer. But he heard that 'Gentle George' Etherege was among the missing; he had been appointed English resident at Ratisbon the year before. Neither Dorset nor Sedley now frequented the wineshops as late as of old; much of their time they spent darkly in the packs and sects of great ones brewing confusion to Catholic James.[1] Buckingham had retired to his country house in Yorkshire, broken but not subdued. The King had sent a priest to try and convert him; the Duke, basting his arrogance with his own fat, ridiculed the wretch and sent him flying.[2]

But Wycherley found living in Bow-street, three doors from his own lodgings, a new neighbour and friend who was more a Plain Dealer than himself, and no less a firm Jacobite (though a Protestant). Dr. John Radcliffe in his thirties had come down from Oxford in 1684. On his arrival in town he was said to have employed a legion of porters to call his name at all the coffee-houses, that he might become known;[3] within a year he was earning twenty guineas a day and five guineas consultation fee. And now he was physician to Princess Anne. The Doctor dressed

[1] Pinto, 172.   [2] D. N. B. (Buckingham).
[3] Physic and Physicians, I, 355.

in lilac velvet with yellow basket buttons. He had
hazel eyes fond of the sidelong look, his chin was
double from drinking seven-year-old beer at home
and his cheeks ruddy from ennobling himself with
claret in the taverns. He always wore his left glove.
He regarded both physic and physicians with contempt, and declared that the whole art could be
written on one sheet of paper.[1] It was his delight to
cure wives whose husbands hated them, but when an
elderly lady who had spoken in disdain of his talents
was taken gravely ill and endeavoured to get him
to prescribe, Radcliffe refused, observing 'he neither
knew what was good for an old woman, nor what an
old woman was good for.'[2]

One of the ways to gain the favour of James II
was of course to adopt his religion. There were in
1686 many like Julie d'Angennes who believed that
one should be a Catholic if for no other reason than
that the King was: one should thereby prosper at
least while alive; after death, one might gamble as
to the everlasting felicities. But men like Buckingham and Dr. Radcliffe cared no whit for the smiles
of James. Obadiah Walker, Master of University
College, Oxford, where Radcliffe had studied, was
employed to make the eminent young physician a
Catholic. Radcliffe said to him: 'Being bred up a
Protestant, and having continued such at Oxford,

[1] MacMichael, 15–16, 28–29.   [2] 'Physic and Physicians,' I, 90.

where I had no relish for absurdities, I see no reason
to change my principles and turn Papist in London."[1]
Likewise, Buckingham, though no longer a man of
means, trumpeted his independence. He was through
with Whitehall. The proselyting of the King only
angered him. And Wycherley, in the singular stead-
fastness of his friendship still devoted to the Duke
remote or near, rich or poor, wrote some new verses
'To the Duke of Buckingham, a Man of great
Mind, reduced to a little Fortune,' and said: 'Secure
of soul, thou canst all fortune brave, Scorning to be
false expectation's slave.'

So great a man as Dryden, on the other hand,
found it tactful to begin to go to mass. By the end
of the year London noticed that the poet-laureate
had become a Catholic. But London did not discover
so generally that hunger of the body rather than
hunger of the mind had wrought this change:[2] Dryden had lived pinched by want for several years.
He could almost say with Emperor Hadrian that his
pallid little soul would soon be joking no more. And
how could change in a man's religion harm his soul?
The intelligence of Dryden was above any such
timidity.

It is very probable that the peculiar episode of
Wycherley's third conversion, his re-conversion to
Catholicism, occurred near this time. The poet is

[1] MacMichael, 28–29.   [2] D. N. B. (Dryden).

said to have been one of the renegades who passed over to the Roman Church in 1687.[1] However, in this day when there were few men of prominence forswearing Protestantism who were not therewith crooking the knee to James, the Plain Dealer, in religion as well as in secular adherence, did not become a Jacobite because of expectations. He gave his loyalty whole, out of gratitude for his release from the Fleet.[2]

Yet Wycherley was a sick man too, and he may have felt furthermore the need of certain spiritual support which he thought only Catholicism could give. Having been a Catholic before the Restoration, he at least had some memories of what there was for him in that faith. He had come out of prison having suffered from apoplexy, as the malady was understood at the time, but even though he was writing no plays he desired to live as much as ever in the way of the outward world, which was the way of Drury Lane. Health, so necessary for the old life, might follow upon devoutness.

If Dryden was seeing much of Wycherley now, the poet-laureate as a new convert may easily have bent him towards the creed of the King. Dryden in any case was keeping in touch with his regained friend, for writing to Etherege—who was still legate to Bavaria—in February, 1687, he said: . . .

[1] Beljame, 214; De Grisy, 46.   [2] Lansdowne, Memoirs, 6.

'In short, without apoplexy, Wycherley's long sickness, I forget everything to enjoy nothing.'

Dryden was passing through perhaps the most trying time of his life. Notwithstanding his laureateship he was earning hardly enough by his writing to keep out of neediness. Etherege had asked for news of the wits; but Dryden had to reply that, even without apoplexy, he had forgotten everything. 'Can you expect news from Covent Garden out of such a man?'

But the gesture of embracing Catholicism under James II, like imitating his prowess on the golf links, was with a great many people a fad, considered a smart thing to do to astonish one's friends, as it sometimes is today. Grandsons of grim Puritan forefathers alike with men who had never worshipped any Deity at all forsook their heresies to carry rosary and scapular and kneel awfully at the King's mass. The reverence with which some of the neophytes regarded their adopted religion emerged when Lord Sunderland cross-questioned Joe Haynes —the comedian dearest to Wycherley's heart—on his conversion:

'As I was lying in my bed,' Haynes protested solemnly, 'the Virgin appeared to me and said:

' "Arise, Joe!"

'You lie, you rogue!' Sunderland broke in. 'If it had really been the Virgin she would have said

'Joseph,' if only out of respect for her husband.'[1]

These faddists all fared well enough as long as a Catholic King could retain his throne. But they who depended upon the lasting favours of James swam with fins of lead. The Duke of Buckingham, for whom a thatched hut was become a mansion, died in 1687, and it was a sign of the times that he was buried in Westminster Abbey with enough cloth of gold to envelop the whole funeral of Charles II two years before. Charles, dislodging statecraft to make room for his conscience, had died an eleventh-hour Catholic.

Wycherley, saddened by losses in the ranks of his friends, still found London in these first years of his freedom not destitute of amusement. He was still the great Plain Dealer, and Drury Lane bore witness to that by thronging to another production of his masterpiece at the Theatre Royal in 1686.[2] Then Sedley, of whom he had heard nothing for so long, tarried in his political plots, and turning his eyes of Puck again to authorship produced at the same theatre, in May, 1687, a second comedy, 'Bellamira, or The Mistress.'[3] This play bore a double interest for Wycherley: its original suggestion, like the original suggestion for 'The Country Wife,' came from the 'Eunuchus' of Terence; and the character of Bellamira was based on the life of none other than Bar-

---

[1] Davies, III, 267.   [2] Cambridge Hist., VIII.   [3] Pinto, 168.

bara Villiers, again a woman talked about over the
tea-cups in St. James's Square. Perhaps 'Bellamira'
prompted another revival of Wycherley; the King's
Troupe in 1688 played 'The Country Wife' again,
and the pit rose in their seats to the satiric wit of
Sparkish and Horner.

Wycherley, an accepted favourite of the King,
whose allowance was enabling the poet to live,
though frugally, in his well-loved Covent Garden,
and to work away at verses and prose writings, was
on the point of making lively new friends amongst
the coming men of letters when Revolution up-
turned Whitehall. King James fled, carrying with
him the last royal patronage to be enjoyed by Will
Wycherley, poet. The pension stopped. It had gone
on, not as the King said as long as Wycherley chose
to live in England, but only as long as James himself
did.

Parliament assembled to meet William of
Orange, a Protestant, two days before Christmas.
There was now nothing for Dryden and the rest of
the abjurers to do but to remain Catholic—inconstancy and indecision must stop somewhere. No very
sincere welcome nor display of confidence would
have greeted their return to the Protestant fold.
Mulgrave relinquished the post of Lord Chamberlain to Dorset, now a fat and melancholy statesman
in the new regime. Dryden to his consternation had

to give up the laureateship, which through Dorset's influence went to merry old Shadwell, but the Earl from his own pocket proceeded to pay the salary of the post to Dryden as if no change of government had occurred. Wycherley's comment on the new laureate was: 'He knew how to start a fool very well, but he was never able to run him down.'

The £200 annuity granted Wycherley by James II had been hardly enough to sustain a poet so prodigal. But when even this much of a pension ceased to come in, Wycherley again found himself in penury almost as embarrassing as his plight before he went to gaol. James had fled in November. He was intercepted and brought back. He escaped again on December 23, and this time the revolution-ists let him go. In the very same week—Christmas week—George Wycherley, mercilessly ignored by his father, died in the Fleet. He was only thirty-seven, but gaol fever was no respecter of young years. And George's dramatist brother in this emer-gency was quite without money to pay for a funeral.

I am at this point able to present two new letters by Wycherley, found in the ancient manor of Lev-ens, where they were deposited in tin boxes in the time of William and Mary, letters which are not only earlier than any others known to be written by the poet, but which appear to fix the hitherto ob-scure year of Wycherley's release from prison. It would appear that Wycherley had drawn his pension through Colonel James Grahme of Levens, Privy Purse to King James II, who kept offices in Whitehall. Colonel Grahme, like the King an intimate friend of Katherine Sedley, Countess of Dorchester,[1] was next younger brother to Richard, Lord Preston, an associate of the Earl of Clarendon in plots against William of Orange. At forty, the Colonel was a handsome courtier, tall, thin, with a long nose and a countenance rather melancholy, but he was a mirror of fashion, and his dry humour was celebrated for setting St. James's Palace into wavelets of mirth. Now, however,—Christmastide, 1688 —with his sovereign in flight, Colonel Grahme's levity was of course smothered by his caution, a trait useful to Jacobites who rather desired to keep their heads on their shoulders. And, when Wycherley asked the late Keeper of the Purse for more money, Grahme seems to have held a purse no longer.

The first of the two new letters is in correction to one written previously by Wycherley (and not found at Levens), which miscarried and fell into the hands of the Colonel's younger brother, Fergus Grahme. Fergus, who on the evidence of letters at Levens was generally begging for his own needs, took it upon himself to reply to Wycherley, who then had to write the Colonel once more:

[1] Pinto, 205.

213

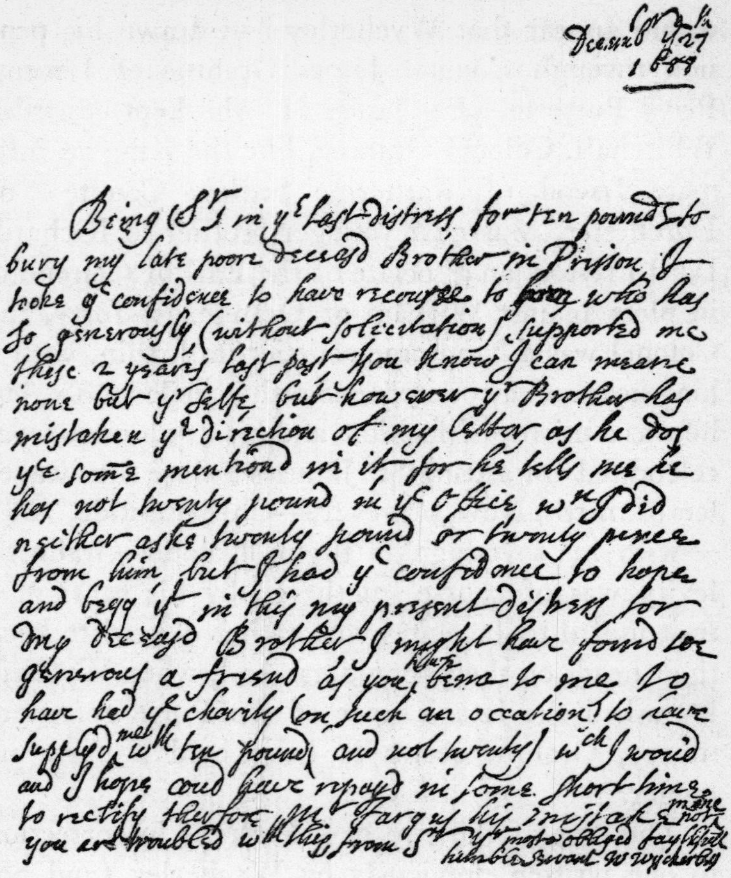

December the 27th 1688 (handwritten)

[handwritten letter in old script]

In current spelling:

December the 27th, 1688.

Being, Sir, in the last distress for ten pounds to bury my late poor deceased brother in prison, I took the confidence to have recourse to him who has so generously (without solicitation) supported me these two years last past. You know I can mean none but yourself. But however, your brother has mistaken the direction of my letter, as he does the sum mentioned in it, for he tells me he has not twenty pounds in the office, which I did neither ask twenty pound or twenty pence from him. But I had the confidence to hope and beg it in this my present distress for my deceased brother. I might have found so generous a friend as you have been to me to have had the charity (on such an occasion) to have supplied me with ten pound (and not twenty) which I would and I hope could have repaid in some short time.

To rectify therefore Mr. Fargus his mistake, not mine, you are troubled with this, from Sir,

Your most obliged faithful humble servant,

W. WYCHERLEY.

The superscription is: 'To Col., the Hon'ble J. Grahme, Whitehall, and not Mr. Fargus.'

Wycherley, by addressing this second letter 'and not Mr. Fargus,' was taking care that his appeal should this time go straight to the Colonel. In these tremulous days, when Fergus Grahme himself was about to scurry out of England in the path of James II, the Grahme brothers were probably in the habit of opening one another's letters.[1] In the correspondence preserved at Levens, another brother mentions that he took the liberty to open a letter to the Colonel from 'Coz. Henry,' because 'he had not had news of him.'[2]

It was, no doubt, the King to whom Wycherley

[1] Private information.   [2] Ibid.

in his letter referred through Grahme as having 'so generously supported him' for two years—the elapsed time since the Plain Dealer, in 1686, had been released from the Fleet. It had been 'without solicitation' on Wycherley's part that the King had rescued and provided for him. But now the King, four days earlier than the date of this letter, had stolen away to France, and in his place the Prince of Orange trod the great halls of St. James's. On January 3, 1689, one week after the poet wrote the above letter, George Wycherley was buried,[1] though as Wycherley in his next communication revealed, no funds for the burial were forthcoming from Grahme:

You courtiers, Sir, seldom cease to be friends but you begin to be enemies, and it is a double unkindness as it is a double unhappiness for the miserable deserted man, which I beg your honour and justice will secure me from. For as I got at first your kindness without deserving it, so have I lost it too, without deserving it. And I protest before God, if we were not of late very much given to change, I should a little admire at yours.

And (if I may be believed) I am more concerned for the loss of such a friend than for the loss of his assistance, because the first is a secret upbraiding me with the want of merit to keep his friendship longer, the other but an upbraiding me with the want of good fortune, which often attends the most meritorious.

But I must consolate my want by yours, for if you want

[1] Shropshire Society, 357.

You Courteous(?) [...] seldome ceass to be Friends
but you begin to be Enimys, and y' is a double
unkindness as it is a double unhappyness for y'
misserable deserted man, w'ch J begger y' honour
and justice will secure me from, for as J got
at first y' kindness without deserving it soe have
J lost it too, without deserving it, and J protest
before God, if we were not of late very much
given to change J should a little admire at yours,
and (if J may be believed) J am more concernd for
y' loss of such a friend then for y' loss of
his assistance, because y' first is a secret upbraiding
me w' y' want of merrit to keepe his friend-
-ship longer, y' other but upbraiding me
w'ch often attends y' most meritorious, but J must
consolate my want by yours, for if you want
ten pounds J may y' better beare y' want of such
a somme, for you have as it were relieved my
want in telling me you have not
but yet tho' you want money for y' friend
y'

ONE OF THE LETTERS FROM WYCHERLEY TO COLONEL JAMES GRAHME
OF LEVENS, KEEPER OF THE PRIVY PURSE TO KING JAMES II

*Found in December, 1929, in an old tin box of papers at Levens Hall,
Kendal, Westmorland*   (See over)

I hope Sr you will not kindness for ye
less asystance you can aford him, you sherd
allow him ye more pitty, ye want of wch
and your good company woud make me yt
more misserable (if it were possible for
me to be more) but herewer Sr I may
of late have deserved from you I hope you have
charity enough left, to pardon this trouble
given you whom no want of a new obligation can make to forget an old one;
let me not be so misserable at least as
to loose yr kindness for yr loves a million
in ye opinion of

Sr

Yr most obliged humble servant
W Wycherley

ten pounds, I may the better bear the want of such a sum, so you have, as 'twere, relieved my want in telling me you have not wherewithal to do it. But yet, though you want money for your friend, I hope, Sir, you will not kindness, for the less assistance you can afford him, you should allow him the more pity, the want of which and your good company would have him yet more miserable, if it were possible for him to be so.

But however, Sir, I may of late have deserved from you, I hope you have charity enough left to pardon the trouble given you by him whom no want of a new obligation can make forget an old one. Let me not be so miserable at least as to lose your kindness, for your love's a million, in the opinion of,

Sir,
Your most obliged humble servant,
W. WYCHERLEY.

To James Grahme, Esq.

There is no denying that Wycherley was in distress: in this letter he used the word 'want' nine times. And it is difficult to believe that Colonel Grahme lacked 'wherewithal' to make a loan of ten pounds. Within the same year, 1688, he had bought Levens Hall and its vast estates from Alan Bellingham, spendthrift descendant of the Deputy Warden of the Marches under Henry VII,[1] for £24,000.[2] But if Wycherley appealed to Grahme on account of the King's bounty, the King was gone, and Grahme

---

[1] Bagot, 1. [2] Private information.

apparently was paying out no more money for James
II. On the other hand, it may be gathered from the
context of these letters, that aside from any forwarding of the King's pension, Grahme was a personal patron also of Wycherley. But the Colonel was
a shrewd conserver of money, and probably at this
trying crisis, when the Government was 'very much
given to change,' he had seen enough of borrowers.

Soon after the proclamation of the new king, in
February, 1689, it became known in the coffee-
houses that William III valued neither plays nor
poets. In fact William and Mary announced, almost
as if they considered literature an evil in itself, that
they intended a 'reformation of manners.' Wycherley had been mending, little by little, as he revisited
his old corners in Covent Garden. Now he was left
penniless again, and with no friends at Court.

A third prison loomed up, worse to Wycherley in
some respects than either Newgate or the Fleet. He
must incarcerate himself in Clive Hall. There only
could he go and wait until the political scene quieted
down and manners got unreformed, there only could
he try to persuade his father, between lawsuits, to
hear his protests and allow him sufficient money to
keep up lodgings in town. At the moment, London
was not a prosperous place for a Jacobite.

The Plain Dealer took the mail-coach to Shrewsbury, a jostling three-day journey during which he

was pushed, crowded, and elbowed against such country wives and husbands as he too well knew. From Shrewsbury, the family conveyance bore him seven miles farther on to the family village. Clive was a spot of singularly exhilarating air when the breeze moved down from the long eastward hills, but to Will Wycherley all the breezes of Shropshire were noxious compared to one whiff of stale air in the Rose Tavern.

Wycherley rode down the lane of gray stone houses, waspnest gray, and was looked at by the same sheep-eyed shaggy-haired men and women to whose families the world for centuries had been only Clive. He gained the rise of the road to his father's house, and knocked upon the door which was shaded by the same old oak that spread its great hand of branches, like a blessing, over the ell of the manor. He crossed the same chill threshold and met the same splenetic father as he had left in the days of Cromwell, to go off to France. There was indeed something of the prodigal in this tired fifty-year-old son come home for the first time to stay, but how forgiving would the father be? Would there be any fatted calf, or would Daniel Wycherley play upon the nerves of his eldest-born with the maddening jabs of a man tuning a pianoforte?

CHAPTER VII

WITS-AT-WILLS

'MAY it please Your Majesty,' said Dr. Radcliffe to William III, 'I must be plain with you, Sir: your case is one of danger, no doubt, but if you will adhere to my prescriptions, I will engage to do you good. The rheum is dripping on your lungs, and will be of fatal consequence to you, unless it be otherwise diverted.'[1]

Radcliffe so well 'diverted the rheum,' which was an asthma, that the King a few months later rode forth to war and overwhelmed his uncle, James II, at the Battle of the Boyne. That was on July 1, 1690.

Curiously like the Marquis de Montausier, William III was grave and phlegmatic except in battle, when his countenance was the very sunlight of animation. Again like the Marquis he avoided company: as Montausier shut himself up in his library, so William constantly went off hunting. At forty he was a man of middle stature, thin and weak, sharp-eyed and hook-nosed. So dry and forbidding was his speech that few dared converse with him. He was

[1] MacMichael, 8.

sullen to the point of affront, but for a reason: to conceal his ambition of conquering Louis XIV. There was something Dutch about his manner at table: he once ate up all the green pease, an early-season delicacy, without offering any either to the Queen or to Princess Anne.[1] Englishmen said to one another: 'Is that the way they go on in Holland?'

William and Mary bought Kensington House of the Earl of Nottingham, and to set an example of domesticity to the nation they lived there as in a villa, not as in a royal mansion. Mary, now twenty-eight, was a Queen out of ancient fable. She walked with the majesty of a daughter of imperial Rome, but all day she sat with her ladies and maids of honour in a room she called the Patch-work Closet, where with the wifely industry of Andromache she wrought tapestries and chair-coverings for chambers of the Court.[2] This toil with the spinsters and the knitters was not wholly the occupation of her choice: Mary had read far in divinity and history, and she had hoped to continue her studies. No Queen of the Stuarts, no Queen of England since Elizabeth possessed so cultivated an understanding. But her reading unhappily had been interrupted, for like Leah, Mary was tender-eyed, from a form of ophthalmia. Deprived of books, she exercised her mind by conversation, and became as eager for it as the King was

[1] MacMichael, 26.   [2] Ibid., 11.

averse to it. It was as if the Queen said, 'Let me have men about me who can talk,' and she wearied of anyone who could tell her nothing about the rise of the church or the fall of empires.

It was perhaps as well for Wycherley that he had withdrawn for a time from such a London, from a city now inspired to polish candlesticks and to mind the sanctity of hearthsides. That had not been quite the code of life under Charles II. Yet what was the alternative, the picture of existence offered in Clive?

The poet upon his homecoming was twice as old as his parents. But in spite of all his ailments he was not twice as full of years: he had been cradled in country air, and the power of his strong body and mind to beat down illness left him still unresigned to banishment from Bow-street. It was in comprehension of life and awareness of the world that Will Wycherley was so much older. What had he to say to his family about cabbages and country lawsuits? What had they to tell him of satire and drollery in Drury Lane? Conversation at times was going to be thin: tea an exchange of sharp pettinesses; dinner a solemn and soundless rite.

Daniel Wycherley looked upon his son not as the most brilliant dramatist of the day, but as a renegade and a rake who had brought him more worry than distinction. A certain unsatisfactory return home of this son in 1660 must have recurred to his mind.

Now, the heir to Clive Hall had not only abandoned the common-sense calling of the law, and evidently for his ignorance of it lost the fortune of his wife, but he had come home a Jacobite, a partisan of a Catholic King, of a man who had been thrust out. James indeed had been the instrument of Will Wycherley's delivery from gaol, but was it necessary for a son of Daniel Wycherley to have Catholic sympathies for that?

At the end of December, 1688, George Wycherley had died in the Fleet, because he owed money to his father. Was Daniel now disappointed because William had not gone the same way? At the distance of two centuries and a half it is not easy to judge, without more evidence, the position of Daniel Wycherley. Both of his sons were careless in money matters, yet the father, who squandered his own income in the law-courts, seems to have held himself above reproach. He was a rich landed proprietor. But he had educated these sons to sympathies wide of his own, and his love of money overcame his fatherly affections.

Daniel was like Hamlet's father only in so far as he appears to have had an eye like Mars to threaten and command. He was not so much lord of his manor as tyrant of it, and in giving refuge to the Plain Dealer he himself made it plain that the Master of Clive Hall was still very much a parent whose word was not to be overridden. One of the amiable things he did for this boy of fifty was to set a guardian over him as if he were a boy of five, a sort of keeper who followed Wycherley about and cocked an eye at what he did.[1]

The old father's intentions may have been most charitable; Daniel may have concluded that his son was enough of an invalid to need an attendant. But such solicitude was not so taken by the dramatist. Irritably he wrote a letter to Dryden in town, saying, 'You know I am a chopping minor.'

Wycherley indeed found himself out of one prison and in another. Ill or well, he loathed the country and everything thereof, surrounded as he was by a testy father, a pettifogging mother, one or two obediently dull brothers,[2] and a cluster or squires whose whole life was to drink, shout, snore, and drink again.

'The damned conversation I meet with here!' exclaimed the poet later, as he aged in the incarceration of Clive.[3]

One of his writings, expressive of his apparent scorn for the squires, he addressed: 'To a Great Country-Drinker, valuing Himself upon his Hos-

---

[1] Gildon, 13.
[2] His sister Frances, a housewife, had died in 1678; and his elder sister Elizabeth had died insane because not allowed to marry a Mr. Pyke.
[3] Letter to Pope, January 19, 1708.

pitality, calling Himself Good Company; and having a Handsome Wife, (whom yet He neglected for the Bottle;) and drank for me all the Glasses I refus'd.'

His writing was to be his diversion, to bridge over the chasm until the day should come for him to hasten back to Bow-street. Wycherley kept working at his poems, which he now proposed to publish. Daniel would allow him little money, but if he could put a new book on the stalls in Middle Temple Gate he might gather in from it enough to release him for a time from torment. Another respite from the buzzing of village gadflies was his correspondence. Frequently he replied by an epistle in verse to letters from his friends in town, men who wanted him back and whose company he himself longed for. Unable to talk with the worthy folk of Clive, he conversed with Covent Garden in pen and ink, and he copied his letters to add to his book. He wrote (either to Sir Charles Sedley or to Sir Car Scroope) 'An Epistle from the Country, to my Friend Sir C. S. in Town; in Answer to one of His, wherein He wonder'd, I did not answer His last.' To the plaudits of two Londoners who sent him sympathy in his isolation he responded with: 'An Epistle from the Country, in Answer to one from the Town written jointly by a Man of Wit and Another of Quality':

225

'. . . So Town-Wits, like Town-Rooks, together join,
In Praise o' th' Squire, whose Ruine they design;
Praise him, and his Wit, so maliciously,
But to make more his Pride, or Vanity,
Till that their Praise becomes his Infamy. . . .'

And then, as soon as Wycherley was away from his writing-table in Clive Hall, one can hear the Widow Blackacre in the person of his father coming to life with a vengeance:

'. . . If you talk of declarations, I'll show you one of the prettiest penned things, which I mended too myself, you must know. . . . I'll show you my bill in chancery here, that gives you such a character of my adversary, makes him as black— . . . If you talk of decreeing, I have such a decree here, drawn by the finest clerk. . . . Nay . . . but first I'll read you a letter of mine to a friend in the country, called a letter of attorney.'

So the chickens of the dramatist again came home to roost, and the man who had hatched them was caught in his own hennery.

It was inevitable that Wycherley, for all his vexation, should find his health tending to improve in this pure though suffocating atmosphere of Clive, and it was equally inevitable that from time to time he should extract a few pounds from his penurious father to enable him to run up to town and sharpen his wits. It so happened. He went to London not only

to recapture old friends, but to conquer new ones.
And he found them not so often at the Cock, nor
even at the Rose, but favouring another tavern more
in the spirit of the new reign—Will's Coffee-House,
on the north side of Russell-street where Bow-street
begins. It was a three-storied box of a house, the top
truncated, the base about thirty feet along each
street, and built of cherry-coloured brick (the original colour is still visible to one who will climb a
ladder to the garret). There Wycherley joined John
Dryden, and there he drank success to the younger
writers who were to carry the torch of English
literature into the coming century.

This tavern had been built in 1634, but not until
Will Urwin took charge as host had it become the
mecca of men of letters. Will was renowned for his
wit as well as for his tea and coffee, and he drew in
to his tables and bowls a circle of celebrities whose
shades seem still to haunt the place. Today one sees
the little house of brick blackened with the dust of
hundreds of years. It stands sagging and bending as
if under its burden of memories, while its eight
chimney-pots, cracked and huddled, seem to whisper
of old legends, nimble words once heard from the
fireside below. A mouldering monument, like a half-
sunken tombstone, where day by day poems unwrit-
ten and books unrecorded were spoken by writers
both then and now called great, Will's Coffee-House

is become in these years of grace a shed of creaking stalls for the sacks of a vegetable-monger.

An iron lamp used to swing from the corner of Will's and throw its light into the shop of a woollen-draper who occupied the street-floor. Behind this shop, in Bow-street, a door opened into a corridor to dark stairs, which with two turnings led up to Will's. At the top of the flight one passed into the Room of the Wits, with its fireplace of white marble and its window-casings a foot deep which gave upon an iron balcony over Russell-street. The company sat not in boxes, but at narrow tables about the room: at three o'clock, the popular hour, there would be a knot of philosophical mutes called the Grave Club in one corner; four or five wits called the Witty Club, raking the ashes of the old poets, in another; and at a third the Rabble, a parcel of boy-faced beaux in red stockings, who peeped into Will's once a day with two or three second-rate sayings,[1] and from whose table one overheard the crow thus chiding blackness: 'Damn me! how can he write? He's a raw young fellow newly come from the University!' or, such *arrêts litteraires* as, 'Shakespeare? hang me the mouldy rogue! I nauseate him.'

Presiding over the Rabble was Ensign Swan, formerly a clergyman in Cambridge, where he had lost his fellowship because he refused to take the oath

[1] Robinson, 101 ff; Timbs, 272.

of allegiance after the Revolution. But he put off the curate's cloth only to put on the clown's costume, and he came to Will's a most egregious punster and dicer.[1] Wycherley, before he had many times heard the lamentable jests of this man who played with words as he played with dice, set down some doggerel which he called 'A Panegyric on Quibbling; to the, that way, Ingenious Mr. Swan,' saying, 'My Goose-Quill shall raise to the Skies my Swan, Tho' some think me a Goose, but for my Pain,' and gravely commending the curate for taking no money, 'So you, Swan, though an Arch-Bird with your Jest, With your Wit ne'er, Swan, feather'd your own Nest.'

It was the sort of nonsense verse which the Plain Dealer might have written in Will's at the height of the hubbub, when snuff-boxes were snapping, coffee-bowls rattling on the tables, long clay pipes sending billows of smoke against the brown walls, and almost befogging one group of men from the sight of another. Hour upon hour, talk of cards, dice, love, learning, and politics jostled the air, until the bellman cried the talkers down at two o'clock in the morning.[2]

Wycherley, but for his empty purse—he was so generous that it was always empty within a day or two after it was full—and the necessity to replenish

[1] Summers, III, 286.   [2] Wheatley, III, 517.

it at Clive Hall, so began one of the happiest phases of his life. He quitted the taverns—there were still a few—thronged only with fops in silver-threaded coats, fringed gloves and knee-tassels, flaxen wigs from Paris, the taverns where the air was like a perfumer's shop, the only tobacco was violet-scented snuff, and the conversation was the very dialogue of the silken young men of his own plays.[1] He had outgrown all that.

And he had outlived the ambition he once felt to be seen at Court. Royal disregard and years of misery, admittedly of his own making, had followed upon his dancing attendance there. Royal patronage, true enough, had rescued him. But if we may judge by his satirical poems against the Court, and they are not a few, Wycherley had found Whitehall a hoax and a snare to which poets were lured only to enliven the frolics of the great, and then, not being face-cards, discarded. Yet he avoided William III mainly because he was so grateful to James II, as Lord Lansdowne has recorded:

'In the turn of times which has since happened, it is not for want of friends, nor powerful solicitations, that he remains in obscurity; he can never forget the generosity of that unfortunate prince, and as in another reign he chose to be a victim to love, he now chooses to be a sacrifice to gratitude.'[2]

[1] Macaulay, III, 345 ff.   [2] Works, 435.

Lansdowne himself, now a young man of twenty-five with aspirations to play-writing, was one of Wycherley's new friends at the coffee-house, and like Wycherley he too had been in favour with James and was therefore out with William. Like Wycherley again he was living for the moment in a sort of literary retirement.

Day after day Wycherley went to Will's and found old Dryden (senior by nine years), more sleepy-eyed and bloated than ever, seated in the arm-chair of honour to the left of a stone slab before the fireplace. Having taken his mid-day dinner at home and escaped from his frozen-faced wife who was always reminding herself of her nobility, Poet Squab puffed and waddled down to Will's to wage book-battles until long past nightfall. In these hours it was his habit to note down in a table-book, his long nose almost turning the pages, the objections made to his plays by the critics.[1]

John Dennis too was at the Wits' Table, and as a critic he was closely listened to. Dennis, poor as a pedlar, lived in a garret and went to bed in a flannel night-cap.[2] He wore red stockings which matched his red face. Some years before he had come up from Cambridge stuffed with learning; he would write dramas. He did write them, but he could not seem to get them on the stage. Whereupon Dennis turned

[1] Timbs, 272; D. N. B. (Dryden).   [2] Thackeray (on Pope), 314.

231

critic—he was born a critic, but had not wished to own it—and by his fluent discourse, founded upon so wide reading, he gained the friendship of Dryden and Wycherley whom he amused by his tremendous scowls and his cannonading of the lesser wits.[1]

William Walsh, a prince as ever Dennis was pauper, was another of the critical circle. Like Bacon, he always made it a point to be seen in the company of great men. Walsh was splendidly a beau of buckles and lace, was most fond of talking of the ladies, and never married.[2] He liked to pronounce, with little whines for semi-colons, upon the elegance of any bit of writing that circulated in the coffee-house, and after the manner of Dennis and the younger fry he showed scant deference to anyone except Wycherley or Dryden. Walsh usually brought a ballad to Will's. It dealt with sighs. In 1691 he wrote 'A Dialogue Concerning Women.' 'I have tried,' said he, 'in these love lyrics, to present the faithful image of an amorous heart.'

There were endless talks on style; modern English prose, fathered by Dryden, was being born at Will's. And it was not enough that every man one met in the Wits' Room should have songs, epigrams, and satires in his hands; a certain 'Julian' hovered about the house and excitedly distributed copies of lampoons which had been passed to him privately

[1] Courthope, V, 27.   [2] D. N. B. (Walsh).

by their authors.[1] If a youngster of the Rabble, with the help of a scribbler in the room, could write a few verses, or get a pinch from Dryden's snuff-box, or get a cup of wine in edgewise with Wycherley, he strutted into the open air and proclaimed himself a wit. From these scenes Dryden padded home after dark and turned the conversations over the coffee-bowls into his masterly prefaces.[2] From these scenes Wycherley, walking two minutes up Bow-street, returned to his lodgings, thought he ought to write a preface for his next book too, but went to bed.

Lugubrious it was for the Plain Dealer to have to forego the fellowship of wits and rumble back to Clive Hall. Yet the family hearth with a figure like Daniel Wycherley upon it occasionally provided for the whole family an incident amusing if not uproarious. In 1690 the Mayor of Shrewsbury had sued the old gentleman for non-payment of tithes, which the town contended should help to support the minister of Clive Chapel, adjacent to the manor. Daniel for a change had to cease being plaintiff, and learn the new role of defendant.

The case was submitted to the High Sheriff, who in the autumn of 1691 made an award, which Gough reports: 'Mr. Wycherley had a great suite . . . about maintenance for the minister of Clive . . . The case was faire, if his designs had been

---

[1] Timbs, 272 ff.   [2] Robinson, 101 ff.

soe: but to endeavour to prove it a donative, and himself patron, was such an idle thing that his own children laft att it . . . Mr. Wycherley . . . soe bombasted . . . his claim of patronage that he could doe nothing but spend money.[1]

The poet continued through the next year to divide his time between town and country, but without seeing nearly as much of the coffee-houses as he longed for. On one of his dashes to London, early in 1693, as he drew up his chair at Will's he must have been startled to hear his eminently sane friend Dryden heralding a new dramatist as the equal of Shakespeare. Smiling Will Congreve, a lath of a boy in his twenties, had written two comedies, 'The Old Bachelor' and 'The Double Dealer,' which flashed with the fire of his wit like opals. The town was squandering praise upon him. Congreve himself was giddily in love with the 'arch black eyes' of the actress Anne Bracegirdle, a girl of nineteen, and the consummate minx in his character of 'Araminta.' But when Congreve was not explaining his love to Anne he stole a little time to drop into Will's.

It was not wholly as a predecessor that Wycherley had to greet the new genius. For he was in a sense Congreve's contemporary as well, since 'The Gentleman Dancing-Master' at the very time was being performed in the King's Theatre, 'The Plain

[1] Gough, 86–87.

Dealer' had just been acted again in Drury Lane, 'Love in a Wood' was soon to be revived,[1] and that was to be followed by still another production (the fifth) of 'The Plain Dealer.'[2] No other author possessed such enduring stage popularity.

The two dramatists became almost instant friends,[3] as a letter of Lord Lansdowne, to a correspondent to whom he wished to introduce Wycherley, suggests that they well might have: '. . . Congreve is your familiar acquaintance; you may judge of Wycherley by him: they have the same manly way of thinking and writing, the same candour, modesty, humanity and integrity of manners. It is impossible not to love them for their own sakes, abstracted from the merit of their works.'[4]

Four men of letters had now replaced the four noblemen—rakes of a bygone reign—as the companions nearest Wycherley's heart: Dryden was his Buckingham, Dennis was his Sedley, Walsh was his Dorset, and Congreve was his Rochester. For the Plain Dealer, after his vicissitudes, these friends were as wholesome a succession as the succession of William and Mary was for him subsequent to Charles. Never in the history of English literature, it is said, have the leading authors been more united

---

[1] For mention of this revival (1694) and a sketch of Anne Bracegirdle's performance in it as Christina, see Thackeray's 'Henry Esmond,' 178 ff.

[2] Camb. Hist., VIII, 130.   [3] Gosse, 21.   [4] Works, 436.

in friendship and loyalty than in the decade beginning in 1690.[1] Only one rising genius grew to rail
against the concord and merriment at Will's: Jonathan Swift. But Dryden had said to him, 'Cousin
Swift, you will never be a poet.' And Swift then
called the conversation at Will's 'the worst in the
world.' Yet in a letter to Congreve, his fellow-col-
legian from Trinity, Dublin, the Dean betrayed that
he was not above admiring, at a distance, the makers
of that conversation, saying: 'Wycherley and you
and Mr. Bays (Dryden) are the three first poets of
the day, and arbiters of taste at Will's.'[2]

What was the humour of this taste, this conversation, what the words 'so nimble and so full of
subtle flame,' heard round the Wits' Table at Will's
in the sixteen-nineties? Dennis has given a piece of
it in a letter he sent to Wycherley:[3]

'Dear Sir: The last time I was at Will's I had the
mortification to hear that our friend Mr. —— had
met with a disappointment in ——; at which, some
who were present were glad, affirming that success
would have thrown him out of his element; for that
a man of wit is not qualified for business as well as
a blockhead . . . I desire your opinion.

'First, as their (blockheads') brains are a great
deal colder than those of men of wit, they must have

---

[1] Gosse, 117.   [2] Ibid., 47.
[3] October 30, 1695.   Dennis, Select Works, II, 498.

but very strait imaginations and very barren inventions; from whence it follows, that they have but few thoughts, and a few objects fill their capacities.

'2. It is reasonable enough to believe that since they are uncapable of many thoughts, those few which they have are determined by their necessities, their appetites, and their desires, to what they call their fortunes and their establishments.

'3. It is not very bad to conceive that since a blockhead has but a few thoughts, and perhaps but one all his lifetime, which is his interest, he should have it more perfect, and better digested, than men of wit who have the same thought, who perhaps have a thousand every hour.

'4. It is easy to comprehend that since such a one has but a few thoughts, or perhaps but one, which by often revolving in his mind he has digested and brought to perfection, he should readily pass from thought to action. For he must grow weary of thinking so often of one and the same thing; and since the nature of the soul requires agitation, as soon as his little speculation ceases he must act to divert himself.

'5. As a little thought often makes a man active in business, so a little judgment often makes him diligent; for he may well be eager in the pursuit of those things on which, seduced by passion and vulgar opinion, he sets an exorbitant value, and concerning whose natures and incertainty he is not very capable of making solid reflections. For though prudence may oblige a man to secure a competency, yet never was anyone by right reason induced to seek superfluities.

'6. Penury of thought supposes littleness of soul, which is often requisite for succeeding in business. For a Blockhead is sordid enough to descend to trick and artifice, which in business are often necessary to procure success, unless they are more than supplied by a prudence derived from consummate experience, or from a great capacity.

' . . . I apply the word "Blockhead" according to the language of you men of wit, to one who thinks but a little . . . By a man of wit I do not mean every coxcomb whose imagination has got the ascendant of his literary reason; but a man like you, sir, or our most ingenious friend, in whom fancy and judgment are like a well-matched pair: the first like an extraordinary wife that appears always beautiful and always charming, yet is at all times decent and at all times chaste; the second like a prudent and well-bred husband, whose very sway shows his complaisance and whose very indulgence shows his authority.'

Wycherley in these years, whenever he was in town, presided at the meetings at Will's,[1] and the discussion at one of these meetings Dennis humourously

---

[1] Letter of Moyle to Congreve, October 7, 1695.

submitted to the Plain Dealer as chairman of the wits. He seems to have agreed with Dennis, and further to have found in this letter a hint for a satirical poem: 'Upon the Idleness of Business. (A Satyr.) To one who said A Man show'd his Sense, Spirit, Industry, and Parts, by his Love of Bus'ness.' It began: 'Your man of business is your idlest ass, Doing most what he least can bring to pass,' and contained also the couplet, 'Business, the seducer of mankind, Enslaves the body and deludes the mind.' Was Daniel Wycherley quite another story?

Congreve wrote to Dennis, when the critic was once away from town, describing a prank played at another meeting in Will's, 'The Consecration of John Abassus, a Country Poet.' Dennis in his answer to Congreve,[1] 'you who after Mr. Wycherley are incomparably the best writer of comedy living,' regretted his absence from the frolic, and wrote what he imagined the scene there must have been:

'W. was in his kingdom, and I would rather have sat there than in the House of Commons. Would to God I could laugh with you for an hour or two at all the ridiculous things that have happened at Will's Coffee-House since I left it. It is the merriest place in the world. Like Africa, every day it produces a monster . . . as Pliny says, beasts of different kinds come to drink, mingle with one another, and beget

[1] 'Occasional Letters,' 129.

239

monsters . . . My humble service to Mr. Wycherley.'

The characters created by Wycherley in his comedies were yielding him a return of fame compounded. But when Dryden in 1693[1] told how the greatest of Roman satirists had impressed him there were not many who suspected that he would weld Wycherley into the same piece: 'Juvenal is of a . . . vigorous and masculine wit, he gives me as much pleasure as I can bear: he fully satisfies my expectation; he treats his subject home: his spleen is raised, and he raises mine: I have the pleasure of concernment in all he says; and when he is at the end of his way, I willingly stop with him. . . . If a fault can be justly found in him, it is that he is sometimes too luxuriant, too redundant; says more than he needs, like my friend the Plain Dealer, but never more than pleases.' When in the same discussion Dryden touched upon Horace, he evidently alluded to Wycherley again: 'Horace gives his father the best character of a father which I ever read in history;[2] and I wish a witty friend of mine, now living, had such another.' The malfeasance of Daniel Wycherley, it might appear, had penetrated to the coffee-house, and been judged.

'The Old Bachelor' of Congreve was published early in 1694, and some lines in front of the play,

[1] 'Prose Works,' III, 168, 176.   [2] Sat., I, 6–70.

speaking of Dryden and his friends, read: 'His eldest Wycherley in wise retreat, Thought it not worth his quiet to be great.' The retreat to Clive may have been wise in point of health, but Wycherley still submitted to it only because his father denied him the money to live in town, and the 'quiet' of Shropshire was perhaps to an exile from Drury Lane its severest ordeal. Daniel Wycherley was a lawsuit sot. He was still wrangling about the curacy of Clive Chapel, and he had got four of its most recent curates to join him in actually petitioning the House of Lords in the matter of payment of their living.[1] The long suffering heir to Clive Hall thus had to live in a stew of petty, carping, miserly litigation.

John Dennis from his garret in London sought to cheer his friend the dramatist with letters. He said, January 19, 1694, 'Sir, while I venture to write these lines to you I take it to be my interest not to consider you as I hitherto always have done, and as for the future I always shall, viz., as Mr. Wycherley, as a man sent purposely into the world to charm the ears of the wittiest men, and to ravish the hearts of the most beautiful women. No, Sir, that in writing to you I may assume some spirit, I shall at present only consider you as the humble Hermit at Clive; humble even in the full possession of all those

[1] 'Journals,' XV, 104 ff.

extraordinary qualities the knowledge of which has made me proud.'

Wycherley replied on February 4, showing that he still retained that fecundity of pointed illustration which year after year drew playgoers to his comedies:

'Dear Sir, You have found a way to make me satisfyed with my absence from London . . . distance . . . indeed uses to lessen friendship, but gives me the greater mark of yours by your kind letter . . . I value your friendship more than money, and am prouder of your approbation than I should be of titles. For the having the good opinion of one who knows mankind so well argues some merit in me, upon which every man ought to consider himself more than upon the goods of fortune . . .

'But I fear I am forfeiting the character of the Plain Dealer with you; and seem like vain women or vainer men, to refuse praise but to get more . . . as knaves are punctual in some payments but to augment their credit. And for your praise of my humility . . . you have praised that to its destruction . . . like those admirers who praise a young maid's modesty till they deprive her of it . . .

'I have no way to show my love to you in my absence but by my jealousie. I would not have my rivals in your friendship, the Congreves, the Drydens, the Walshes, and the rest of your tavern

friends enjoy your conversation while I cannot . . .
Pray let me have more of your letters . . . for like
a country esquire I am in love with a town wit's conversation.'

Dennis submissively wrote again: 'Generally,
whatever is said is said for the satisfaction of him
that speaks it. But Mr. Wycherley . . . commends
his friend for his friend's sake. You never are witty
to please yourself, to whom wit has so long been ha-
bitual that you are often hardly moved yourself
when you say those admirable things with which we
are transported. But your reason, as the Duke de la
Rochefoucauld says, has been bubbled by your affection.'

Wycherley came up to town in the autumn. He
found another new neighbour and friend in Bow-
street. Sir Godfrey Kneller, whom for his services
as Court painter King William had knighted in
1691, occupied the house next Dr. Radcliffe. They
had just become friendly enemies. The artist had a
garden of exotic plants. Radcliffe asked to cut a door
through their garden wall so that he too could admire them. Kneller complied, but soon afterwards
the Doctor's servants took to walking through and
trampling on rare ferns. Sir Godfrey complained,
and sent word that he feared he might have to brick
up the door. To this, Radcliffe in a rage returned
reply, 'That Sir Godfrey might do even what he

pleased with the door, so that he did not paint it.'

'Did my very good friend Dr. Radcliffe say so?' cried Sir Godfrey to his footman. 'Go you back to him, and tell him that I can take anything from him but physic.'[1]

Wycherley walked on to Will's, only to find that John Dennis himself had retired fifty miles into the country because of illness. The poet then immensely enjoyed stepping into the usual role of Dennis, and sending him 'the news,' together with the customary pirouettings. On the first of December, 1694, he wrote to the critic:

'. . . You tell me you converse with me in my writings . . . but for your truer diversion, pray change my Country-Wife for a better of your own in the country, and exercise your own Plain-Dealing there; then you will make your Country Squire better company, and your Parson more sincere in your Company than his Pulpit, or in his Cups.

'But when you talk of store of delights you find in my Plain-Dealer you cease to be one; and when you commend my Country-Wife you never were more a courtier. And I doubt not but you will like your next neighbour's Country Wife better than you do mine . . . and like her innocence more than her wit, since innocence is the better bawd to love. But enjoy my Wife and welcome in my absence. I shall take it as civilly as a city cuckold.

[1] MacMichael, 15–16.

'I was sorry to find by you that your head ak'd whilst you writ me your letter, since I fear 'twas from reading my 'Works,' as you call them . . .

'I have been very busie this week about law affairs, that is, very dull and idle, tho' very active.

'Your friends . . . whether drunk or sober, good fellows or good wits . . . never are more wits and less poets, that is, less lyars, than when they profess themselves your servants . . . Walsh lives soberly, Cheek goes to bed early; D'Urfey sings now like a poet, that is, without being ask'd. And all the poets or Wits-at-Wills, since your departure, speak well of the absent . . .'

The 'law affairs' alluded to may have been Wycherley's resumption of his case against his wife's family. For the third Earl of Drogheda, after Wycherley upon entering Newgate had relaxed his claim against Lord Radnor, managed in his own lifetime to recover from the Robartes family a part of the Drogheda estates willed away by his enfeebled brother.[1] Therefore with the suit of the peers decided, or nearly so, and Lord Radnor knowing just how secure he stood in property holdings, Wycherley might now more reasonably expect a settlement in his own behalf.

The poet appears to have passed the winter at Clive Hall, but in the spring of 1695 he was again in London, on the heels of the latest revivals of

---

[1] Drogheda, 1680-90.

'Love in a Wood' and 'The Plain Dealer,' both at the King's Theatre. A young friend (probably Dennis) asked his advice with regard to a mistress, who herself was capricious, but whose father also had a way of interfering with the course of true love. Wycherley, having been so little married, was by all the gallants looked upon as widely travelled in the adventure of love. These circumstances perhaps brought him even more into demand as an adviser than his formidable combination of wit and physical comeliness. On April 11 he replied to a letter from the love-wrecked knight:

'Know, my friend, from one sufficiently experienced in love disasters, that . . . the loser is most often the gainer. If you have been deprived of a mistress, consider you have lost a wife, and tho' you are disappointed of a short satisfaction you have likewise escaped a tedious vexation, which matrimony infallibly comes to be, one way or another . . . Your misfortune is an accident which your true friends should rather felicitate than commiserate.

'You told me in your last that you were no more master of yourself. Then how should I help rejoicing at the restoration of your liberty? A man might as reasonably be sorry for his friend's recovery from madness as for his recovery from love (tho' for a time a pleasant frenzy) . . . Your mistress's father has rather been your doctor than your enemy. And you should not be angry with him if he cures your love distemper, tho' by a means a little too violent, for next to his daughter's cure of love his may prove the best . . .

'I own my friendship for you has a little selfishness in it, for now (that) you cannot be so happy as you would in the country I hope you will make us as happy as we can be in town . . . Change of air after a love distemper may be as good as 'tis after a fever. And therefore make haste to town, where a great many doctors have engaged to compleat your cure.

'Your friends will do anything to root out the remains of your passion. The Witty Club will grow grave to instruct you, and the Grave Club will grow gay to delight you. Wh. will turn a philosopher, and I will grow a good fellow, and venture my own health, for the recovery of your good humour. For I had rather be sick in your company than for the want of it . . .'

The French influence—Julie d'Angennes now five years dead murmuring even from her grave—the influence which had swayed Wycherley all his life, thus reasserted itself so far as his correspondence.

Soon after he had sent this letter off the Plain Dealer went away to Shropshire for the summer, where he awaited further news of lover and beloved.

The lover, like innumerable pallid suitors in the same agony who rush from one friend to another to be assuaged, had also written to Moyle and to Dryden. The letter of Dryden in reply has been preserved:[1]

'. . . Having had the honour to see my dear friend Wycherley's letter to him (the young man in love) on that occasion, I find nothing to be added or amended. But as well as I love Mr. Wycherley I confess I love myself so well that I will not show how much I am inferior to him in wit and judgment by undertaking anything after him.

'There was Moses, and the prophets in his counsel. Jupiter and Juno, as the poets tell us, made Tiresias their umpire, in a certain merry dispute which fell out in heaven betwixt them. Tiresias you know had been of both sexes, and therefore was a proper judge.

'Our friend Mr. Wycherley is full as competent an arbitrator: he has been a bachelor, and married man, and is now a widower . . . Yet I suppose he will not give any large commendations to his middle state, nor as the sailor said will be forced, after a shipwreck, to put to sea again.'

Late in the summer Wycherley found that he had to answer another letter from his harassed young friend, who was still distraught, though evidently

[1] Dennis, 'Occasional Letters,' 38.

not yet gone mad, over the same lady. On August 31 the Plain Dealer sent more admonishment from Clive:

'. . . If you but complain to your Mistress as wittily as you do to your Friend, I wonder not at her cruelty, nor that she should take pleasure to hear you complain so long. But, my Friend, have a care of complaining to her with so much true sense, lest it should disparage your true love.

'And indeed that, I fear, is the only cause you are suffered to complain so long without the success which is due to your merit, love, and wit, from one who you say has herself so much. Which with your pardon I shall hardly believe, tho' you are her voucher, if she does not do what you would have her; that is, do you and herself reason as fast as she can, since she must need believe you a warm and sincere lover as much as I believe you a zealous and true friend.

'And I am so well acquainted with love and you that I believe nobody is able to alter your love or advise your reason, the one being as unalterable as the other infallible, and you (for aught I know) are the only man who at once can love and be wise. And to the wise, you know, a word is enough, especially since you gave me a caution against opposing your passion, because it would be in vain.

'If love be in you as in other men, a violent passion, it is therefore a short frenzy, and should be cured like other distempers of that kind, by your friend's humouring it rather than opposing it. Yet pardon me if I prescribe the common remedy of curing one love with another . . .

'Pray give all the honest gentlemen of the Coffee-House, of my acquaintance and yours, my humble service, whom with you I hope to see again within these three weeks at London.'

When Wycherley did come up to town in September (as at other seasons when the London weather was mild and sunny), he sat with Dryden not by the fireside at Will's, but in the window upon the narrow iron balcony overlooking Russell-street.[1] There the greatest poet and the greatest dramatist of the day read and discussed plays together. And hardly anyone now dared write for the theatre in London without first ingratiating himself at Will's, then with Mr. Wycherley and Mr. Dryden in the Wits' Room.[2] Of a summer evening the two captains of wit lingered by the window and discoursed on whether Iago should be tortured in sight of the audience, why a Greek drama was the more tragic for its action of twenty-four hours, or why the literary glory of Italy and Spain had set and the radiance of France had risen to outshine it. Dryden and Wycherly took attentive note of the French theatre of the

[1] Perromat, 45.   [2] Wheatley, III, 517.

age. It was at this time that the 'Esther' of Racine had set all heads bobbing in Paris, and Dryden made public what he and his friend thought as to its adaptation for Drury Lane:

'The play could not possibly have succeeded on the stage, and much less the translation of it, here. Mr. Wycherley, when we read it together, was of my opinion in this, or rather I of his; for it becomes me so to speak of so excellent a poet and so great a judge.'[1]

Dryden knew that Wycherley excelled him in understanding of materials of the drama, but he knew too that he excelled Wycherley as a poet. It therefore seemed to him that if they collaborated upon a play the one could so neatly supply what the other lacked that the result ought to be a sensation in Drury Lane if not in the history of English comedy. He approached Wycherley with the project. Wycherley may have thought it possibly productive of a little too much comedy. But what he saw, at the time, was his own dramatic laurels, as he was wearing them, ever green. Why should he tamper with them?

He declined the offer in a letter in verse, some hundred and twenty-five lines, a tactful poem in which he represented Dryden's talents as too superior to attempt collaboration without injustice to

[1] 'Prose Works,' III, 335.

both writers. And the Plain Dealer ended with a delicate suggestion that he must guard his own standing, such as it was:

'. . . Your Reason's Light would my dark Sense outshine,
And your Poetick Flame extinguish mine.
So when bright Phœbus' purer Rays conspire,
To mix with Smoak, and dull Material Fire;
The Fire, that shone with mod'rate Light before,
O'ercome by too much Lustre, shines no more.'

The spectre of debt had rearisen and shadowed Wycherley ever since he had come out of the Fleet. He always spent more than he had to, and he always needed more than he spent. Friends who were no friends were ever caressing his purse to tell him exactly what victuals and drink they should like bought for them. There were some old prison debts still unpaid[1]—The Captain of the Gaol had been 'good' to him. And in the ten years since the Fleet he had borrowed numerous small sums; visits to London were expensive. This situation must have fomented constant quarreling, in Clive, between father and son, and made the family roof a perpetual thundercloud to live under. Daniel Wycherley was now seventy-nine. Years had flogged him into slow submission, into retirement from his campaigns in the courts. What must he now do to gain

[1] Gildon, 11, 13.

his peace, protect his estates so arduously amassed, and yet silence his heir?

On September 10, 1696, Daniel listed his lands and drew up a conveyance of them. He then called in three friends, and Will Wycherley, and told them he had decided upon a trust, a settlement of his property which would provide for its entail. This settlement,[1] in its essentials, read:

'Daniel Wycherley of the first part; Robert Corbet, Richard Corbet, and Thomas Grant of the second part; William Wycherley, son and heir of Daniel, of the third part.

'Item: £1,000 towards paying the debts of William Wycherley.

'Item: Lands in trust: 1. All that capital messuage and mansion house and lands situated in Clive, late the property of Daniel Wycherley, father of the said Daniel. 2. A messuage and land in Clive once the property of the late Michael Baugh. 3. The Drawwell house in Clive, late the property of William Fetton. 4. A messuage late the property of Joseph Smith in Clive. 5. Another, late the property of Daniel Sturdy, with land in the townships of Sansaw and Clive. 6. A chief-rent of 26s. from the freeholders of Clive. 7. The royalty of Clive wood and

---

[1] I quote from a certified copy (1705) of the Settlement of 1696, here noticed for the first time, and kindly conveyed to me by the Rev. Cunliffe Brookes.

Clive hill. 8. A messuage in Acton Reynald held by
Widow Buckley. 9. Another messuage there held by
Mrs. Walker. 10. Two messuages in Yerton, for-
merly the estate of James Wycherley and bought of
Richard Wycherley. 11. An estate in Houlson lately
the property of James Wycherley. 12. Lands in
Wem, held by Joseph Taylor and John Dickson.
13. Two or three other messuages in Wem. 14. A
messuage in Aston, lately belonging to William
Wolfe. 15. The Pools, a farm in Wem. 16. The
Trench farms in Wem, occupied by Thomas Taylor,
Roger Ireland and John Baugh, with woods, under-
woods, and fishing.

'To be held in trust by Robert Corbet, Richard
Corbet, and Thomas Grant as follows:

'To the use of Daniel Wycherley aforesaid during
the term of his natural life (Daniel was King Lear
with a caution), then all the messuages and lands excepting only those in Clive to the use of William
Wycherley, son and heir apparent of Daniel, for
life, with power to make a jointure on his wife of
any of the lands excepting those in Clive.

'Then to the eldest son of William and his heirs
male, failing which to William, eldest son of John
Wycherley son of Daniel, and his eldest son with
the usual entailing clause to heirs male. Failing such
to Daniel, second son of John Wycherley, and heirs
male. Failing these to Thomas Wycherley of Lacon

in the parish of Wem, son of Thomas Wycherley
son of Joseph Wycherley deceased . . .'

This settlement wrote down William Wycherley
a spendthrift. It revealed Daniel's candid estimation
of his poet son, to whom he even denied the better
half of 'the use' of the estates, that is, the richer
half situated in Clive. And this limitation of 'the
use' measured the father's displeasure at the im-
providence of his heir. Daniel was proud of the
family overlordship in Clive: he thought to per-
petuate it by skipping a generation. Since William
still had no children, the children of the third son,
John, were in line. John Wycherley (next younger
to George who had died childless)[1] had himself died,
a docile farmer, in 1691, and his son William, in the
settlement named prospective heir succeeding the
poet, was now a boy of twelve. The whole estate,
and not merely its usufruct, was to come to him out-
right.

How could Wycherley bring himself to sign an
agreement to be content with only an amputated income from farms in outlying villages? The bait was
the thousand pounds ready money 'towards paying
his debts.' It was a bribe, but it was also a windfall.
To the Plain Dealer it meant, mainly, an immediate
and delicious breathing-spell in Bow-street. He put
his name to the settlement, and fled.

[1] The Countess's little namesake died in 1685, aged 5.

255

Wycherley had also a particular reason for desir-
ing to be in town; he had already begun arrangements for publishing his 'Miscellany Poems,' and he
wished to carry the plans onward. These poems he
had been writing at odd intervals ever since he had
left Angoulême thirty-five years before, but most of
the time he devoted to making verse had come to
him in the Fleet, in rustication at Clive, and especially in London during the past year or two as a
rebound from many inspiriting talks at Will's. Now
in Covent Garden once more, he gave the wheels another turn towards bringing out his book. And a
little later, at the top of a column in *The London
Gazette*, issue of November 30-December 3, 1696,
the following advertisement in piquant bookseller's
English appeared:

'Mr. Wycherley's Miscellany Poems, Satyrs,
Epistles, etc., printed in folio by way of subscrip-
tion, for the benefit of the author; for which proposals having been already made, have received encouragement from the nobility and gentry.

'They who design to promote this undertaking are
desired to send in their first payment, with their
names, to Sam Briscoe, Bookseller in Covent Garden: for it is designed to print no more books than
for subscribers only, so that gentlemen must not expect 'em, except they send in their first payment before the book is put to the press, which will be with

all possible speed. Proposals are to be had at most booksellers in London and Westminster."[1]

It seemed good to Wycherley to be liberated, to be back in Bow-street for a longer stay, back at the Widow Hilton's with his man after sixteen years of misfortunes and mail-coaches: the eternal pounding up and down the two-hundred-mile post to Shrewsbury. He appeared older than fifty-six: prison had obliterated the benefits of Montpellier, and anxiety since his imprisonment had worked more harm than the fresh air of Clive had done good. Sometimes in the morning he looked like a man at the end of a long day's walk, over hills. His gaiety was gone. Yet those qualities of vivacity which in his rakish days he had developed to such an extraordinary degree[2] so persisted that even now his mind, save for occasional seizures of amnesia, seemed no less alert than the minds of many of the younger Wits-at-Wills.

While he was waiting for sufficient subscriptions to his poems to come into the hands of Sam Briscoe, Wycherley could be found nearly every afternoon at the coffee-house. Men became wits by sipping coffee or wine with the Plain Dealer,[3] who over a glass was as civil to D'Urfey the songster as to Dryden the laureate,[4] and who was more discursive of contempo-

---

[1] For permission to copy this notice I have to thank Mr. Thorn-Drury.

[2] Dennis, 'Usefulness of the Stage,' 31–2.

[3] Wheatley, III, 517.   [4] Gildon, 14.

rary manners than of pontifical wise saws. He made
no laborious effort to please, nor tried to shine by
that pert sprightliness which only mystifies. John
Dennis watched him intently, with steady affection,
and wrote: '. . . I must confess that I have no great
opinion of that which men generally call humility:
in most men humility is want of heat; 'tis phlegm,
'tis impotence, 'tis a wretched necessity, of which
they who lie under it vainly endeavour to make a
virtue. But in a man of Mr. Wycherley's make, 'tis
choice, 'tis force of mind, 'tis a good, 'tis a generous
condescension, and what force of mind is there not
requisite to bend back a soul, by perpetual reflection,
which would be always rising and eternally aspiring
by virtue of its inborn fire?'[1]

Wycherley had paid off a desk-full of old debts,
and his thousand pounds was ebbing blithely away
when, early in 1697, came help whence he had almost ceased to hope for it. The poet now saw the
finish of his last lawsuit: the relatives of the Lady
Laetitia paid him £1,500 for his rights in her estate.[2]
This was not quite the same thing as getting the
Countess's jointure, but the Robartes family, like
the lord of the manor of Clive, had a way of taming
lesser litigants. The poet may have reflected that if
this sum had been given him in 1682, when he had
no less right to it, it would have paid twice over the

[1] 'Select Works,' II, 491.   [2] Gildon, 13.

debt that cast him into prison. But the autumn of life was now encroaching upon Wycherley. He made no more protest. Without the least malice in the world he determined to send to the young Earl of Radnor a presentation copy of his poems,[1] containing verses to the Lord Chancellor, with some outspoken allusions to Laetitia, the aunt who had been so valuable to the house of Robartes in spite of the lawsuit brought by the Droghedas.

But the stars in their courses fought against the publication of the 'Miscellany Poems.' Delays unforeseen arose to drive writing and printing out of the Plain Dealer's mind. In the spring he was called to Shropshire because of the alarming illness of his father. The family were not kept long in doubt. On May 7, 1697, the doors of the chapel of All Saints, Clive, opened for the burial, beneath the chancel, of Daniel Wycherley.[2] His last words, in faint sarcasm, might have been this advice to fathers: Do not educate your son to be more a gentleman than yourself unless you have a mind to struggle up to his level.

[1] Mr. Thorn-Drury. [2] Summers, I, 57.

CHAPTER VIII

THE BRIGHT-EYED URCHIN

WYCHERLEY was resting at Clive in 1698 when a literary earthquake shook Covent Garden and sent its tremors far into the provinces of the midland. The cause was the pamphlet 'A Short View of the Immorality and Profaneness of the English Stage,' by Jeremy Collier, M.A.——he wished the world to know he had *not* left the University 'without taking a degree.' Collier denounced Dryden, Congreve, and lesser dramatists without much mercy, but aside from condemning certain characters in 'The Country Wife' and 'The Plain Dealer' his treatment of Wycherley was rather cautious. He said:

'. . . Some people appear coarse and slovenly out of poverty: they can't go well to the charge of sense. They are offensive, like beggars, for want of necessaries. But this is none of the Plain Dealer's case. He can afford his Muse a better dress when he pleases . . . I must own the Poet (Wycherley) to be an author of good sense.'

Yet faithful John Dennis, who spent an enormous part of his life writing letters of denial, resentment, and vilification, thought Collier undervalued the

Plain Dealer, and he retorted with 'The Usefulness of the Stage,' in which he swept to the defense of his friend:

'Mr. Wycherley being indeed almost the only man alive who has made Comedy instructive in its fable, almost all the rest being contented to instruct by their characters . . . the best thing that he (Collier) can afford to say of the greatest of our Comick Wits is, that he is a man of good sense . . . How unworthy was it . . . to take no notice of those extraordinary qualities which are peculiar to him alone—his wit, his penetration, his satyr, his art, his characters, and above all, that incomparable vivacity by which he has happily equalled the ancients and surpassed the moderns!'[1]

Collier was attempting to preach the funeral sermon of Restoration drama to a congregation that would not sit still. Had William III not carried through his reforms in manners? Kensington House undoubtedly was no Whitehall. London undoubtedly was no longer the London of Charles II. But over the theatre hung the crimson twilight, apparently unfading, of a generation past.

Wycherley himself evidently had the good taste to pay no heed to Collier. At all events he was in-

---

[1] Congreve also had paid tribute to Wycherley in the prologue to 'Love for Love':

'Since the Plain Dealer's scenes of manly rage,
Not one has dared to lash this crying age.'

terested in other things. Fondness for the theatre had in Wycherley long since given way to the poetical impulse, and though he well knew his verses no more showed him at his best than the verses of Swift or the prose of Donne showed what those men were going to live by, he was resolute in his purpose to publish the 'Miscellany' to prove that there was a strain of something in him besides giggles and mockery. As for his dramatic reputation, the public in spite of Collier continued to demand revivals of his comedies. On that score, Wycherley rested content.

But at the end of the seventeenth century, to assemble poems in sequence for the printer was one thing and to marshal enough subscribers to clear the bookseller's risk was painfully another. Postponement followed postponement, whilst authors who were friends of the author waited expectantly, if not with too much foregone confidence. Dryden wrote to Beau Walsh in May, 1699, mentioning a concerted plan to welcome the book at Will's: 'Mr. Wycherley's Poems will not come out until Michaelmas Terme: if his versification prove as well as his wit I shall believe it will be extraordinary. However, Congreve and Southern and I shall not faile to appear before it, and if you will come in he will have reason to acknowledge it for a favour.'

This letter was perhaps the last service which the great poet undertook for his closest friend. John

Dryden died in the following year. He was buried in the Abbey, but without an epitaph. Wycherley in mingled defiance and resentment at this neglect was moved to write that Dryden's verses alone would make his name lustrous, 'as Dust of Diamonds makes the Diamond shine.'[1]

Two or three more years dragged on, while Wycherley was racked on the one hand by the tergiversations of his bookseller Briscoe, and on the other by comments against his poems from certain of his acquaintance at the coffee-houses. Not a few of his sheets of verses from time to time had circulated amongst the critics at Will's and the Rose: they expected from a man like Wycherley something approaching the brilliance of his plays: the poetry fell short, and so did commendation of it. However praiseworthy the subjects of some of the poems were, lines here and there were considered defective in numbers and rhythm. Charles Gildon noted: 'As the conduct of some of his acquaintances of Will's in regard to these poems was by no means agreeable to Mr. Wycherley, it caused a coldness between them, especially on the part of Wycherley, who could not but resent a behaviour he thought the effect of either ignorance or envy.'[2]

Meantime the King died, after a fall from his horse while hunting. Dr. Radcliffe had predicted

[1] Summers, IV, 154.   [2] Gildon, 13.

the time four years previously. William had suffered from boils, which his Dutch doctor Bidloo treated with powdered crabs' eyes.[1] Dropsy ensued. 'I would not have Your Majesty's two legs,' said Dr. Radcliffe, cheerfully apprehending fatality, 'for your three kingdoms.'[2] But William III died having achieved his purpose: he restored the liberties of England.

Princess Anne became Queen at thirty-seven. Unlike Queen Mary, Anne was so silent that she rarely spoke save to answer a question. She was therefore companionable for her husband, Prince George of Denmark—blonde, brave, and gentle—who was a man of few words in English and still less in French.[3] But Anne did resemble her sister Mary in one point: weak eyes. Thinking Queen Mary had neglected hers, Anne made a hobby of her own, and laid herself open to the impositions of every quack in the kingdom. Two, a tailor and a tinker, she allowed to call themselves her 'sworn oculists,' and the tailor she knighted.[4] She was frail-minded, querulous, crotchety, and self-indulgent. Understanding all this, her physician, Dr. Arbuthnot, returned the perfect answer when the Queen asked him the time of day. He said, 'Whatever it may please Your Majesty.[5] It must be remembered

[1] MacMichael, 11.   [2] Physic and Physicians, I, 88.
[3] MacMichael, 27.   [4] Jeaffreson, I, 110, 113.   [5] MacMichael, 26.

that the Age of Anne marked the beginning of an age of intrigue, because the succession to the throne was so in doubt. Politicians found it hard to stay honest, and therefore literary men, soon mingling freely with them, discovered in themselves the same difficulty. And Arbuthnot was medical, political, and literary.

As if to mark the new century, Wycherley paused in his negotiations for his book long enough to have his portrait painted again. He went to his next-door neighbour in Bow-street, Sir Godfrey Kneller, whose fee was fifty pounds. But Kneller was a pupil of Rembrandt, he had painted ten reigning sovereigns, and he was now at the top of his accomplishment in art.[1] Sir Godfrey told the Plain Dealer, who was 'not unvain of his face,' and 'unequal to his own venerableness,' that he would make a very fine head without a wig. 'It was drawn at first,' according to Spence, 'with his little straggling gray hair; he could not bear it when done, and Sir Godfrey was obliged to draw a wig to it.[2]

The finished picture showed Wycherley now to be a man with shortish gray hair, and a mouth still determined, but with hooked wrinkles near the corners. Between his eyes two upright lines clove his forehead. Though he looked distraught and somewhat drawn, he sat nobly erect as in his youth, wear-

[1] D. N. B. (Kneller).   [2] 'Anecdotes,' 335.

ing no longer the staid gown of a Templar, but a white shirt open loosely at the neck. His most arresting feature was his eyes, deep and haunting as the eyes of a tragedian, and eloquent of adversity.[1] But in a poem he wrote to Sir Godfrey, he said: 'So to the life you paint, that ev'n you make The painted canvas seem to move and speak; Moving the passions, speaking to the eye, You make us guilty of idolatry.' Though Wycherley penned these verses on the occasion of a portrait Kneller did of the poet's mistress, the tribute was the sincere feeling of one artist for another.

Wycherley now took his poems out of the hands of Briscoe, the shifty bookseller, and gave them to another shop. At long last the book appeared, in 1704: 'Miscellany Poems: as Satyrs, Epistles, Love-Verses, Songs, Sonnets, &c.,' and underneath the title, 'These Poems printed for C. Brome, J. Taylor, and B. Tooke, at the Gun at the West End of St. Paul's, the Ship in St. Paul's Churchyard, and at the Middle Temple Gate, Fleet-street.' The printer had asked the poet for his portrait to use as a frontispiece. Wycherley would have none of the Kneller likeness of him as he now was, but he engaged the skilful engraver Smith to make a mezzo-tinto of the Lely portrait done thirty-five years before, showing

[1] This portrait now belongs to Lord Sackville, and is at Knole Park, Seven-oaks, Kent.

the author as a handsome beau of the town. Beneath this engraving he caused to be printed, half deploring, half explaining, the line from Virgil, 'Quantum mutatus ab illo!' He grieved over his old portrait as a young man; he was heartsick over his new portrait as an old man. But he then in good humour wrote, for the first poem in the book after the dedicatory, 'The Author to the Book-Seller, who desired his picture before his Book, in Front of his Follies, pleading the custom for it':

. . . Each author puts the best face on his book,
That buyers might on both more kindly look. . . .
All Lyers, Cheats, Historians, Poets, Quacks,
Divines, Diviners in their almanacks,
Or books, tho' but more to their own disgrace,
Look, in effigie, buyers in the face. . . .'

Wycherley touched upon his luckless relations with Briscoe in a letter to Lord Halifax, a subscriber, to whom he sent a copy of the book in May, 1704, soon after it had appeared in St. Paul's:

'My Lord, Since presents of this kind are seldom made without apologies for making them, yesterday Dr. Garth told me that your Lordship did me the honour to subscribe to this book, which I never knew before, for the knave ye bookseller who should have printed this scurvy miscellany broke for the credit of ye book before he printed it and never told me

what he had received or from whom; so robbed me
of the subscriptions which I suppose he thought his
due for not being accessory to my shame in publishing so scurvy a book.

'But (My Ld) lest this should seem an epistle
dedicatory, I conclude it assuring your Lordship if
I had had the confidence to have prefixed any illustrious name before it, your Lordship's might have
been in danger, tho' I seldom use my friends so
scurvily as that comes to . . .'[1]

The Plain Dealer of course did not believe his
book to be so bad as he intimated to the noble lord.
He knew that to exchange Muses, to forsake Thalia
for Euterpe, was not quite so safe as to meander
from one lady to another in Chatelin's French ordinary, but he also knew that he had written not
wholly without the drive of inspiration. So he felt
the sting of his critics. He thought most of them had
run down his work on hearsay, and he resolved to
forestall their further objections by taking out of his
cupboard some old utensils of satire. To the Miscellany of some hundred and eighty poems, which
he dedicated 'To Vanity, Greatest Friend of the
Muses,' he wrote a 5,000 word preface, 'To my
Criticks ante manum, Who were my Criticks before
they were my Readers,' and quoting Horace five
times[2] for his purpose, said:

---

[1] Perromat, 47.
[2] Epist. II, 11 (twice); Epist. II, 1 (twice); 'De Arte Poetica,' 388.

'If thou wou't but own thy Want of Wit to write, I will my Want of Judgment for Writing too much . . .

'An Ill Poet obliges the Ill-Natur'd World better than a Good One, since the Carping Readers who are made Good Criticks by Bad Authors would take it ill of a Good Author to be well Pleas'd . . .

'Criticks, like Hypocrites, will own some small Imperfections to have a Pretence to the Virtue, Honesty, and Sincerity of Self-Accusers; to prove their Wits good, will own their bad Memories; to magnifie their Fancies, will lessen their Judgments, will own their Flegm, or Slowness of Thought, and call that their Mature Consideration which was their Crude Stupidity . . .

'Wit in the city is Craft, where they call Cozening, Cheating, or Betraying a Man, Out-witting him; amongst Lawyers, Wit is . . . Impudence and Lying, which are the Supports of their Reputation; amongst Little Courtiers, 'tis called Address, which is Fraud and Flattery; amongst Men of Honour, and the Great, 'tis Policy, which is Treachery and Villainy amongst the Poor and Little Men . . .

'As all the most Thoughtless, Stupid, Brutal Animals seem by Nature designed more for preying on their Fellow-creatures than the sagacious or tractable, so are the heavy, laborious, thick-skulled brutes

of men, who are least fit for Thought or Contempla-
tion, designed most for Drudgery, or Business in the
World, which is amongst men as amongst beasts,
preying on one another . . .

'As the braying of the ass is much louder than the
neighing of the horse, and the hollowing or whoop-
ing of the Owl much louder than the notes of the
Nightingale . . . so is it amongst mankind, the
Human Asses and Owls are always louder in publick
as they less deserve to be heard . . . such is the
noisie mischievous Screech-Owl, the would-be wit,
called the Critick . . .

'Criticks, the vermin, I say, of Parnassus, associate with men of sense not out of friendship, but
malice to them, call themselves judges of men's
sense and reputation when they are but lazy mur-
therers of them . . .'

That was Wycherley behind his pen, when he
could still be as bitter as when he created Horner
and Manly; but one must see him also behind his
cup of wine. A letter of this period 'from a French
gentleman in London to his friend in Paris, containing an account of Will's Coffee-House,' said: 'Mr.
Wycherley is one of the politest Gentlemen in England, and the most civil and affable to Strangers,
especially to those of our Nation, for whom he has
an Esteem; he is a little shy and reserv'd in Conversation, but when a Man can be so happy as once to

engage him in Discourse, he cannot but admire his profound Sense, Masculine Wit, vast Knowledge of Mankind, and noble but easie Expressions . . .'[1]

But in the outpouring of invective in his preface, aside from its being a reply to the gossip about his versification, Wycherley made no allowance for the change in public taste in poetry. His plays continued to be popular—all four of them were revived over and again—and if audiences still liked such plays why should not readers like verse, 'Love-Verses' bearing on situations of the same sort? One reason was that the stage was among the last things to be touched by the reform in manners. The kind of lyrics written by Rochester in the time of Charles (and Wycherley included in his book many pieces he too had written when he was a young man well-gloved) was no longer relished. No one could object to such inspired poems as 'The Invocation to Fortune,' or 'Upon the Impertinence of Knowledge' or 'To a Witty Man of Wealth and Quality.' Of the two last, it has been left for a living poet, Mr. Drinkwater, to confute Georgian and Victorian critics and say, 'Technique apart—and how far apart does not matter—this might be Milton speaking.'[2] Wycherley however overbalanced these laudable themes by poems to a proud mistress, a jilting mistress, a peevish mistress, a scornful mistress, a painted mistress,

[1] Boyer, 'Letters,' III, 217.   [2] Drinkwater, 45 ff.

a conceited mistress, an affected mistress, a diffident mistress, a mercenary mistress, an antiquated mistress, an impertinent mistress, a false fickle mistress, and a mistress said to be an hermaphrodite. The poet let his verses of this flavour so outnumber those in keeping with the decorum now fashionable that some of his readers did not appraise the book by the best work in it. Sovereigns of England had come and gone too fast for the Plain Dealer. The reign of Queen Anne saw men shamelessly beginning once more to love their own wives. The home and the hearth were exalted as a novelty. Indeed virtue was as modish under Mary and Anne as levity had been under Charles and James, and the kitchen-hearth, perhaps because Anne was so monumentally fond of food,[1] was the altar at which the women of Britain repented. Diet was yet to come.

Nevertheless Wycherley remained extremely incensed at his detractors. Certain minor figures at Will's, whom the poet had not taken notice of before, leapt into the breach and praised the 'Miscellany.' Wycherley was too ruffled by his critics not to accept this shallow deference, and whilst in his vexation he laid himself open to one of the strangest friendships in the history of English letters. A brawny man of sixty-four, now so despondent that he thought he saw death stealing up to his side, ad-

[1] Teaffreson, I, 140.

mitted to his company a hobgoblin of sixteen, and lived through the excitement of the association to see his ugly dwarf write the most beautiful poetry of the age.

Alexander Pope was born with a tubercular spine.[1] He was so frail that as a boy he had to be lifted in and out of bed, wrapped in flannel and fur, and by day he wore a bodice of stiff canvas to keep him from collapsing in a heap. The canvas served well when once a mad cow trampled upon him at play. He was protuberant before and behind and when he started to rise from a chair his elbows shot above his head like a spider's. At the age of nine he believed himself a poet, because in school at Twyford he wrote a satire on the master which was tart enough to earn him a beating.[2] Alexander neither cried nor laughed at that; he scarcely ever laughed under any provocation.[3] As early as 1700, before he was twelve years old, he began to hunt out the lions of literature. He made a friend carry him to Will's so that he could peer into the Wits' Room and see Dryden. Then he went back home to Windsor Forest, where the Popes lived amidst a colony of Catholic Whigs, and schemed for another visit to town.

The boy grew vain and wilful. Peals of admiration from his elders, whom his father—a retired

[1] Medical Library, IV, No. 4. [2] Courthope, V, 26 ff.
[3] Thackeray (Pope), 311.

linen-draper turned gentleman—did not repress,
echoed round him. Upon hearing Alexander speak
one soon forgot his twisted body: his voice in common conversation was so naturally musical that
friends calling upon his father always ended by in-
quiring for 'the little nightingale.' He was given to
writing rather smooth verses, for which he seemed
to have caught a knack, and he had the elfin impudence to desire at once to set up for a wit and a poet.
He was barely sixteen when he prevailed upon one
of his father's suburban friends, Sir Charles Wogan,
to take him up to town, for all his cropped hair and
his country dress, and introduce him with his poems
at Will's.[1]

When the exquisite William Walsh in his seat at
the Wits' Table first looked upon this little 'pale,
crooked, sickly, bright-eyed urchin,'[2] he must have
stayed his bowl of coffee in mid-air. The boy looked
like Punch, this four-feet-six-inches of contortion,
but he wormed his way into notice and wrung from
the wits their shocked interest. His custodian Wogan
thought it worth a trial to fit out little Pope in
clothes comformable to his appearance in London.
And from this time the dwarf from Windsor strewed
the footsteps of his rising with obeisance to men of
renown.

Among the Catholics who were intimate friends

[1] Timbs, 272.   [2] Macaulay, 'Comic Dramatists,' xxxviii; Gildon, 13.

of the Popes and had settled near them was Anthony
Englefield, of Whiteknights, long a patron of poets.
One evening in the early winter of 1704 Wycherley appears to have been calling upon Englefield
and was there introduced to Pope. The Plain Dealer,
ripe for fresh acquaintance, found the boy poet
agreeable, while Pope was delighted to achieve
meeting with a dramatist whose plays were the talk
of four reigns. Wycherley chatted in coffee-house
manner upon writers and writings, and is said on this
occasion to have 'done justice to his dead friend Mr.
Dryden.'[1] The imp of fame was enthralled.

It was from just such a man of the world as
Wycherley that Pope thirsted to take lessons, and
when the great man went back to Bow-street the boy
followed him, telling his parents that he wished to
go up to town to study French and Italian.[2] He
sought out Wycherley, wandered round his lodgings,
and perched on his door-step like a toad not to be
moved even by the spear of Ithuriel. Occasionally he
got into the house, where he seems to have given
rise to some consternation amongst friends of the
dramatist. One of them, Charles Gildon, long afterwards wrote:

'. . . I was once to wait upon Mr. Wycherley
and found in his chamber this little Æsopic sort of

---

[1] Letter of Pope, falsely dated (1704) five years before it was written.
[2] Courthope, V, 77.

animal . . . I confess the gentleman was very silent all my stay there and scarce uttered three words on any subject we talked of, nor could I guess at what sort of creature he was, and should indeed have guessed all the pretences of mankind round before I should have imagined him a wit and a poet.

'I thought indeed he might be some tenant's son of his, who might make his court for continuance in his lease on the decease of his rustic parent, but was sufficiently surprised when Mr. Wycherley afterwards told me he was poetically inclined, and writ tolerably smooth verses . . .

'Though Wycherley's pique at that time to greater men had made way for his admitting such a wretch as this into his conversation and intimacy, yet he was all his life besides more cautious of his friendships. The brightest and most excellent always esteemed him and he them, having all along a contempt for pretending coxcombs.'[1]

Wycherley in truth took compassion on this misshapen oaf, this little crooked man who so often walked a crooked mile in the winding streets of London to sit at his feet. Up and down Covent Garden, over and under the New Exchange, in and out of the coffee-houses, Pope trotted after the Plain Dealer[2] like a dachshund. They sat before the assembled

[1] Gildon, 13 ff. passim.
[2] Letter of Pope to Cromwell, Oct. 19, 1709.

Wits-at-Wills. There the elder poet suffered his disciple, chin cupped in his hand, to gaze raptly up at him as a cherub to a saint, whilst Wycherley dispensed his masculine wit like Falstaff and Pope piped applause like Falstaff's page.

The imp had written in the Virgilian manner four pastorals, on the seasons, and he submitted them to his friend. Wycherley thought both the poems and their preface (which pretended to elegance) astonishingly good, but to confirm his impression he tested them beneath the whining semi-colons of Beau Walsh. That fastidious gentleman straightened up with a start, and invited Pope to come to stay at his house in the country.[1] The pastorals then circulated through the hands of the newer critics in Russell-street: Lord Lansdowne, Sir William Trumbull, Lord Halifax, Dr. Garth; all were friends of Wycherley.

Lansdowne, who all his life sailed alternately in or out of favour whenever a new monarch began to reign, on the death of King William had emerged from the dark and now stood in the light of Anne.[2] From talking to Wycherley he learned what good dramaturgy was, then went off and wrote bad plays. But like Dennis, Lansdowne could speak with point on what was right or wrong in the works of other men. Sir William Trumbull, retired diplomat of

[1] *Athenæum*, Oct. 3, 1857. [2] D. N. B. (Granville).

Easthampton Park near Windsor, and friend of the
Popes, was a Fellow of All Souls'; his criticism
therefore was respected. Lord Halifax was a lesser
Walsh, a pretender to taste rather than possessed of
it. Like a man who merely owns books he would
say, 'There is something in that passage which does
not quite please me; be so good as to mark the place;
and consider it a little at your leisure. I am sure you
can give it a little turn.'[1] Yet Halifax was a patron
of letters, and his suffrage would be valuable. Dr.
Samuel Garth, from Peterhouse, Cambridge, was a
wit, free, affable, and benevolent. He was as unwilling as Dr. Radcliffe to leave a dinner for a patient,
and he wrote more poems than he administered pills.[2]
His judgment upon all sorts of writing was steady.

These gentlemen without any dissent upheld the
commendation of Wycherley regarding Pope's pastorals. What Lansdowne thought precisely came
out in a letter to one of his intimates, a letter which
began as a defense of Wycherley's 'Miscellany':

'It is certain that he (Wycherley) is no master of
numbers, but a diamond is not less a diamond for not
being polished . . . In my friend, every syllable,
every thought, is masculine. His Muse is not led
forth as to a review, but as to a battle; not adorned
for parade, but execution; he would be tried by the
sharpness of his blade, and not by the finery. Like

[1] 'Physic and Physicians,' I, 220.   [2] Ibid., 214.

278

your heroes of antiquity he charges in iron, and seems to despise all ornament but intrinsic merit . . .

'Name your day and I will bring you together. Let it be at my lodging. I can give you no Falernian that has outlived twenty consulships, but I can promise you a bottle of good old claret that has seen two reigns . . .

'He shall bring with him, if you will, a young poet, newly inspired, in the neighbourhood of Cooper's Hill, whom he and Walsh have newly taken under their wing; his name is Pope; he is not above seventeen or eighteen and promises miracles. If he goes on as he has begun, in the pastoral way, as Virgil first tried his strength, we may expect to see English poetry vie with the Roman, and this swan of Windsor sing as sweetly as the Mantuan . . .'[1]

It was in this same year in which Wycherley and Pope met, 1704, that Wycherley seems first to have considered going to Bath for his health. Queen Anne had sojourned there in 1703, and Bath had since become a fashionable resort for Londoners as well as a cure. John Caryll, one of the minor wits in the Rabble at Will's, who was also neighbour of the Popes at Binfield, Windsor, asked Wycherley to come and stay with him in the country, and the poet sent this reply, together with a copy of his new book:

[1] Works, 436 ff.

'I have received the honour of your letter, and in it your most obliging invitation to your house, for which I think my obligation very great . . . if I can get away from the Bath, time enough, you may be in danger of a troublesome visit from me, who should be as proud of the honour of your conversation as I should be pleased and instructed by it . . . As to ye scurvy present I make you, I wish there were anything in it could entertain you; perhaps in the country where ye Gazettes are welcome, nay, and a letter from a London taylor would be acceptable, (unless it were accompanied with a dun) my damned book may be admitted, at least be less impertinent.'[1]

Wycherley was inclined to brood somewhat over the alleged defects of the 'Miscellany.' And Pope was sympathetic. Having thus far gained the genuine interest of the Plain Dealer by a tangible show of his own merit, the gnome fed this friendship with sweets for the age's tooth. He is said to have made his 'courtly reflections' on such of the wits and critics as he discovered to be not too solidly rooted in Wycherley's good graces.[2] This sort of fawning he kept up through the year 1705, while Wycherley looked on, half in amusement, half in a doze, rather as a basking old dog shakes off the antics of a puppy. But the dramatist was always exquisitely polite.

[1] Summers, II, 242. [2] Gildon, 15.

Pope then proceeded to institute a correspondence with his patron. It would be for him a channel in which to air his precocity. Wycherley during this time had continued to read the boy's poems, and he was not loath to acknowledge in them talents much superior to his own in point of rhythm and polish. Now he had already done Pope a priceless service in providing him with social experience in London, and if the young man was to make added demands upon his attention by letters, it was fair that Wycherley should ask Pope to read and criticise some of the dramatist's verses in return. The first positive evidence that Wycherley entertained this idea was in his letter to Pope dated March 22, 1706.

According to Pope, however, several letters passed between them in the previous year. These are trustworthy[1] only in so far as they may suggest something of Wycherley's sentiments and activities at that time. The Plain Dealer appears to have been correcting a few of his madrigals for 'a great man'— possibly with a view to publishing a second volume. Again,[2] he compared his association with Pope to a saying of old Sir Bernard Gascoigne: 'that when he was grown too old to have his visits admitted by the

---

[1] The story of Pope's duplicity in falsifying and fabricating his correspondence, not only with Wycherley, but with Addison and Swift (in order to make his genius appear more sensational), belongs rather to the life of Pope, in later years.

[2] April 7, 1705.

281

ladies he always took along with him a young man to ensure his welcome to them and escape rejection, because otherwise his visits would not be scandalous.' Pope with his melodious voice and bubbling wit was usually more welcome to the ladies than a youth comely but tongue-tied.

The little poet repeatedly urged Wycherley to visit him in Binfield. Wycherley, an 'obstinate lover of the town,' replied by inviting Pope to 'his forest of London, where wild and tame beasts pursued one another out of either love or hatred, where one might see a pack of spaniels called lovers in hot pursuit of a two-legged vixen, who only fled the pack in order to be singled out by one dog.'[1]

But the first letter of Wycherley not tampered with, the letter of March 22, 1706, appears to have been written from Clive, and it alluded to Wycherley's friend and physician, Dr. Radcliffe, and again to the prospect of his going to Bath, although the Plain Dealer seemed chiefly to object to Pope's lavishing upon him the painted flourish of his praise. Wycherley said:

'My Great Little Friend . . . you try my patience . . . in the beginning of your letter; not by the many lines in it, but the too many compliments you make me for nothing; in which you prove yourself, (tho' a sincere friend) a man of too much fiction

[1] November 5, 1705.

. . . your letter is like an author's epistle before his book, written more to show his wit to the world than his sincerity or gratitude to his friend, whom he libels with praise . . . I know not whether I am more complimented than abused; since too much praise turns irony, as too great thanks for small favours turns ingratitude . . .

'If you would have laid some wit to my charge, you must have told me that I showed (at least) some when I intended to submit all I wrote to the infallibility of your wit, judgment, and censure, who are my Pope . . .

'I have some thoughts of going from hence to the Bath, being advised to it by Dr. Radcliffe when I was at London as likewise by my doctor here (if I would be thoroughly well) . . .

'My humble service to your Mother and Father, as likewise to that factious young gentleman Mr. Englefield, and tell him if I am come into Berkshire I will make him holloa as loud in the tavern at Reading as he did at the Coffee-House in London, till he dances with his own dairy maids . . .

'Now after all I must lay a penance upon you, which is to desire you to look over that damned Miscellany of Madrigals of mine, to pick out (if possible) some that may be so altered that they may yet appear in print again, I hope with better success than they hitherto have done . . . In the meantime once more farewell, My Dear Little Infallible.'

Pope took some of Wycherley's poems, with a view to smoothing out some of the lines in them, though his father, quite callous to the good offices Wycherley had bestowed upon his 'infallible' son, begged him not to do it.

'You'll do nothing,' insisted the elder Pope, 'but get enemies by it.'[1]

Alexander was not exuberant over the task, although he himself for over a year had shown no hesitation in requesting Wycherley to read and comment upon his own work. But the truth was that from the age of eighteen, as Pope every day grew more and more conscious of his own power, he grew less and less mindful of any debt he owed his literary grandfather, and his friendship began to wear the garb of duty as well as the costume of pleasure. Pope amended and improved certain verses of the dramatist, and of this exercise he said:

'. . . Some I have contracted, as we do sunbeams, to improve their energy and force; some I have taken quite away, as we take branches from a tree, to add to the fruit; others I have entirely new expressed, and turned more into poetry . . .'[2]

Yet this virtuoso was not altogether frittering away his time in thus serving the man who had led

[1] Spence, 336.   [2] April 10, 1706.

him through the mazes of literature in Drury Lane. He studied Wycherley's wit. And he did not abstain from plucking a few flowers out of his friend's garden as he glanced up and down its trellises. He put aside a line from the prologue of 'The Plain Dealer' which he thought he could use one day; it was a neat thrust at human hypocrisy: 'And with faint praises one another damn.' Then he was especially taken with Wycherley's 'Panegyrick on Dulness'; he tinkered with this poem in great glee, beat it into one shape after another, broke it in pieces and pounded them together again, tossed it back to Wycherley,[1] and when he got ready he sat down and wrote his own 'Dunciad' out of the debris.

By reason of his very youth Pope clung to the glamour of Wycherley's fondness for him, and never ceased exhorting Wycherley to visit him in Windsor Forest. The dramatist always excused himself; he could not be pried away from his chair at Will's, where he was now become the undisputed potentate of wit. Since the death of Dryden the perfervid temper of the discussions there had cooled a bit, but Will Urwin still remained coffee-house king. Wycherley, in his brown wig, glass buttons on sleeves and coat, and square-toed Queen Anne shoes, convalescing both from the attack on his poems and the attack on his health, was again enjoying town life

[1] Pope to Wycherley, November 20, 1707.

as of old. Except upon an imperative call he utterly refused to go down to Shropshire; he sent his man. Though the air of Paradise might fan his father's house, though angels might wait upon his whims, he would not stay in Clive. His servant had to keep rushing off to the country with an empty satchel and rushing back with it full of pounds sterling. Wycherley's purse was a sieve.

In November, 1707, he wrote to Pope to say he was sorry Pope's father would not let the young man come to town (Alexander's parents believed a child of nineteen, well or ill, not too old to coddle), for so much comedy was likely to be acted by 'the two great playhouses of the nation—the Houses of Parliament.' It was a gay season in London, 'when everybody of the two Nations, almost, was in it.'

There were two reasons, then, for the frequency of letters between the poets: one was that they were constantly urging each to visit the other, and neither accepting the invitation; the other that they had to exchange views on the editing of Wycherley's poems. Pope in his rustic den seldom had anything very human to say, and never anything that might beget a smile, while Wycherley—always the writer of comedy—sprinkled his letters with amusing observations on his age-old diversion: London life.

Pope wrote that besides 'rectifying the method, connecting the matter, and mending the expression

and versification' in his friend's poems (a rather ex-
aggerated table of remedies),[1] he had also to omit
the repetitions. This last hinted at Wycherley's impaired memory. But one of Pope's wisest suggestions was that Wycherley reduce many of his ideas
to single maxims, like la Rochefoucauld's, and this
the elder man eventually did.

From Shrewsbury in January, 1708, Wycherley
wrote to thank Pope for a New Year's letter: . . .
'I must confess my journey was very tedious to me,
by reason of the season . . . but necessity (which
made the old mare to trot) made me jog down into
Shropshire, having two farms of some considerable
rents thrown up into my hands which might have
been unlet . . . for this whole year following, had
I not come down, nor had I stayed above, would my
tenants have Come Down With the Ready . . .

'Since your letter tells me you are forced to keep
your chamber upon so melancholy an occasion as
that of your sight being so obscured . . . pray look
to your eyes . . . since you may spoil your eyesight
. . . but you can hardly improve your reason's in-
sight . . . it is recompensed by the strength of your
imagination and inward penetration as your poetick
forefathers were from Homer to Milton . . . do
not read so much as you do (since you have learned

---

[1] Details of this letter (November 29, 1707) rest on the authority
of Pope alone.

287

enough) . . . Take my advice, rather, to losing
your eyes by gazing on the fair Shepherdesses of
your plains, than by poring on the fairest impressions
of your authors . . .'

Jacob Tonson in this year proposed publication of
his sixth volume of 'Miscellanies,' and Pope wrote
to Wycherley to say that he intended to make his
first bow to the public by contributing his pastorals
to that book. The Plain Dealer, still in the country
at the end of February, replied:

'. . . I am pleased with the good news of your
going to print some of your poems, and proud to be
known by them to the public for your friend; who
intend (perhaps the same way) to be reveng'd of
you for your kindness by taking your name in vain
in some of my future madrigals . . . to let the
world know my love or esteem for you are no more
poetick than my talent for scribbling. But of all the
arts of fiction, I desire you to believe I want that of
feigning friendship.'

Pope was dedicating his third pastoral, Autumn,
to Wycherley, and Wycherley spoke further of his
'revenge' in two letters to his friend in May and
July: 'I have made a damned compliment in verse
upon the printing your pastorals, which you shall see
when you see me.—If you suffer my old dowdy of
a Muse to wait upon your sprightly lass of the plains,
into the company of the town, 'twill be but like an

old city-bawd's attending a young country-beauty to town, to gain her admirers, when past the hopes of pleasing the world herself.'

Wycherley, with his verses in Tonson's book, was to stand at the door of the Temple of Fame and bow the new member in, but Pope was to have the privilege of reading beforehand the speech of welcome. For two years, now, Pope had been the corrector of Wycherley's poems.

About a month before Christmas, 1708, the dramatist in another letter gave a glimpse of his 'boarding-house life' in fashionable London, insisted also upon his shrimpish little friend coming to visit him, and lamented the sadness of a coffee-house acquaintance, Titcombe (who Pope thought led 'a beastly laughable life'), together with his own sadness because of the death from an asthma of the Queen's consort, Prince George of Denmark:

'. . . . I desire to know when you will come to town to make Titcombe and me bear the Prince's departure from this life the better, for which the whole town is going to be sad, as far as black cloth and crape or muslin will show their sorrow; for I believe the truest mourners are the silkmen, the lacemen, the embroiderers, and players, who (they say) must shut up their shops for these six months . . .

'Titcombe himself is now a sadder fellow than ever, so that the only way to relieve the general sadness here is for you to come to town . . . the chamber next mine is empty and Mrs. Bambro's table is now no more full of guests than meat, so that . . . you are sure to be welcome to everybody here that knows you . . .'

Pope appears in the ensuing winter to have burst the parental fetters and scampered to London. One can hear his birdlike voice fluting in the bended ear of the Plain Dealer. Both evidently celebrated their renewed 'Nunc est bibendum' without counting the flagons, for Pope upon his return home protested his 'want of health,' and Wycherley replied complaining of 'the collick.' The dramatist observed that if he could keep off a cold he should be content to do without the philosophy which sickness may teach a man, and be 'a good hardened blockhead,' with health, but without thought or sense. In his brawny benignity he added, 'I yet hope your great, vigorous, and active mind will not be able to destroy your little, tender, and crazy carcass.' Pope did not care to hear animadversions upon his 'carcass.' He could not rise to the honesty of a chuckle. He was an agelast.

But Wycherley himself, at sixty-nine, was still unable to shrink from merriment. On the twenty-ninth of April (1709)[1] he went with a Mr. Balam, obscurely illustrious in being a friend of a friend of

[1] Letter to Pope.

Pope and therefore 'literary,' to the old Painters' Tavern in Upper Thames-street near St. Paul's, a house of conviviality historic even in the day of Chaucer. The night grew jovial and brightened into morning. Wycherley and Balam, while still able to recognize each other, started downstairs. But Balam, because he thought himself sober, was somewhat drunker than Wycherley, and insisted upon leading the poet down. Wycherley with a profound bow refused this polite aid; the two then descended in safety. When they reached the second flight of steps, going into the street, Balam, still the conscientious Samaritan, turned short upon Wycherley to help him lest he fall, and both tumbled helterskelter. That made the night a success.

'Balam turning back upon the Ass, not the Ass upon Balam,' wrote Wycherley later, 'he fell upon me, and threw me backward, with his elbow in my stomach and the hilt of his sword in my eye bruised me so sorely I was forced to keep my bed for two days, with a great pain in my side which by the help of surgeons is but lately gone, so that I have been almost a fortnight in pain . . .'

Wycherley however during this springtime had some reason to feel complacent. As soon as the half-year period of mourning for Prince George had elapsed the theatres reopened, both 'The Country Wife' and 'The Plain Dealer' were revived, and

'The Country Wife' was called for in Drury Lane several times over, enough to give the author 'third night receipts.' Only a fortnight prior to the little soirée in Painters' Tavern a benefit performance of 'The Country Wife' was given with resounding applause for the actress Mrs. Bicknell, who herself acted Margery Pinchwife, while Colley Cibber in the character of Sparkish did what he could to approach the classic humour of Joe Haynes.[1] Wycherley was still the favourite satirist of two generations.[2]

A critique of this performance appeared in the second issue of *The Tatler*, which had been founded a week before by Dick Steele. Under the heading 'Will's Coffee-House, April 14,' Steele wrote:

'. . . The Poet, on many occasions, where the propriety of the character will admit of it, insinuates that there is no defence against vice but the contempt of it: and has, in the natural ideas of an untainted innocent, shown the gradual steps to ruin and destruction which persons of condition run into, without the help of a good education to form their conduct. The torment of a jealous coxcomb, which arises from his own false maxims, and the aggrava-

[1] Summers, II, 5.

[2] The latest revival of 'The Plain Dealer' was given on May 22, 1929, for the teaching staff of Yale University, by the society of Zeta Psi. The latest run of 'The Country Wife' was in June, 1926, at the Lyric Theatre, Hammersmith, with Mr. Baliol Holloway and Miss Isabel Jeans.

tion of his pain by the very words in which he sees her innocence, makes a very pleasant and instructive satire.

'The character of Horner, and the design of it, is a good representation of the Age in which that comedy was written: at which time love and wenching were the business of life, and the gallant manner of pursuing women was the best recommendation at Court. To this only it is to be imputed that a gentleman of Mr. Wycherley's character and sense condescends to represent the insults done to the honour of the bed without just reproof; but to have drawn a man of probity, with regard to such considerations, had been a monster, and a poet had at that time discovered his want of knowing the manners of the Court he lived in, by a virtuous character in his fine gentleman, as he would show his ignorance by drawing a vicious one to please the present audience.'

Steele, now thirty-seven and the embodiment of Irish blarney in scarlet and gold lace, was noted all over town for his experiments in love. After the pattern of Wycherley he had himself pursued and married a widow of fortune. Nor had these escapades by any means alienated the Court from 'Rollicking Dick.' The age of Charles II was scotched, but not killed, and though Steele spoke of those times almost as if they were a geological epoch gone by, there were some manners of the Restoration not yet become fossilized.

To show patriarchal indifference was not in the character of Wycherley. But to Pope he wrote[1] only that the coffee-houses were being entertained 'with a whimsical new newspaper called the *Tatler* which I suppose you have seen, and is written by one Steele, who thinks himself sharp upon this Iron Age, since an Age of War, and who likewise writes the other *Gazettes*, and this under the name of Bickerstaff.'

Dick Steele really held Wycherley's genius in great regard, as he revealed in another issue of *The Tatler* in his comments on certain pretenders to belles-lettres then rampant in London: 'The town has for half an age been tormented with insects called "easy writers," whose abilities Mr. Wycherley described excellently well in one word: "That," said he, "among these fellows is called easy writing which anyone may easily write." '

On May 2, 'Tonson's Miscellany' was published. In dedicating his third pastoral, 'Autumn,' to Wycherley, Pope thus addressed the old poet:

'Thou, whom the Nine, with Plautus' wit inspire,
The art of Terence, and Menander's fire;
Whose sense instructs us, and whose humour charms,
Whose judgment sways us, and whose spirit warms.

[1] May 17, 1709.

294

Oh, skilled in nature; see the hearts of swains,
Their artless passions, and their tender pains!'

The contribution next the pastorals was Wycherley's 'damned compliment in verse,' which, it appears, the Plain Dealer had submitted to Pope like any other of his poems. 'To my Friend Mr. Pope on his Pastorals' read in part:

'. . . Young, yet judicious; in your verse are found
Art strengthening nature, sense improved by sound. . . .
But wit and judgment join at once in you,
Sprightly as youth, as age consummate too:

Your strains are regularly bold, and please
With unforced care, and unaffected ease. . . ."

As Pope published only an 'extract' from the two letters of Wycherley which mentioned these verses, and suppressed the remainder, it is difficult to estimate how far his hand went in shaping the verses to their form in Tonson. There were more than fifty lines, and if Dennis and others were too severe in accusing Pope of writing all,[1] the rhythm and antithesis, so seldom facile in the couplets of Wycherley, did tend to disclose Pope as embellishing the garlands that bedecked himself. Tuberculosis may impel its victim to pernicious practices. In Pope it engendered an appetite for trickery, which as he

[1] Courthope, I, 21-2.

grew older he indulged more and more in order to sate his deepest passion: love of fame. Pope warped by phthisis, Wycherley weakened by apoplexy: it was one pathological case face to face with another.

If Wycherley ceased to write to Pope for any length of time, Pope made inquiries about him through their mutual friend of the coffee-houses, Henry Cromwell. Urging Cromwell to go and see the Plain Dealer, Pope said: 'Wycherley will be sure in less than a quarter of an hour's conversation to give enough wit to atone for twice as much dulness as I have troubled you with.'

Cromwell was a Lincolnshire gentleman of property, who hunted foxes in the country and ladies in the town.[1] Sometimes he combined town, country, and ladies by going to Bath. When he was not trying to be an author he could be original, but always in both verse and voice he was a courageous captain of compliments.

In May, 1709, Pope sent with a letter to Cromwell a copy of Sappho's poems which he had previously promised to Wycherley. This letter, which seems to have asked for news of Wycherley, Cromwell would not let the Plain Dealer see, though he did disclose to him a part of its contents. Wycherley wrote banteringly to Pope on June 4, explaining that he could not come for a visit to Windsor Forest because in the

[1] Ibid, V, 75.

five weeks since his orgy with Balam he was only just rid of the pain in his side, 'who thought at this age I should nevermore have had pain there.'

He continued: 'I find by your letter to Mr. Cromwell you have disposed of the Sappho (you promised me) to him, so that you have a mind to give me jealousy. But it is rather of your friendship than of the love of your Sappho, since he refused to let me see your last letter to him, who would be a lover or a friend by his rude civil ceremony, too much for woman or man to bear. So that I dare swear your ladies (his acquaintance) whom you desire him to salute in your name are Irishwomen, by their intimacy with and friendship for him, more than their names.

'Otherways his hard face would render ineffectual all the soft things he could say to them in praise of theirs; who never discommends anything and is only a Satyr in his face, not in his tongue, and like the Devil tempts living Eves to sin by his creeping advances, clinging embraces, since the more he bows and creeps to them, the less they see his face, which like the Devil's were enough to frighten them from what his tempting tongue would persuade them to.

'Thus he is damned to perpetual flames of love here without hopes of his Fool's Paradise in love; yet like the Devil is still tempting women to his love to the augmentation of their persecution and his

despair. All this I say a little peevishly of him because he would not let me see your letter; but so
much for him who looks like a Devil, loves like a
Tormentor, and damns like a Critick, because he is
damned himself . . .'

Wycherley, in spite of his life benefice of his
father's farms allotted him under the settlement of
1696, was finding himself in these years in a finan-
cial pinch. Perhaps not unreasonably he considered
that old Daniel had been unjust in shutting him off
from all benefits of the more valuable half of the
estate—the holdings in Clive. It was of course to be
admitted that the poet in the lifetime of Daniel had
made no secret of his hatred for his birthplace; the
lord of the manor had enough truculence in him on
that account alone to exclude his son from all connection with such a 'despised' spot. Young William
Wycherley, heir apparent and nephew to the Plain
Dealer, was now twenty-five. To him Wycherley
made overtures (with a view to obtaining money to
clear more debts) about transferring part of the Clive
income to himself, since he considered he had been
unfairly deprived of it.[1] Such reasoning left the
nephew dry-eyed.

The alternative was for Wycherley to marry
again. He could then liquidate from what fortune his
wife might have of her own, and recompense her

[1] Spence, 18; Perromat, 81.

with the widow's jointure on the estate as provided in the settlement. But when he reminded his nephew of this expedient, young William still remained bleak. He appeared to be utterly without feeling for his uncle or for the honour his uncle had brought to the family; it was as if old Daniel on his death-bed had thriftily adjured the boy to be pitiless.

The late second marriage of Wycherley's friend and coæval, Sir William Trumbull (at sixty-seven), reminded the poet of his own thoughts upon the matter, and in August, 1709, he wrote to Pope: 'Pray present my most humble service to Sir W. Trumbull, for whom and whose judgment I have so profound a respect that his example had almost made me marry more than my nephew's ill carriage to me; having once resolved to revenge myself upon him by my marriage . . .'

Yet Wycherley so dreaded the prospect of a second pandemonium in his house that he did nothing about another wife. Phantoms of his winter-minded Laetitia came back to shake his peace. In one of his later poems, 'On Orpheus's Descent to Hell,' he wrote that Orpheus sang because he was a widower; that Eurydice was the only beast whom the harper's music could never control; and that she was kept in hell in order to make sure that the discord down there would last.[1]

[1] Summers, IV, 188.

At this point the interchange of quips and civilities between Wycherley and Pope broke off. Wycherley had either fallen ill, or he doubted the sincerity of Pope. Perhaps he had both reasons. Pope was worried, and he wrote, with apparent emotion, to Cromwell (August 29, 1709):

'I have not heard these two months from Mr. Wycherley, though I have written to him twice. I am since told he has been ill, which I am very much concerned for, and fear is the occasion of his silence since his last letters, which were the kindest in the world. If you happen at your return to find him in town it will be very obliging to let me know of it.'

Cromwell did not find Wycherley, for Dr. Radcliffe in September had bundled him off to Bath for the waters.

Pope was conscience-stricken. He wrote to Cromwell again: 'My concern for his friendship will excuse me . . . if I vent a part of my uneasiness to you, and tell you that there has not been wanting one to insinuate malicious untruths of me to Mr. Wycherley, which I fear may have had some effect upon him.'

However, any disagreement in the air must have blown out to sea, for Wycherley resumed writing in February, 1710, felicitating Pope upon coming shortly to London: 'I must needs tell you in the style of the wise Recorder of London, who told King

James after the death of King Charles he came to him with sorrow in one hand and grief in t'other (tho' he meant joy), so your letter brings me sorrow in one sense and joy in another; sorrow for your indisposition, and joy that it will not hinder you from coming to town.'

Pope was afflicted with headaches, his lifelong ailment. Wycherley insisted that the little man visit London, where 'he could have his head ache to some purpose.' Pope came, got his head attended to thoroughly in the coffee-houses, and when he returned to Binfield he wrote that for all his punishment he would rather be 'sick in town in Wycherley's company than well in the country without it.'[1]

During this spring Wycherley sent his friend another sheaf of poems to correct, saying: 'Be most kindly unmerciful to my poetical faults, and do with my papers as you country gentlemen do with your trees; slash, cut, and lop off the excressness and dead parts of my withered bays, that the little remainder may live the longer; and burn the bulk of my writings to encrease the value of them by diminishing the number of them, as the Dutch burn three parts of their spices (from the Indies) to add to the value of the remainder . . .'

The old poet had now a set object in reviving his requests to his censor. He wanted the world to see

---

[1] Repeated by Wycherley (to Pope) April 1, 1710.

that he had not held himself in petulance over criticism, and that as he had risen above the failure of 'The Gentleman Dancing-Master' and gone on with his burly pen to make his conquest of comedy, so could he surmount the fiasco of his 'Miscellany' and prove that since then he had trimmed his talents. It was not too exciting to be known in London either as the defunct author of living comedies or as the living author of defunct verses. Wycherley therefore designed another volume of poems. Ten days after he had reopened with Pope the subject of editing his work he wrote again, on April 11:

'. . . I beg you to give yourself the pains of altering or leaving out what you think superfluous in my papers, that I may endeavour to print such a number of them as you and I shall think fit, about Michaelmas next. . . . Be severe to them, that the Criticks may be less so, for I had rather be condemned by my friend in private than exposed to my foes in publick. . . . By your tuning my Welsh harp[1] my sense may be the less offensive to the nicer ears of those criticks who deal more in sound than sense. . . .'

Pope answered within a few days, and Wycherley wrote again. To this last the young poet did not reply. He had complained of Wycherley's repetitions in his poems, due to lapses in the memory of

[1] Wycherley like his friend Samuel Butler was born near the Welsh border.

the author. Pope was now complaining also of the repetition of Wycherley's anxious requests. But in one particular the memory of Pope had evidently begun to fail: he seemed no longer aware that it was Wycherley in his bountiful kindness who had taken him up and sponsored him when all London had stared at him as a crab-gaited freak.

Wycherley on April 27 waited no longer, and wrote: '. . . Having not yet received any answer . . . I doubt your old pain of the headache has prevented it. . . . You give me an account in your letter of the trouble you have undergone for me in comparing my papers . . . with the old printed volume, and with . . . that bundle you have in your hands, amongst which (you say) you find numerous repetitions. . . . I would not have you give yourself more trouble about them. . . .

'All that I desire of you is to mark in the margent . . . matter, or sense, or any thoughts or words too much repeated . . . you will most infinitely oblige me, who almost repent the trouble I have given you, since so much. . . .'

Pope was now twenty-two years old and he was ably paddling his own literary canoe. He was on the straight course to become the most quoted living poet, and he rather acted as if he were confident of it. He looked upon the carpentering of Wycherley's poems as a chore, and he was no longer a chore-boy. On the second of May he wrote a letter which he meant Wycherley to read between the lines:

'. . . It really is my opinion, and desire, that you should take your papers out of my hands into your own; and that no alterations may be made but when both of us are present; when you may be satisfied with every blot as well as every alteration and addition, and nothing be put upon the papers but what you shall give your own sanction and assent to at the same time. . . .'

Pope ended by again counselling Wycherley to turn the greater part of his poems into single maxims and reflections in prose, after the manner of 'your favorite Rochefoucauld.' He said it would be an easy task for Wycherley himself to do.

This was the final letter of the published correspondence between the greatest poet of the rising generation and the greatest satirist of the generation gone down.

Wycherley did not answer it.

Three months of silence elapsed. In August, Pope naïvely wrote to Cromwell: 'I know myself guilty of no offense, but of doing sincerely what he bid me.'

It was as if Pope twisted the lion's tail when nobody was looking, then, when the lion resented it, turned to bystanders with his shining, lashless, motionless eyes and innocently inquired:

'What's he growling about?'

CHAPTER IX

OLD LION IN SATIRE

In monolithic loneliness Wycherley lived on, last column of the peristyle of 'confident young men' that once surrounded King Charles. Embrowned relic of a Temple to Aphrodite, he was swept by the wind of an age that was new. He was seventy.

The London he now saw was something too much a London of faces unseasoned. Since the calendar had marked 1700, all three surviving personages with whom the Plain Dealer was once a fellow-player on and off the proscenium in Whitehall had died: Sedley, cheeriest old blade of them all, with eyes of Puck and scarf of gauzy lace, was dead from grief over the loss of his only son, a love-child by Ann Ayscough; Dorset was gone, that 'first gentleman of the Court,' incredibly gouty at the last, and incredibly dull, having lived and died on five thousand dinner-parties; Barbara Villiers, whose defiant loveliness for half a century vanquished London and baffled Paris, had swollen into a cistern of dropsy, and succumbed. Not that these onetime friends had for a generation been anything to Wycherley, but while they lived—a glimmer of the old London, the radiance of his spangled nights, abode with him. Now the circus had departed. He trod its tent-ground quite alone.

Wycherley was ill, and Dr. Radcliffe ordered him again to Bath. He did not object to Bath. It was pleasanter exile than Clive Hall, where the fatherly nephew made his lair; it was pleasanter exile than Tunbridge, where the ghost of Laetitia Isabella might be flouncing up and down the Pantiles. He had already made fleeting stops in Bath—it was at the elbow of one route to Shropshire—but now he went down there and lingered. Bath seemed to be a place to get well in magnificently. Bath amused the father of English modern comedy.

It was the one English town which turned back the clock. Under William III and Anne nearly every other corner in the kingdom had been swept with the broom of propriety, but Bath—whose streets echoed by day to the patter of coquettish damsels and by night to the zig-zag step of young noblemen in their cups—Bath still wore a smile left over from the throaty laughter of Charles II.[1] It was really the only town where Wycherley might imagine himself living again his brawny years, where he could again saunter gracefully, chat affably, bow gallantly. There was talk about its 'Golden Age' now under way. That had begun, it appeared, with

[1] Perromat, 79, 80.

the visit of Queen Anne to Bath in 1703, and two years later had taken visible form after Beau Nash had descended upon the Pump-room and walked out muttering.

Nash was an Oxonian and a Middle Templar. In London he had been a conductor of pageants, a practised expert in tinsel. As the supply of pageants was none too steady he turned gamester; then Bath attracted him as a field for both of his pursuits. Almost immediately upon his appearance there he succeeded as Master of Ceremonies a Captain Webster, who had just been killed in a duel, and the beginning of Nash's reforms was as sudden as his taking his office. He forbade duels.[1]

Nash knew three priceless assets to a man of sense: dress, manners, and style. He looked upon the scene of Bath and saw it neither dressy, mannerly, nor stylish. In dress he himself lost no time in setting the example: he got an enormous white beaver hat to wear as a symbol of his office; for street costume he put on embroidered satins which would beggar the wardrobe of a Persian prince. He lifted his chin and dropped his eyelids until gentlemen even taller than himself felt they had to stoop to look up at him. With the pinnacled majesty of Moses announcing the commandments he dictated laws of taste: he abolished the wearing of

[1] D. N. B. (Nash).

swords; he proclaimed that stockings and shoes, not boots, were the thing for the Parades and at the green table of play.

In a dog-eared old canvas booth, season after season, men and women had been drinking chocolate and rattling dice between sips. Beau Nash waved his wand over this hut and turned it into gorgeous assembly rooms of red plush and tinkling chandeliers. He inspected lodging-houses. He found gentlemen staying in rooms like garrets, unpainted, uncarpeted, curtained with cobwebs, musty from dead air, with nails sticking through crossbeams to jab unwary heads, yet rooms considered sumptuous if they stemmed the draughts with coarse hangings of wool, and almost regal if they possessed one or two creaky rush-bottom chairs which fainted away if sat upon. The Master gave terse orders that such coops be refitted, on pain of having them condemned, and for every room he fixed a tariff.

Nash's chariot was a sight to dream on: he might have talked it away from the Fairy Queen herself on the very morning after Cinderella had ridden in it. The sun picked out this coach to shine upon as it hummed down the South Parade, drawn by six greys and turreted by lackeys with apple cheeks blowing into French horns. To match this extravaganza Nash had an indoor display as well: he collected snuff-boxes from every country where snuff was used, quite as if he intended to dedicate a museum to the dainty vice they fostered.[1]

At the time Wycherley came to stay for the cure, Beau Nash, having repaired the streets of Bath in 1706, was planning to adorn them with stately buildings and drives in Queen Square, the Royal Crescent, and the North and South Parades. But there was one street-scene which the dictator made no attempt to improve upon: the ancient town-market. It was held on Wednesday and Saturday. In the midst of the shopping avenues there was a broad oblong clearing arrayed with wooden stalls. At dawn, red-wigged bandy-legged farmers steamed into their slots with barrows of guinea-fowls in crates and turnips in sacks. Their fat wives tumbled after, panting, and in a trice stood triumphant behind tables, barking the virtues of their plums and marigolds, or sweeping a warty hand over a sea of mushrooms. By breakfast-time the air in the whole market-place was viscid, earthy, and onionish, like air in a cellar. But to the invalids at Bath, those who came to the Pump-room nearby for bulging joints and cold sciatica, Wycherley among them, this air, this market and the fresh pungency of it, was a tonic after the air one had to breathe in eighteenth-century London, and none knew the worth of such homeliness better than Beau Nash himself.

[1] Barbeau, passim.

Wycherley on the advice of Dr. Radcliffe as well as for his outward entertainment[1] now determined to spend at Bath as many weeks each year as he had money to pay for. Upon occasion his vexing estates in Shropshire drew him northward, and he did return to town for long stays in order both to catch up on the gossip of the coffee-houses and to push forward arrangements for his second book of poems. To all purposes, the game of letter-writing played by himself and Pope ceased in 1710. Between battles with medicine-bottle and empty purse Wycherley chose thenceforth to proceed alone in authorship. Pope for his part continued to distribute his guiltlessness about town through the agency of Henry Cromwell, and sincerity, like many a time-conquered memento, went to the auction-room.

Pope wrote to Cromwell in October: 'I thank God there is nothing outside myself I would be at the trouble of seeking except a friend—a happiness I once hoped to possess in Mr. Wycherley: but 'quantum mutatus ab illo!' I have for some years been employed much like children that build houses with cards, endeavouring very busily and eagerly to raise a friendship, which the first breath of any ill-natured bystander could puff away.'

There seemed to be still, at least to the mistrusting mind of Pope, a mysterious unnamed person in

---

[1] Perromat, 80.]

the background. But that person was possibly Pope himself, his other self, a twin dwarf of sinister plots who racked by disease frustrated the goodness in his soul. Within a fortnight, again nipped by the fang of conscience, he insinuated once more to Cromwell (letter of October 28, 1711):

'I hope it will be no offence to give my most hearty service to Mr. Wycherley, tho' I perceive by his last to me I am not to trouble him with my letters, since he there told me he was going instantly out of town and till his return was my servant, etc. . . . I do not know to this hour what it is that has estranged him from me: but this I know, that he may for the future be more safely my friend, since no invitation of his shall ever more make me so free with him. . . . But I pardon his jealousy, which is become his nature, and shall never be his enemy whatsoever he says of me.'

After six years of acquaintance with the Plain Dealer, Pope had achieved almost complete metamorphosis from supplication to condescension, as these lines written in November suggested: 'I am heartily sorry for poor Mr. Wycherley's illness, and it is to his being long indisposed that I partly attribute his chagrin. I wish he may enjoy all the happiness he desires, though he has been the occasion of my enjoying much less than I did formerly.'

Wycherley, lonely but dogged, worked away at

his book in the obscurity of Bow-street. Infections of mind and body were making him by inchmeal a disease, yet he wrote, crossed out, wrote again, and on his drill-ground of white paper he daily drew up the ragged regiment of his wit. In an apology, the Introduction to his new poems, he set forth some of his feelings:

'Worn as I am with age, and harassed by fortune, I find many of my vices still faithfully troublesome, and amongst the rest that impertinent itch of scribbling, which has betrayed so many authors to ridicule, and almost undone our notions of reason and common sense: tho' at the same time I must own the lust of writing, like a man's other lewdness, should forsake us in our state of impotence. But we grow most vicious when we have least power left to be so, as beggars become most importunate the more strenuously we deny them. . . .

'One great mischief pursues all compositions, and that is, that no man can please the few wise who would please the many. Now he who makes it his aim to please the few wise must consequently be damned by the vulgar, and undo his bookseller: and he who writes down to the level of blockheads may possibly have his worthy labours vended to the conviction of his own good sense, and the contempt of all good judges . . .

'If we speak well of ourselves we but provoke the

world, which loves contradiction, into a scrutiny of our faults; if we speak ill of ourselves 'tis understood that we do it but that others might think well of us. . . . So that the bully-scribbler, like the bully in company, is beat out of his bravadoes only for assuming them; and the coward-scribbler, like the coward in company, is beat for raising the dispute and then not daring to defend it. . . .

'My pretensions are but small in the province of poetry, and the title of poet is the least of my ambition, for I have found poetry and poets such different things that the men who were the most proud of the possession have been most ashamed of the name.

'What I have produced of late years, want of health and too much leisure must in part be answerable for. I made my study, like a young wife, the amusement of my melancholy, and it cannot be wondered if I should desire to cherish its issue . . . Ill authors, like indulgent parents, are most fond of their weakest offspring, and therefore all are fondest of those begotten in their age.'

There was a time when Wycherley had looked into the Court, and written; now he had nothing left to examine but himself, the cleaned-out cupboard of his heart. Still he fought on.

Pope, on the contrary, was at this time as buoyed up by confidence as Wycherley was weighed down

with misgivings. Bent double in his bookish den he
was whittling out proverbs for his 'Essay on Criticism.' Whilst he was dipping his pen in acid Pope
thought it would be timely in this essay to scoff at
superannuated gentlemen, 'shameless bards impeni-
tently bold,' who persisted in writing poetry at the
instigation of a toothless Muse. The fiends of malice must have danced when they saw Pope polish off
these lines:

> 'In sounds and jingling syllables grown old,
>   Still run on poets in a raging vein,
>   Even to the dregs and squeezing of the brain,
>   Strain out the last dull droppings of their sense,
>   And rhyme with all the rage of impotence. . . .'

The 'Essay on Criticism' was published in May,
1711. There was no proof that its excoriation of old
versifiers was pointed at Wycherley. But as one
critic[1] has asked, 'Whom else could the lines suit at
that period? . . . If Wycherley was intended,
what must we think of Pope, who could wound in
this manner his old friend, for whom he professed
so much kindness and who first introduced him to
notice and patronage?'

Wycherley in any case was too big of heart to dis-
til a grudge against the rising genius, and he was
too masculine to embroil himself in a womanish

[1] Bowles.

314

quarrel. There can be no doubt that he was irritated, as a dying coal glows red under the assault of the bellows, but in the autumn, when he went down to Bath again and put his spirits in tune, he seems to have declared a general amnesty to the world. Yet such was the character of the Plain Dealer, before he had ever seen Bath, or even before his memory had begun to play him tricks.

He called upon Beau Cromwell, who had gone down for both the waters and the ladies, and Cromwell (October 26) dutifully reported the incident to Pope:

'Mr. Wycherley visited me at the Bath in my sickness, and expressed much affection to me: hearing from me how welcome his letters would be, he presently writ to you . . .

'I could not possibly be in the same house with Mr. Wycherley, tho' I sought it earnestly; nor come up to town with him, he being engaged with others; but whenever we met we talked of you. He praises your poem (the 'Essay on Criticism')[1] and even outvies me in kind expressions of you. As if he had not wrote two letters to you, he was for writing every post; I put him in mind he had already.

'Forgive me this wrong; I know not whether my talking so much of your humanity and tenderness to

[1] This "praise" is on the authority of Pope only, who published the correspondence.

me, and love to him, or whether the return of his natural disposition to you, was the cause, but certainly you are now highly in his favour: now he will come this winter to your house, and I must go with him; but first he will invite you speedily to town.'

One might have thought Cromwell was a sort of detective engaged by Pope to report everything Wycherley said about the little man in Windsor Forest. The truth probably was that Cromwell had succeeded the Plain Dealer as Pope's most favoured correspondent, and naturally Cromwell in his rôle of little friend to the great lost no chance to record his meetings with them. However, there was of course a certain liking on the side of Wycherley as well. When he drove up to London from Bath early in November he went to call upon Cromwell. Their talk as usual turned to Pope, and this is Cromwell's account of it to him:

'Mr. Wycherley came to town on Sunday last, and kindly surprised me with a visit on Monday morning. We dined and drank together, and I saying, 'To our loves,' he replied:

' " 'Tis Mr. Pope's health."

'He said he would go to Mr. Thorold's and leave a letter for you.'

Wycherley, ill or well, could never harbour any sense of hurt. Pope purred his satisfaction over this news of his old friend, and replied: 'I am highly pleased with the knowledge you give me of Mr. Wycherley's present temper, which seems so favourable to me. I shall ever have such a fund of affection for him as to be agreeable to myself when I am so to him, and cannot but be gay when he's in good humour, as the surface of the earth (if you will pardon a poetical similitude) is clearer or gloomier, just as the sun is brighter or more overcast.'

Pope then evidently decided to be 'disagreeable' to himself. Wycherley in this month of November invited him several times to town, and Pope, though he had come to congratulate himself on the polish of his manners, taught him by his father the linen-draper, did not bother to acknowledge these letters. But his perennial Cromwell, perhaps with a spot of truckling at the same time he seemed to aim at a reconciliation, rather kept to the shelter of a middle course, writing on December 7:

'Mr. Wycherley has, I believe, sent you two or three letters of invitation, but you, like the fair (ones), will be long solicited before you yield, to make the favour more acceptable to the lover . . . He is much yours by his talk; for that unbounded genius which has ranged at large like a libertine now seems confined to you . . .'

There was never any further mention of Wycherley in the letters between Pope and Cromwell.

The rendezvous for men of letters in Covent Gar-

den now shifted. Since Wycherley for several years
had gone to Bath more and more, the wits cast round
for a new leader to follow, found him in Joseph
Addison, and with Addison left Will's Coffee-
House to follow whither he should lead.

In 1712 Addison, at forty, was at the top of his
achievements in English prose, and just beginning
his applauded sketches and lampoons in *The Spectator*. He was a tall, fair man, with eyes of the liveliest light blue, and like Aristophanes he could
drink no end of wine without ever getting flustered.
His dress was as plain as he could make it, usually of
a tawny colour; this aversion to showiness made his
wit the more remarked. Addison set up his man,
Daniel Button, in a coffee-house across Russell-
street from Will's, and even Swift and Pope bestowed their patronage upon Button; Swift, whom
Addison sometimes upset in conversation, and Pope,
who was nettled by the humour of the Spectator as
he was nettled by the humour of Wycherley, and
who once in a huff went back to Will's.[1] But though
Pope with his exquisite 'Rape of the Lock' had now
plucked the highest laurels in poetry, the wits stayed
with Addison. These men continued to pour their
praise and affection upon Wycherley whenever he
did come amongst them, and they continued to defer
to him, saying: 'You may behold old excellent Cas-

[1] Spence, 263; Courthope, V, 74 ff.

sius (Wycherley), who in our comedy has furnished more wit than could Plautus and Terencius in their whole compositions.'[1]

Wycherley no doubt accepted such tributes with gratitude, but he was now growing month by month more infirm, and having outlived nearly all his friends and the age he had thrived in as well, he gave himself over increasingly to solitude—except when he took his walks at Bath—in his lodgings at Widow Hilton's. He narrowed down his reading to a few of his oldest favourites: Montaigne and Rochefoucauld, Seneca and Gracian, and over these books he read himself asleep.[2] But he had a purpose in choosing such authors: he had adopted Pope's advice, and was turning many of his verses into prose maxims, to fill up the book which was still not ready for the printer. The writers he was devoting himself to got him into aphoristic mood. But he had no solemn idea that these pills of wisdom of his own were bitterly important, when he defined them:

'Maxims are to the mind what a stick is to the body when too weak to support itself; those of a superior reason and capacity have no need of the first, as strength and bodily vigour despise the assistance of the latter.'

Wycherley at this stage was living to reflect. From the haystack of experiences in his brain he had

[1] Manley. Vol. III.   [2] Spence, 18.

only to pluck a straw and ruminate upon it. What he produced was a sort of impersonal diary—some of it doubtless old coffee-grounds from talks at Will's:

'A little piece of kindness oft gains a friend, and a great one as often loses him again.

'Fine books in the possession of a blockhead are evidences of his ignorance; as fools are ever exposed by good company.

'Revenge proceeds always from the weakness of a soul that is not able to support an injury.

'Old men are as fond of their crazy bodies as old villagers are of their crazy cottages; and still, like the others, are for renewing their lease.

'Believe your friend honest to make him so, if he be not so; since if you distrust him you make his falsehood a piece of justice.

'An old friend is often used by mankind like an old horse; they hackney him out in their service, and when he's past his drudgery, leave him to die in a ditch.

'Conversation augments pleasure and diminishes pain, by our having sharers in either; for silent woes are greatest as silent satisfactions least; since sometimes our pleasure would be none but for telling of it, and our grief insupportable but for participation.

'Every little Club thinks wit confined to it, as every small Sect of godly professors think to monopolize salvation.

'If it be wisdom to choose a profession that will be sure to maintain us, then all men should be parsons; for they living on the sins of the people follow a trade that can never fail.'

Sometimes the old Plain Dealer's memory did not awaken in the morning when he did, and he would write down one or two maxims which he had read in French or Latin only the night before, thinking them his own. Or in the course of a morning's work he would repeat on one page the same adage he had penned upon another. When a friend calling in Bow-street and reading over Wycherley's manuscript noticed such an error and showed it to the author, the old gentleman, vexed, would say: 'Gadsso, so it is. I pray you, blot it out.'[1]

Still he made some three hundred original maxims, and in writing this short prose, not entirely different from lines of dialogue such as glowed in the plays of his prime, Wycherley was ending his creative career in a task rather more diverting than it would have been if he had kept to poems. To Pope, for prescribing this medicine to soothe his 'itch of scribbling,' the old dramatist must have given repeated thanks. There was that residue, at least, left over from a painful intimacy. Wycherley had learned to patch pain with proverbs.

Pope in 1713 was twenty-five, and he had grown

[1] Spence, 2.

rather less solicitous about Wycherley's opinion of
him. He was now a busy Londoner, developing a
power of ridicule in order to inoculate himself
against it. He had become a sort of politico-literary
ferret, he delighted in sniffing out plots, schemes,
and intrigues concerning the Government, and he
hardly drank tea, it is said, without a stratagem. On
the stilts of his fame as a poet he patted the back of
Bolingbroke, Oxford, Peterborough,[1] with one hand
because like himself they were schemers, with the
other because unlike himself they were nobly born.
He eddied and whirled in the intrigue that swept in
billows from Kensington House to St. James's. His
poem 'Windsor Forest' was now ready to publish.
To whom would it be astute to dedicate it? Pope
chose a gentleman who was both a peer and a poli-
tician: Lord Lansdowne, Secretary for War.

On the 28 of July, 1714, Queen Anne, who from
girlhood had refused to dine sparingly and in consequence was racked with gastritis ("blue devils"),
gave way to a fit of illness more severe than usual.
Dr. Radcliffe, though the Queen had long dismissed
him her service, was summoned. Such was the super-
stitious belief in his mere presence that it was
thought he could kill whom he liked and keep alive
whom he liked. Radcliffe now sent word from his
country house, Carshalton, Surrey, that he had

[1] Thackeray (Pope), 296, 305, 308.

'taken physic and could not come.'[1] On August 1 the Queen died. And as Radcliffe a score of years before had been charged with killing Queen Mary, whom he attended at her death-bed, he was now charged with killing Queen Anne, whom he did not attend. Maniacs at large sought to assassinate him.[2] The Doctor stayed in the country, read Genesis, and observed 'he found Moses a clever fellow; if he had known him a little sooner, he thought he would have read him through.' But within three months Radcliffe himself was dead, of the gout.

In the autumn Wycherley and Pope were in Bath at the same time. They were occasionally seen somewhere standing together—venerable Wycherley like a grandfather towering a foot and a half above the little tight-skinned dude whose persimmon lips ever thwarted a smile. To a lukewarm degree Cromwell had reconciled them, but there was no rebirth of the old cordial greetings. Pope was taking his mounting acclaim with some self-esteem, and to buttress his dignity he kept pitting his strength of ridicule against his dread of it, while Wycherley, who like all born humourists mocked at gravity when it became too ponderous, seems to have exasperated the ablest poet in England by playing iconoclast, though he thrust some of the very sentiments Pope had put in writing back into Pope's own long teeth. Pope on

[1] Jeaffreson, I, 160.   [2] Ibid., 163.

September 25 wrote from Bath to his neighbour in Binfield, John Caryll, who was also Wycherley's friend:

'. . . I walk about here as innocently, and as little dreaded, as that old Lion in Satire, Mr. Wycherley, who now goes tame about this town . . . He that dares to despise the great ones of this age, to deny common sense to Ministers of State, their small portion of wit to the poets, who live by it, and honesty to maids of fourteen . . .'

Jets of vitriol like this are rather more akin to Pope than to Wycherley. A troop of Wycherley's friends, from Rochester to Dennis, had discovered no such spleen in the Plain Dealer. If Wycherley thus talked to the sour little man from Binfield he could have been laughing up his sleeve at Pope, the man who never learned to laugh.

Pope had not been kind. How could he long be kind to anyone? His deep and spongy brain shrank up his heart to the size of a sparrow's eye.

Yet Wycherley was now severely and chronically ill, and under the added burdens of years and poverty his tongue no doubt sharpened. In body he was tormented with gravel, in mind with his inability to remember his plans from one day to the next. As for money, his rents came to him only half-yearly, and he was out of funds long before his pockets were replenished. These hardships and maladies at last unseated his good humour,[1] and younger friends whose distresses he himself had so often dissolved now found Wycherley upon occasion fretful and impatient when they tried to cheer him.

The Plain Dealer returned to London, where in his rooms at the Widow Hilton's he was to endure the nightfall of his life. He did not gain strength. And there was no Dr. Radcliffe now to husband it for him. The Pump-room at Bath had done much to prolong and alleviate his days. But it seemed now that the waters were less effectual.

Again the project of marrying wound its way through Wycherley's thoughts. He had often told Pope he would marry again as soon as his life was despaired of.[2] Should he not despair of it now? He had told another friend that 'he was resolved to die married, though he could not bear the thought of living married.'[3] Should he have to, for very long? Life to him now, at seventy-five, was only a vision of a churchyard, and the poet knew that if his battalion of ailments did not soon overthrow him another marriage would. For years unpaid bills had blown about him, like autumn leaves in Lincoln's Inn Fields. He was anxious not only to see his debts cleared while he lived,[4] but with the help of a wife's dowry to pass his final days with coals on his fire and

[1] Perromat, 46.   [2] Spence, 18.
[3] Pack, 13.   [4] Ibid.; 'Shropshire Society,' 347.

bread in his cupboard. His bargain was fair: in exchange for the fortune of the woman he should wed, he would convey to her the jointure on the Wycherley estate as provided in his father's settlement.

From the woman's point of view there is no such thing as an unmarriageable man. Wycherley, like many elderly men whose experience has not been tethered by married life, well comprehended that women thought so. He was no more ashamed of marrying than he was afraid of dying, and by the light of a philosopher's lamp in Bow-street he meditated upon his impending funeral and his impending wedding with equal serenity.

In this year came the end of the seventy-two-year reign of Louis XIV. The French King had lived the same span of life as Wycherley, having been born only two years before him. The King had come to Angoulême as a boy when Wycherley was there as a boy, he had come to Holland a conqueror in battle when Wycherley was there a conqueror in comedy, and now both King and poet in their third scene of life had dwindled to nothingness. How long, how very long it seemed, that the old King had ruled a Continent. Wycherley, not long before, had been thinking of him, and wrote:

'. . . Fortune, like all other jilts, leaves those in their age who were her favourites in their youth; which truth I myself (as unworthy as I am) have experienced sufficiently, as well as Lewis the Grand (now the Petit). However, far be it from me to lessen by any impertinent popular reflection so great a Prince, who like his device, the Sun, from having been all the first part of his days in glory, may set at last in a cloud.'

Yet Wycherley, in all his penury and wretchedness, enjoyed in this dimming year one recompense, one tribute, which even the King of France at his brightest could not have gathered: his name was again in the eye of the people as the great master of satire. 'The Country Wife' was performed in May, 1715, at the Drury Lane, with a cast who could only shed lustre on the old author. It was the most talented company seen in this play since its first night, when Charles Hart and Joe Haynes had woven all their skill into the lines Wycherley set them. Now Barton Booth appeared as Pinchwife, and Colley Cibber again acted Sparkish admirably. The lively Mrs. Bicknell repeated her triumph as Margery, while 'Jubilee' Norris, foremost mimic of the day in 'helpless husband' parts, was Sir Jasper. But the one whom London wanted to see above all was the famous Hester Santlow, as Alithea. On the stage she was soft-voiced and elegantly prim, a Diana of discretion. Yet everyone knew her to be as public in her private life as she seemed private in her public life, for she had been the unruly mistress of the Duke of

Marlborough (young Jack Churchill of the old days).[1] That association may have made Mrs. Santlow feel singularly allied to Wycherley, who with her friend the Duke had once shared the favours of Barbara Villiers.

Still the glory of this revival of one of his masterpieces brought no known relief to Wycherley, bolting his doors against creditors in Bow-street. Tributes appeased no hunger. That was the irony in the lot of the dramatist, however great, two centuries ago. The dejected Plain Dealer could only wander through his rooms and look with emotion at his first portrait, by Lely, the young portrait which showed him in the bud of his dramatic genius. It still bore the legend from Virgil which he had pinned at the bottom, to be printed under the engraving in the 'Miscellany Poems.' Day upon day the old poet gazed upon the image of such gallantry —the ease, the ardour, the brilliance, the liveliness of it—fetched a rueful sigh, shook his head, and murmured 'Quantum mutatus ab illo!'[2]

Before the end of the summer appeared a man who was to play in the last days of Wycherley a fantastic part. He was a Captain Thomas Shrimpton, cousin to the poet, and his nearest living relative on his mother's side. He began, at a time when few others were showing any solicitude, to be a frequent

[1] Summers, II, 6. [2] 'Shropshire Society,' 348.

caller in Bow-street, and to him Wycherley naturally confided. The poet at first proposed that his
cousin and his heir join and raise a thousand pounds
to discharge his debts; such a partnership was defunct almost as soon as it was broached.[1] Then Wycherley disclosed the plan he had of circumventing
both his nephew and his debts by an eleventh-hour
marriage. Shrimpton intently gave ear. And without
delay his cousin commissioned him to find out a lady
who would be willing to exchange her fortune for a
jointure in Clive.

Taking it upon himself to produce a bride, the
Captain shortly brought to the Widow Hilton's a
young woman called Elizabeth Jackson, from St.
James's, Westminster. She was the daughter of 'Mr.
Joseph Jackson, gent.,' who however appeared to be
a stationer of Hertingfordbury. According to neighbours, 'her manners and conversation were coarse
and unrefined,'[2] and she was reputed not only the
mistress of Shrimpton, but to be with child.[3] Wycherley looked upon the lady with favour.

On the word of Captain Shrimpton, the desira-
bility of Elizabeth rested upon two things: her
father was 'very conversant' in the house of Lord
Chancellor Cowper, and (rather more to the point)
she had a fortune of one thousand pounds, part of

[1] Gildon, 21.   [2] 'Shropshire Society,' 349.
[3] Wheatley, I, 229.

which would come to her at marriage.[1] Wycherley's apoplectic weakness and his amnesia had so enfeebled him that he was on the verge of agreeing to anything that Shrimpton proposed.

It was autumn. The fog and the sulphurous smoke in Bow-street[2] were no tonic after the sunny parades of Bath. To torment him still further, his servants, taking advantage of his unwatchful eyes, broke faith with Wycherley and forced him ever deeper into debt. Barnes, his man, then fled the house. One day in the middle of November, as the poet sat lonely and penniless in his rooms, almost at the very moment when his genius was again being exploited and the actors of Lincoln's Inn Fields were rehearsing 'The Plain Dealer' for autumn production, officers of the law entered Mrs. Hilton's and arrested him. He was apprehended for a debt of thirty pounds.[3]

This little drama, ludicrous if it had not been catastrophic for its victim, must have carried back the old gallant to a similar scene thirty-three years before when he was escorted to Newgate for the same offense. But whereas he was then imprisoned as a result of having married, he was now in custody as a result of not having married. It was enough to wring gall from his satirical soul.

Shrimpton is said to have come to the rescue, at

[1] Oldfield; letter from Shrimpton.
[2] Dennis, 'Familiar Letters,' January 19, 1694.   [3] Oldfield.

length borrowed the thirty pounds, and set his cousin at liberty. Wycherley then sent the Captain down to Shropshire to collect funds for him, insisting that his nephew had conspired with tenants to keep back his rents. But Shrimpton upon his arrival at Clive Hall apparently found the estate so tangled up with mortgages and interest, demands and counter-demands, that he was able to bring back to London only a very slim purse for the downcast landlord.[1]

Wycherley now made all haste to bring about his wedding, which he swore should be performed even if it were on his death-bed. Shrimpton, at this juncture a constant attendant in the Widow Hilton's house, readily put forward Elizabeth Jackson, and to her the tired old poet raised no objection. On the twentieth of December she came to his lodgings, ostensibly full of sympathy for him because his nephew refused in any way to help. Elizabeth was in wedding clothes, which Shrimpton himself probably paid for. Wycherley had secured a special license, but being unable to walk to a church he sent for John Harris, assistant curate of St. Paul's, Covent Garden, to come to Bow-street.[2]

The ceremony was accomplished. The old man then lay down, in abundant relief that by this grotesque act he had both obliged his creditors and taken

[1] Ibid. [2] Perromat, 82.

unto himself a woman who seemed to show towards him a certain tenderness. As for the momentary Mrs. Wycherley, it can be said at least that she granted her affection as part of the bargain.

Elizabeth evidently did bring to her dying husband enough money to discharge what he owed. And Wycherley thereupon fulfilled his own promise by making over to his wife the jointure upon his estate, £500 yearly. This lien he gave upon the Trench Farm, near Wem, 'with woods, underwoods, and fishing,' about one mile north of Clive. The Trench Farm, acquired by Daniel for £800 from Lord Stafford, about 1642, was the scene of much of Wycherley's childhood.[1] He could hardly have chosen it for the stationer's daughter out of sentiment, but more likely because the Trench was among the most valuable of the nine properties listed to his use in the Settlement of 1696.

Before Christmas Day the poet began to fail noticeably, and he had to totter to his bed. It was a sombre holiday-time in the old rooms in Bow-street, the rooms which had seen joys and sorrows not so much, but rather so many elations and so many miseries, because Wycherley had there known the peaks and the bases of life, more than mere ups or downs. At the Widow Hilton's he had lived as bachelor, husband, widower; and now he could be

[1] Garbet.

called even none of these. Round the corner, and only ten minutes' walk through Prince's-street to Lincoln's Inn Fields, his play, the great comedy which had made him and by whose title he delighted to sign himself, had renewed only a few nights before its victory now forty years old. In its cast, as Olivia, had been another celebrated mistress of the day, Letitia Cross, said to have been mistress to Peter the Great while he lived in England.[1] But neither kings, nor mistresses, nor the laughter in the pit, nor friends forgetful and vanished, nor even the pile of blotted poems on his dusty table, could hold for Wycherley any meaning further.

As his life was ebbing away Pope did come to see him, twice. And the greatest poet in England scurried forth from Bow-street without emotion, to tell his friends that he had found Wycherley 'less peevish in his sickness than he used to be in his health.'[2]

On Friday night after Christmas, the old dramatist, a dramatist to the end, called his young wife to his bedside. He told her he had one request, the last he should make, and he entreated her not to deny it him. Elizabeth assured her compliance.

'My dear, it is only this,' said Wycherley gravely, 'that you will never marry an old man again.'[3]

Humour, that soft nurse through his life, that

[1] Summers, II, 93.
[2] Letter of Pope to Blount, January 21, 1716.   [3] Ibid.

dominant passion which always reached for Wycherley with a long arm if he strayed, had come at the last to tug at his pillow, even whilst death stalked back and forth atop the coverlets.

In the morning—it was the thirty-first of December and the year itself was dying—Wycherley sent for a friend of his to draw his will. In it, perhaps hearing again the twenty-four violins in Whitehall as he dined with King Charles, perhaps seeing the gray bedchamber in Bow-street swim with possessions he had so often moved amidst, and loved, but himself had none of, he bequeathed to his wife, with whatever else he had, 'all his ready money, plate, and jewels.' It was a poet's dream.

The only other person he named in the will was Shrimpton, as executor. When the document was written out, Wycherley approved and signed it, then lay back content.

About two hours later—the short winter day was unfolding its blanket of dark, and it would soon be candle-time—Will Wycherley died. It was so easy for him. It was as if breathing had grown superfluous . . . and there was no more need . . . to go on.

So came peace on New Year's Eve to Bow-street.

Had they asked Wycherley where he desired to be buried he would have answered in the words of his own Horner: 'Oh, amongst friends, amongst friends.'

334

Almost next door, just a spot of a walk past Will's Coffee-House and across the cobbles, stood old St. Paul's, that Westminster Abbey of Covent Garden. It was full of buried laughter. Joe Haynes, Yorick of the taverns and the great Sparkish of Wycherley's play, lay there; and nearby, just touching the outer wall, old Samuel Butler, whom Wycherley had tried to fend from starvation, himself not dreaming he should live to walk within its shadow; even there was the tomb sacred to Peter Lely, who had painted Wycherley in his brawny days when maidens ogled him and widows pursued him—the beau garçon of Drury Lane. And now the cold vault in St. Paul's gaped wide again, while they bore in the man from Bow-street.

He was a great lover, if only he had ever loved.

READING FOR WYCHERLEY AND HIS TIMES

d'Aigrefeuille, Charles. *Histoire de la Ville de Montpellier.* 1877.

Archives de la Ville de Montpellier. Tome IV.

Ashton, J. *The Fleet: Its River, Prison, and Marriages.* 1888.

Athenæum. Jan., Oct., 1857; Sept., 1860.

Aubrey, John. *Letters Written by Eminent Persons.* 2 vols. 1813.

Bagot, Josceline. *Colonel James Grahme of Levens. A Biographical Sketch of Jacobite Times.* 1886.

Barbeau, M. *Une Ville d'eaux Anglaise au XVIIIe Siècle.* Paris, 1904.

Beljame, Alexandre. *Le Public et Les Hommes de Lettres en Angleterre au XVIIIe Siècle.* Deuxième edition. Paris, 1897.

Biographia Britannica. 6 vols. 1747.

Biographia Dramatica. 3 vols. 1812.

Boissonade, P. et Bernard, G. *Histoire du Lycée d'Angoulême.* Angoulême, 1895.

Boswell, Eleanore. *Wycherley and the Countess of Drogheda. Times Literary Supplement,* November 28, 1929. (Correspondence.)

Bourgoin, Auguste. *Valentin Conrart et Son Temps.* Paris, 1883.

Boyer. *Letters of Wit, Politics and Morality.* 1701.

337

Boyer. *History of Queen Anne.* 1722.

Brett, A. C. A. *Charles II and His Court.* 1910.

Burnet, Gilbert. *History of His Own Time.* Edit. 1903.

Character of a Town-Gallant. London, 1680.

Churchill, G. B. Editor: *The Country Wife* and *The Plain Dealer.* New York, 1924.

Cibber, Theophilus. *Lives of the Poets.* 4 vols. 1753.

Collier, Jeremy. *A Short View of the Immorality and Profaneness of the English Stage.* 1698.

Courthope and Elwin (See Pope.)

Cousin, Victor. *La Société Française au XVIIe Siècle.* Paris, 1858.

Cunningham, Peter. *The Story of Nell Gwyn.* Edinburgh, 1908.

Cyclopædia of Biography. Conducted by Charles Knight. 2 vols. 1858.

Dalton, Charles. *English Army Lists.* 1661–1714.

Davies, Thomas, *Dramatic Miscellanies.* 3 vols. 1784.

Delort, André. *Montpellier au XVIIe Siècle.* 2 vols.

Demogeot, J. *Histoire de la Littérature Française.* Paris, 1884.

Dennis, John. *Letters upon Several Occasions.* 1696.

Dennis, John. *The Usefulness of the Stage.* 1698.

Dennis, John. *Original Letters.* 2 vols. 1721.

Dennis, John. *Select Works.* 2 vols. 1721.

Dictionary of National Biography.

Doran, J. *Annals of the English Stage.* 1865.

Downes, J. *Roscius Anglicanus.* 1708.

Drinkwater, John. *Mr. Charles of England.* 1926.

Drogheda, Anne, Countess of. *The History of the Moore Family.* Privately printed. 1906.

Edinburgh Review. January, 1841.

Egerton, William. *Memoirs of the Life of Mrs. Anne Oldfield.* 1731.

Evelyn, John. *Diary.* Edited by Wheatley. 4 vols. 1879.

Fanshawe, Lady. *Memoirs of Ann, Lady Fanshawe.* Edited by Herbert Fanshawe. 1907.

Fléchier. *Recueil des Oraisons Funèbres.* Paris, 1767.

Foster, J. *Men at the Bar* and *Inns of Court Registers.*

Gaetschenberger. *Geschichte der Englischen Literatur.* 3 vols. Prague, 1859.

Garbet, Samuel. *History of Wem.* (circa 1740.)

Garonne. *Histoire de la Ville de Montpellier.*

Genest, John. *Some Account of the English Stage.* Bath, 1832.

Gentleman's Magazine. 1811, 1812, 1850, 1871.

Gildon, Charles. *Memoirs of the Life of William Wycherley, with a Character of His Writings by Lord Lansdowne.* Curll, 1718. (Recently discovered by Mr. Thorn-Drury.)

Gosse, Edmund. *Life of William Congreve.* New edition, 1924.

Gough, Richard. *History of the Parish of Middle.*

Grahme, Col. James of Levens. *The Correspondence of Colonel Grahme and His Brothers, to* 1689. (MSS.)

Granger's Biographical History of England. Vol. I. 1806.

Griffith, A. *Chronicles of Newgate.* 1884.

de Grisy. *Histoire de la Comédie Anglaise au XVIIe Siècle.* Paris, 1878.

Hamilton, Antoine. *Memoirs du Chevalier de Grammont.* English translation. Notes by Scott.

Hargest, W. G. *Wycherley and the Countess of Drogheda. Times Literary Supplement,* November 21, 1929.

Harleian Society Publications. *Visitation of Shropshire.* Vols. 28–29. 1889. Also 1396, fo. 328 (Wycherley of Clive).

Hatton. *A New View of London.* 1708.

Haynes, Jo. *The Life of the Famous Comedian, Jo. Haynes.* 1701.

Hunt, Leigh. *Dramatic Works of Wycherley, Congreve, Vanbrugh and Farquhar.* 1840.

Inderwick, F. A. *Calendar of the Inner Temple Records.* 3 vols. 1901.

Jacob, Giles. *Poetical Register.* 1723.

Jeaffreson, J. Cordy. *A Book about Doctors.* 2 vols. 1860.

Johnson, Samuel. *Lives of the Poets. Life of Rochester.* 1811.

Journals of the House of Lords. Vol. XV.

Klette, Johannes. *William Wycherleys Leben und Dramatische Werke.* Münster, 1883.

Krause, Hugo. *Wycherley und Seine Französischen Quellen.* Halle, 1883.

Langbaine, Gerard. *Lives and Characters of the English Dramatic Poets.* Oxford, 1691.

Lansdowne, Lord. *The Genuine Works in Verse and Prose of the Rt. Hon. George Granville, Lord Lansdowne.* 1736.

Letters of Friendship, and Several Other Occasions. Written by Mr. Dryden, Mr. Wycherley, Mr. Congreve, and Mr. Dennis. 1700.

London Gazette. November 30-December 3, 1696.

Longueville, T. *Rochester and Other Literary Rakes of the Court of Charles II.* 1903.

Macaulay, Lord. *History of England.* Vol. III.

Macaulay, Lord. *Comic Dramatists of the Restoration.* (In W. C. Ward's introduction. See Ward.)

MacMichael, William. *The Gold-Headed Cane.* New York, 1915.

Magne, E. *Voiture et les Origines de l'Hôtel de Rambouillet.* Vol. I. Paris, 1912.

Magne, E. *Voiture et les Années de Gloire de l'Hôtel de Rambouillet.* Vol. II. Paris, 1912.

Magrath, J. A. *History of the Queen's College.* 2 vols. Oxford, 1927.

Manley, Mrs. *Court Intrigues . . . from the Island of New Atalantis.* 1711.

Manley, Mrs. *Secret Memoirs and Manners of Persons of Quality. . . . From the New Atalantis.* 1720.

Medical Library and Historical Journal. December, 1907. (Article by Jacobson.)

Memoires et Observations faites par un Voyageur en Angleterre. 1698.

Monspeliensia. *Publications de la Société des Bibliophiles de Montpellier.* 1899.

Montausier. *La Vie de M. le Duc de Montausier. Ecrite sur les Memoires de sa Fille.* 2 vols. Paris, 1729.

Notes and Queries. July-December, 1860.

Nouvelle Biographie Universelle. Paris, 1861. Vol. 36.

Pack, Richardson. *Miscellanies in Verse and Prose.* 1719.

Pack, Richardson. Introduction to the *Posthumous Works of Wycherley.* 1728.

Pepys, Samuel. *Diary,* edited by H. B. Wheatley. 1904.

Perromat, Charles. *William Wycherley. Sa Vie—Son Œuvre.* Paris, 1921.

Physic and Physicians. A Medical Sketch-Book. 2 vols. 1839.

Pinto, V. de Sola. *Sir Charles Sedley. A Study in the Life and Literature of the Restoration.* 1927.

Pitt, Moses. *The Cry of the Oppressed.* Printed for Moses Pitt. 1691.

Pope, Alexander. *Works.* Edited by Courthope and Elwin. 9 vols. 1871–86.

Quaas, Curt. *William Wycherley als Mensch und Dichter.* Rostock, 1907.

Robinson, E. F. *Early History of Coffee-Houses in England.* 1893.

de Rosset. *Les Portraits des Plus Belles Dames de Montpellier.* 1660.

Roux, Amadée. *Montausier et Son Temps.* Paris, 1860.

Shropshire Archæological and Natural History Society. *Transactions.* Second Series, Vol. II. Shrewsbury, 1890.

Société Archéologique de la Charente. *Bulletin,* 1899.

Spence, Rev. Joseph. *Anecdotes, Observations and Characters of Books and Men.* 1820.

Summers, Rev. Montague. Editor: *The Complete Works of William Wycherley.* (First Collected Edition.) 4 vols. 1924.

Taine, H. *Histoire de la Littérature Anglaise.* Paris, 1863.

Tallemant des Réaux. *Historiettes.* 2 vols. Paris, 1854.

The Tatler.

Thackeray, W. M. *English Humourists of the Eighteenth Century.*

Timbs, J. *Curiosities of London.*

Tinsley's Magazine. Vol. 32. (Article by Malloy.)

Vialles, P. *La Cour des Comtes de Montpellier.* 1921.

Villemain. *Choix d'Etudes sur la Littérature Contemporaine.* Paris, 1857.

Voiture, V. de. *Familiar and Courtly Letters.* 1700.

Voltaire. *Lettres Ecrites de Londres sur les Anglais.* Œuvres, 1876.

Walpole, Horace. *Letters.* Vol. 14.

Ward, A. W. *History of English Dramatic Literature.* 2 vols. 1899.

Ward, A. W. Editor: *Cambridge History of English Literature,* Vol. VIII, *The Age of Dryden.*

Ward, W. C. *William Wycherley. Plays.* Edited with Introduction and Notes. (Mermaid Series.)

Wheatley, H. B. *London Past and Present.* 3 vols. 1891.

Wilmot, John. (The Earl of Rochester.) *Poems on Several Occasions.* 1685.

Wood, Anthony à. *Athenæ Oxonienses.* New Edition, 1820.

Wootton, C. W. *Chronicles of Pharmacy.* 2 vols. 1910.

DOCUMENTS IN THE PUBLIC RECORD OFFICE FOR THE
CASE OF BARNABY V. WYCHERLEY

Chancery: Proceedings C5. (Bridges' Division, 1613–1714.) Bundle 454, number 72. Also C5. 583/78, and C5. 96/93.

Town Depositions C24. 1053–10, and C24. 1061–148.

Six Clerks' Depositions, C22. 327–39.

Decrees and Orders Entry Books (for 1680–81–82): C33. 253, C33. 255, C33. 257.

Affidavits C31. 49/264 and Register 23.

Masters' Reports: in Vols. 205 and 208.

Common Pleas: Docket Books for 1679 and 1685.
King's Bench: Docket Books for 1680–1 and Coram
Regem Roll for Michaelmas Term 1680, part 2,
553.
Fleet Prison: Commitment Book 1a. Entry beginning:
Willus Wicherley Comissus fuit prisone de le ffleet sep-
timo die Iulij anno regni Dni nri Iacobi scdi nunc Rx Angl
&c primo p Cur dci dni Regis de Banco virtute bris de
hend corpus vic Hertf direct. . . .

INDEX

345

Index

Racan, Marquis de, 8
Racine, his 'Esther,' 251
Radcliffe, John, 205, 206, 220, 243, 244, 263, 264, 282, 306, 322, 323
Radnor, Lord, 245
'Rape of the Lock,' 318
Réaux, Tallemant des, 9
'Rehearsal, The,' 97, 102
Richelieu, 4, 153
Richmond, Duke of, 141, 159, 160
Robartes, Charles, 181
Robartes, John, 147, 165
Robartes, Laetitia Isabella, see Drogheda, Countess of
Roche, Mme. la President de la, 155
Rochefoucauld, de la, 10
Rochester, Earl of, 50; in attack on Dutch, 52; marriage of, 54, 55; masking made popular by, 75; intercedes in behalf of Wycherley, 82, 83; his praise of Wycherley, 111, 124; illness of, 142; quoted, 173; death of, 172, 174
Roebuck, the, 130
Roger of Wycherley, 41
Rose Tavern, 38, 100

Sablieres, 153
Sailsbury, 137
St. Evremond, 71
St. Paul's Church, 37, 38, 334
Saintes, royal reception at, 24
Salop, Daniel Wycherley appointed Justice of Peace for, 54
Sandwich, Lord, 70
Santlow, Hester, 327, 328
Sappho's poems, 296, 297
Sedley, Katherine, see Dorchester, Countess of
Sedley, Sir Charles, 55, 102, 182, 205, 210; arrested, 56; plays criticised by, 58; intercedes in behalf of Wycherley, 82, 83; death of, 305

Shadwell, laureateship given to, 212
Shaftesbury, 137
Shakespeare, 101; grand-nephew of, 60
'She Would if She Could,' 57
Sheppard, Fleetwood, 183
'Short View of the Immorality and Profaneness of the English Stage, A,' 260
Shrewsbury, Countess of, 79
Shrimpton, Bethia, 14
Shrimpton, Thomas, 328–331, 334
'Sir Martin Mar-all,' 86
'Sir Salomon,' 91
Smith, the engraver, 266
Spain, peace proclaimed, 156
Sparkish, 34, 104–107
Spectator, The, 318
Spence, quoted, 265
'Spouse I do Hate, A,' 60
Spragge, Sir Edward, 52
Sprat, Mr., 97, 102
Stanhope, Philip, (Earl of Chesterfield), 68
'State of Innocence,' quotation from, 127
Steele, Dick, 292–294
Stewart, Frances, 69, 141
Sunderland, Lord, 209
Swan, Ensign, 228
Swift, Jonathan, 236, 318

Tatler, The, 292–294
Theatre du Petit-Bourbon, 25
Thorn-Drury, G., 47 n.
Titcombe, 289
'To a Great Country-Drinker,' 224
'To a Witty Man of Wealth and Quality,' 271
'To all you Ladies now at Land,' 48
'To King Charles II on His Return,' 37
'To my Friend Mr. Pope on his Pastorals,' 295

350

Index

Wycherley, Henry, 184
Wycherley, John, 255
Wycherley, William, 3, 210, 211,
315, 316, 318, 319; ancestry, 10,
11; description of, 11, 12; education, 12, 13, 16, 17, 27; and
Julie d'Angennes, 17–27; religion of, 22, 28, 33, 207; return to
England, 26–29; at Oxford, 30–
34; listed in the Bodleian, 31;
becomes member of Inner Temple, 33; life in London, 34 ff.;
manners of, 41; plays, 42, 59–
66, 85–92, 102–111; on town-
gallants, 43–45; presumably on
staff of Ambassador to Spain,
45–48; visit to Holland, 48; in
English navy, 51, 52; poems by,
51, 53, 194, 207, 225, 229, 256,
262 ff., 310–311; cup donated
by, 54; portraits of, 57, 128, 158,
265, 266, 328; and Barbara Villiers, 72–78, 81, 93, 94, 139,
and Buckingham, 82–85; a captain-lieutenant, 84, 85; strained
relations with father, 92, 93;
presented to Court, 94, 95; and
Charles II, 95, 96; moves to
Covent Garden, 99; acquaintances among nobility and
writers, 101, 102; disliked visiting Shropshire, 108; hailed as
'the Thalian bard,' 111; and
Dryden, 127, 250–252; his protest in favor of Buckingham,
137, 138; taverns frequented by,
140, 141; at Tunbridge, 143 ff.;
and Lady Drogheda, 145 ff.,
155, 158, 159; illness of, 150,
151, 324; at Montpellier, 154–
157; ring sent to, 155; return to
London, 157–159; appointed
tutor to Duke of Richmond,
159; evades tutorship, 162; marriage to Lady Drogheda, 162–
169; King's displeasure with,
167–169; marital difficulties,
167 ff.; friendships strangled,
167–172, 182, 196; wife's death,
177, 178; Drogheda-Radnor
suit, 179–183, 245, 258; finan-
cial difficulties, 180 ff., 204, 212
ff., 229, 252, 298, 324, 328, 330;
his life parallel to Julie d'Angennes, 185; at Newgate, 186–
190; at Fleet Prison, 191–204;
James II orders release of, 203;
re-conversion to Catholicism,
207; letters of, 212–217; return
to Clive Hall, 218, 219; father's
attitude toward, 222–224; visits
to London and Will's, 226 ff.;
to Dennis, 242, 244, 245; letters
to a love-wrecked knight, 246,
247, 249, 250; father's settlement on, 254, 255; at fifty-six,
257; Collier on, 260, 261; letter
about, 270; and Alexander
Pope, 275 ff., 290, 301, 310 ff.;
correspondence with Pope, 281,
282, 286 ff., 310; with Balam at
Painters' Tavern, 291; contem-
plates second marriage, 298,
299, 325, 326, 329, 330; break
in correspondence with Pope,
300; birthplace of, 302 n.; at
seventy, 305; at Bath, 306 ff.,
323; his maxims, 319–321; failing memory, 321; marriage to
Elizabeth Jackson, 331; arrested, 330; death of, 332–335
Wycherley, William, (son of
John), 298, 299; Daniel Wycherley's settlement on, 254,
255

York, Duke of, 49, 97, 198